Duplicate Bridge Direction

Duplicate Bridge Direction

A Complete Handbook

Alex Groner

BARON
BARCLAY BRIDGE SUPPLIES
Louisville, KY 40241

This book is dedicated to my favorite partner.

Library of Congress Catalog Card Number
67-29818

18th Printing 2012

Devyn Press, Inc.
3600 Chamberlain Lane, Suite 206
Louisville, KY 40241
1-800-274-2221

ISBN 978-0-939460-56-4

Contents

Foreword

THE SEEDS OF THIS BOOK were sown in a London club in the year 1857. Some of the regular losers at whist, the great-grandfather of our modern game of contract bridge, were fed up with the constant winners. "It's bad enough to lose so often with the horrible cards we pick up," said the losers, "but it's even worse to listen to all the patronizing advice you chaps hound us with. If our cards were exchanged, we would be doing the advising, and you would be listening to us humbly."

"Let's try just that," said Henry Jones, known under his pseudonym of Cavendish as the greatest whist authority in the world. "We'll exchange cards and see what happens."

That night two rooms of the London club were used for the first duplicate tournament in history. In the first room, two of the regular winners played a hand of whist in the usual way against two of the losers. Before they played the cards, however, a group of assistants wrote down the cards held by each player. When the hand had been finished, other assistants reconstituted the hand and took it to the other room. This time the cards of the regular winners were held by two of the chronic losers of the club; and the cards held by the "poor" players in the first room were given to two "good" players in the second room. Meanwhile, the original four players in the first room went on to play another hand.

After a few hands had been played in this way by the eight participants, it became evident that the good players in the first room won more with their good cards than the poor players who held those same cards in the second room. Similarly, the good players in the first room lost less with bad cards than the poor players who held those same cards in the second room.

The experiment marked the death of an excuse: that a loser was unlucky rather than unskillful. And it marked the birth of a new game: duplicate whist.

Today, the descendant of that new game, duplicate contract bridge, is played daily or almost daily in hundreds of communities in the United States and Canada. You will find duplicate games when you travel in Europe, or South America, or the Far East; and you can while away your traveling time at duplicate bridge if you go by ship or train. Duplicate bridge is a pastime, a challenge, a means of improving your game -- even, for many fanatics, a way of life.

Duplicate games need more than just cards, equipment and players. The other indispensable element is the director. Generally, club duplicate games are neither better nor worse than the people who direct them.

The old-line club director, who grew up with the game, learned his craft by making mistakes. Some of those mistakes meant an evening of confusion and frustration for his patrons as well as for the director; it was an expensive way to learn.

Fortunately, there is no need for new directors to go through the mill in the same way. With the publication of DUPLICATE BRIDGE DIRECTION it is possible for an experienced bridge player to become a competent club tournament director painlessly.

In this book the subject of duplicate bridge direction is carried step by step from the very simplest -- but necessary -- information to some of the most complex concepts of the game. This is done so gradually as to be almost imperceptible, and the reader finds himself learning more than he expected.

This is not the first book on duplicate club direction. The works of General Alfred M. Gruenther (a lieutenant when he wrote his book) and of George W. Beynon are milestones in the history of tournament bridge. But this is the most readable book on the subject, perhaps because Alex Groner was a professional writer for many years before he became fascinated by tournament bridge.

Although DUPLICATE BRIDGE DIRECTION makes a pleasant evening's reading, it is far more than that. It is as thorough a reference book as any club director will ever need, and it is probably the first director's guidebook to include a comprehensive index.

The book also has a number of welcome innovations. One is the orderly arrangement of all the most common tables and master sheets, in a series of appendices. The text includes just enough tables to demonstrate their use, and has references to all the materials in the appendices. Most of the master sheets have been prepared in a new and very useful form, which enables the director to follow the movements by the table numbers as well as by the player numbers and the board numbers.

I cannot imagine any club director who would want to get along without a copy of this book on his shelf -- right where he can reach it on a moment's notice. But I also cannot imagine any serious student of the game who would fail to read this book carefully -- just to gain a clear understanding of the workings of his favorite sport. I have been both a club director and a serious student, and I know that if this book had been available years ago I would have been spared many of my grievous errors and would have had the pleasure of learning my job while reading a quite delightful text.

--Alfred Sheinwold

Preface

NEW HORIZONS OF EXPERIENCE await the bridge player who has never played duplicate bridge before. The transition from rubber bridge play to duplicate is nearly as great as that from auction bridge to contract -- and is certainly as novel and exciting and as stimulating.

Duplicate is perhaps best enjoyed by those who have already sharpened their skills at rubber bridge, and who are looking for additional challenges in the game. It introduces new dimensions to both bidding and play, and different perspective to scores and potential scores. But, more important, it offers the opportunity to compare results with those of others who have held identical hands in identical deals. Inevitably, duplicate bridge opens new vistas of improvement in bidding and play.

By removing from bridge the largest single factor of chance -- the deal of the cards -- duplicate becomes a vastly better test of skill than rubber bridge. But this does not mean that all the elements of luck have been eliminated. In any particular deal, one set of opponents may be substantially better, or worse, than another. In any given situation, some quirk on the part of one player may make a shambles of the most skillful efforts on the part of the other players at the table.

Even given a fair degree of uniformity in the abilities of players in a duplicate game, chance still has a role to play. Some styles of bidding and play are better adapted to certain types of hands, less effective with others. Of the billions of possible bridge hands (actually 635,013,559,600) and the trillions and the quadrillions of possible deals in the deck (precisely 53,644,737,765,488,792,839,237,440,000), the run of the cards could well favor one style or system over another in the 20 to 30 deals usually played at a duplicate session. Even if some pair were to bid and play all its own hands perfectly during the course of play, they have no control over the distribution of their opponents' cards; in every bridge deal there are 10,400,600 different ways that the opponents' cards can be divided between them, and some of these distributions are likely to foil even the most able players.

Nevertheless, duplicate is far superior to rubber bridge as a test of skill. The rubber bridge player is likely to contend that the luck factor will gradually diminish over a long career of play. And so it should. The point is that chance always plays a smaller part in duplicate, and that the elements of luck balance each other out over a much shorter period of time.

Some forms of duplicate have quite a considerable advantage over others in measuring the real abilities of the players. Team-of-four contests, for example, are better tests than pair contests, and pair games in turn are usually superior to individual tournaments in this respect. By the same token, however, the team-of-four contest measures the combined abilities of four players, without differentiating the separate ability of each pair or individual as well as pair contests and individual duplicate games do.

Some duplicate games, as it will be seen later in this book, offer "more perfect" comparisons than others do. The ideal is to have every pair play every hand, and meet every other pair in the field some time during the course of the session.

The real value of this kind of perfection is minimal, except perhaps in indulging a tournament director's whim for mathematical elegance. Much more important in testing skill is the number of comparisons that can be made on each hand, on the quite valid assumption that the more times a hand is played, the less important the factor of luck becomes. No amount of symmetry or elegance can ever overcome the flukes that are bound to come up in the ordinary course of playing 20 or more bridge deals.

Duplicate bridge will invariably be a disappointment to those who come to it in quest of an infallible measure of skill. But for those eager to find new experiences in the game, it offers, in addition to an almost endless variety of hands, a similar variety of opponents during the course of an afternoon's or evening's play. This combination of social and intellectual stimulation is usually all the reward that most duplicate players seek.

1

Mechanics of Duplicate Play

A DUPLICATE BRIDGE GAME requires a minimum of two tables, or eight players, and the practical maximum is determined only by the space available for the game. The minimum is determined by the fact that more than one group of players must play the same bridge deals. (Deals, not hands; a bridge hand consists of just 13 cards, while a deal consists of the four hands in play.)

For reasonably comfortable play, the space provided should allow placement of tables on eight-foot centers, thus requiring 64 square feet for each table. The room for the ordinary duplicate game of a dozen tables or so should be rectangular, rather than square, and an arrangement of tables in two rows is usually most serviceable.

Ideally, the room should be well-lighted, sound absorbing and well-ventilated. In practice, the rooms all too often harbor shadowy corners, they echo and amplify the sounds of scraping chairs and partnership discussions, and they are characterized by a charcoal blue pall of tobacco smoke almost from the time the games gets under way. Any bridge club worth its weight in traveling score sheets will constantly be on the lookout for better quarters, or for ways to improve its housing. Many bridge clubs now ban smoking, except during "hospitality breaks," when those who wish may smoke in designated areas.

The director should designate one side of the room as North. This need not be geographical or compass North. But once the North position has been chosen, it is wisest to keep it in the same place for succeeding duplicate games, especially if many players are likely to return.

When the North position has been selected, all tables automatically take on the same orientation. The side of each table closest to the North wall will be the North position for that table. When table guide cards are used, they will indicate the proper positions on each table. Directors should watch out for those free spirits who insist on turning their guide cards around in other directions. ("George is the only one who can keep score, and he doesn't like to look into the light").

What for the rubber bridge player has always been an arrangement of Nancy, Edna, Sam and Walter now becomes the placement of North, East, South and West. This is not just to emulate the bridge hands in the newspaper columns, but rather to fulfill a very special purpose in duplicate bridge whose meaning will soon become clear.

A Game of Movement

What is frequently most enervating to the beginning duplicate player is the movement that goes on between rounds of play -- the moving of cards and the shifting of people from one table to another. When there are more than three tables at play, the newcomer looks at all this seemingly random commotion -- in which he must perforce take part -- as a plot to confuse and distract him from his concentration on the game.

The point is that duplicate is a dynamic game, a game of movement. In order for different groups of players to play the same deals, and for partnerships to play with a wide assortment of opponents, there must be motion of either something or someone or of both. These movements are known as changes and they form the basis for much of the excitement and variety of duplicate bridge.

It is not really necessary for the player to understand what is happening in a change, other than to know his own relatively small role. The director, however, must have an overall sense of what should be taking place throughout the room. A practiced director learns to spot and correct errors in the movement before such mistakes really result in confusion.

Duplicate Equipment

Some reference has already been made to table guide cards and to traveling score sheets. These are items of equipment especially designed for duplicate bridge.

In addition to the function of telling "which way is North," the guide cards also designate the table numbers, and give instructions concerning the movement of cards and players. These are described in Chapter 3. Traveling score sheets are specially printed score slips, on which are entered the scores of different groups of players on any particular deal. Since these score sheets relate to the cards they accompany, and since the cards move, the score sheets necessarily move -- or travel -- with their cards. These will be described more fully in Chapter 4.

The basic items of equipment that are desirable for the average duplicate game are the following:

A set of duplicate boards and carrying case
A set of Howell movement guide cards
A set of numbered table cards
A pad of traveling score sheets
Pencils
A pad of recapitulation sheets
Enough playing cards to supply one deck for each board
A supply of private score cards

The reader should already know what pencils, playing cards, and carrying cases are like. The nature and function of recapitulation sheets and private score cards will be treated in detail in Chapter 4.

That leaves just the duplicate boards -- perhaps the single key item of equipment in duplicate bridge -- and certainly an essential part of the language of the duplicate player.

The Duplicate Board

In order to move a bridge deal from one table to another, it is possible to reassemble each of the four hands and move them to the appropriate table. Sloppy, perhaps, but possible. Soon, however, any perceptive person would see that it would be much neater to put rubber bands around each of the hands, and transfer them in that way.

Eventually some enterprising soul would design and build a wooden tray, with separate compartments, or pockets, into which each of the hands could be slipped. And as the game of duplicate became more popular, it would be worth somebody's while to design and manufacture more attractive and durable trays of aluminum. The next logical improvement was to design trays of lightweight plastic.

This is approximately the genesis of the modern duplicate board, pictured here, and the fact that it is called a "board" rather than a "tray" stems from the fact that the earliest widely-accepted models were made of wood.

As can be seen from the accompanying photo, the duplicate board has more functions than just to serve as a convenient method of transferring bridge deals from one table to another. The boards have three other pieces of information that would be unnecessary in rubber bridge, but are vital to duplicate. These are (1) the number of the deal, (2) the dealer (and thus the one who starts the bidding auction) and (3) the vulnerability situation.

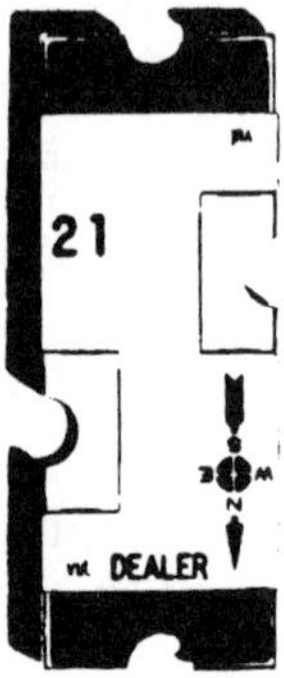

Because hands are dealt out just once, but played many times, at duplicate, the position of the dealer must be a matter of record. And because each deal at duplicate is a thing unto itself, unrelated to any other deal or the results achieved in any other deal, vulnerability must be arbitrarily assigned -- and this too becomes a matter of record.

A small compass rose on the face of the duplicate board indicates the positions of North, East, South and West, with an arrow pointing toward North. The number of the board and the position of the dealer are very clearly marked. Less clear, particularly on worn boards, are the smaller "vul." designations, which show which pairs are vulnerable; on modern boards, however, the bottoms of the pockets that hold vulnerable hands are painted a bold, conspicuous red.

To dispense some measure of even-handed justice in the matters of dealing and vulnerability, these will follow a regular pattern of rotation on a set of boards. Thus North will be dealer on Board 1, East on Board 2, South on Board 3 and West on Board 4; on Board 5, the deal starts with North again.

The vulnerability cycle is slightly more complex. On Board 1, neither side is vulnerable; on Board 2, North-South is vulnerable; on Board 3, East-West is vulnerable, and on Board 4, both sides are vulnerable. The rotation does not resume on Board 5, however. Instead, it moves ahead one notch, and North-South is vulnerable on 5, East-West on 6, both on 7, and neither on 8. On Board 9, a notch is skipped again, and East-West is vulnerable, then both on 10, etc. It is not necessary for either the players or the director to be familiar with the dealer or vulnerability patterns, although it is sometimes helpful to the director in checking scores.

In the parlance common among duplicate players, each deal is called a "board," and this has given rise to such expressions as "a good board," "that board was a disaster" and "top on the board." Because the distinction between hand and deal is largely unfamiliar, and therefore awkward, this book will adopt the terminology of board in referring to a duplicate deal, and the terms tray and board will be used interchangeably to indicate the piece of physical equipment itself.

The Deal, Bidding and Play

At the start of a duplicate game, the cards are removed from the trays, shuffled and dealt at each table. They are ordinarily dealt into four piles, rather than around the table, since they are being prepared for the trays, rather than for the players. It is sometimes the practice for the first board to be dealt to the players around the table, to avoid the redundancy of placing the cards in their respective pockets, only to have the players take them out again.

The shuffling and dealing chore is usually divided between the opposing pairs on the first round of play, although this is not required. What is required, however, is that at least one member of each pair be present while the cards are being prepared for play. On subsequent rounds of play, of course, there will be no dealing and shuffling (except in special cases in certain movements), since the players will get their appropriate cards from the trays. There is only one shuffle for each board in a duplicate game.

When a player gets his cards, whether dealt to him on the first round or taken out of the tray, his first act must be to count them, to make sure there are no more and no less than 13. This is a ritual that becomes automatic for the seasoned duplicate player, and one that the director should require -- especially if there are a number of players in his game who are new to duplicate. The act of counting, while it may seem tiresome, is well worth the effort in helping to avoid troublesome fouled boards.

The auction for a partnership begins, just as in any bridge game, as soon as either partner looks at his cards. The player designated as "Dealer" on the tray is the first to call. The bidding then proceeds as it normally would in any bridge game. Normally -- except that the rules of bidding, and specifically the Laws covering duplicate bidding,* are far more rigorously observed than in the rubber bridge games played in the cozy surroundings of a living room.

When the auction has ended and the contract has been reached, play begins. As in any other bridge game, the player to the left of the declarer is the first to play a card. Here the resemblance to other bridge games ends.

Instead of playing his card to the center of the table, the player places it directly in front of him. Indeed, the center of the table is already otherwise occupied. Resting there is the now empty tray from which the cards have been taken, still pointing its arrow to North, still recalling who was the dealer, and still proclaiming the conditions of vulnerability. Underneath this tray may be other trays, whose cards have been already played or are yet to be played on this round. And all the trays are likely to be nestled in the center of a table on a guide card. Somewhere on the periphery of all this will be a discreetly folded traveling score sheet.

In making the opening lead, the card must be placed face down, giving the opening leader's partner and declarer an opportunity to ask questions about the bidding — and making certain that the questions will not influence the choice of an opening lead. The dummy then comes down, just as in any bridge game. The declarer then announces (or in rarer cases, touches) the card he wants played from the dummy. His partner then places the card directly in front of himself on the table. The other players, in order, play their cards by placing them face up in front of themselves.

When a trick has been fully played, there is no pile of cards in the center of the table. Instead, each player must look to the four positions if he wishes to review what cards have been played to the trick.

After the four cards are played to a trick, each player turns his

* Laws of Duplicate Contract Bridge, revised 1990. Paperback $5.00; American Contract Bridge League, publisher.

card over and leaves it in front of him. The four cards are not gathered up by the winner of the trick. Instead, each card is pointed in the direction of the winner of the trick. The same thing is done on subsequent tricks, so that each player may keep a personal record of the progress of the play, in terms of tricks won and lost. As the cards are played and turned face down, they are placed in an overlapping position, both to conserve space and to facilitate a rapid count of the number of tricks won and lost. So long as he keeps his own card face up, any player (but not the dummy) may request that the other players expose their cards played to that trick, and they must comply. When he has absorbed all he wishes to know, he indicates that the cards may be turned over again by placing his own card face down.

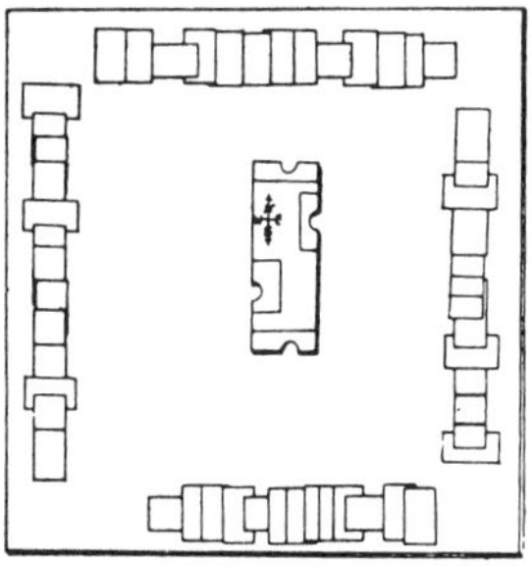

When the board has been fully played, the top of the card table should look something like the accompanying drawing. Each player has his own record of tricks won and lost, and the records of all players should match. If there are discrepancies, and some question is raised, the cards may be turned back up in the order played, so as to review the full play. In the board shown, North-South has won ten tricks and lost three, whatever the contract was, and the results may now be entered on the score sheet.

At this point, each player may gather up his own hand and place it back in the proper slot in the tray. Out of consideration for the players who will next get this board, he should first count his cards again. This final ritual act of counting is one more honored in the breach than in the observance, although it is actually more important than the earlier count. It is in the late stages of play on a board that players frequently grow casual about the cards. The cards themselves seem to have an annoying propensity for sliding over a few inches when they are near the corner of a table, so that a card or two from the North hand looks as though it really belongs to East.

A correction of misplaced cards by players who have just finished a board is usually quite simple. A correction by those who are just starting a new board is obviously more difficult, requiring the presence of the director and necessitating a certain amount of delay.

When a board has been completed, it is placed under the other boards on the center of the table (sometimes face down, although this is hardly necessary for players experienced enough to remember which boards they have already played). The next board is then played, and then the next, until all the boards on the table have been played. The round is over.

This is virtually all that your players will need to know about the mechanics of duplicate play. As director, you will have to know a good deal more. But it will be of immeasurable help to you if most of your players get to know quite well the basic principles of duplicate play, and have some sense of the hazards of violating them.

2

The Duplicate Director

THE SUCCESS of any duplicate game -- as a test of bridge skill, as a source of intellectual stimulation, and as a pleasant social experience -- depends in very large part on the duplicate director.

It is the director, more than anyone else, who sets the tone for his game. His friendly greeting to players as they arrive helps establish a good initial mood. If he remains cheerful, pleasant and relaxed, his players will tend to take on some of the same qualities, almost as if by osmosis.

A competent director will become thoroughly familiar with the mechanics of duplicate bridge, with the movement of boards and players, and with a wide variety of special situations that are likely to arise. By taking over all these technical concerns, he leaves the players free to do what they came for: concentrate on their bridge game.

It is this faculty of concentration that helps bring out the most competent -- and sometimes brilliant -- bidding and play. A good director will certainly want his game known for as much competence and brilliance as he can find. But excessive concentration by his players can also cause some of his major headaches.

Concentration is time-consuming, and there will always be some players who insist on using far more than their reasonable share of time. After all, they may argue, the laws of bridge put no time limit on thinking. Nobody as yet has put clocks on bridge tables, such as tournament chess games use. True. But too much time out for thinking by any single player slows up a duplicate game. Furthermore, when concentration has no real purpose, opposing players may become annoyed. And worst of all, inferences drawn from long hesitation may constitute unfair and improper communication between partners. Or their opponents may suspect that this is the case, whether it is or not.

Let's face it, duplicate bridge is a highly competitive game. And competition has been known to arouse some of the baser emotions in the human breast, or wherever base emotions are lodged. This hazard of bad feeling lurks constantly at a duplicate game, threatening to rob the players of their pleasure -- and, more important to the director, threatening to put a pall of ill-will over the game itself.

What can the director do about it? A number of things.

First of all, when obvious bad feeling erupts among his players, the most effective action the director can take is to try to slow down the adrenalin flow by kidding them out of their differences. If this fails to work, he can make mental notes about repeated offenders, and eventually warn them that they may not be welcome at his games.

Next, the director has to strive for complete fairness. He should be thoroughly familiar with the laws of duplicate bridge, as well as the ethics and proprieties of the game. The rulings he makes, when he is called on for rulings, must be designed with the equities of the situation in mind, and should seek to restore the players to the position they would have had if no offense had been committed. The laws of bridge, of course, prescribe the penalties for infractions, and these must be followed. But in the case of improper actions, rather than illegal ones, the duplicate director is allowed a wide range of discretion in deciding what penalties it would be most fair to exact.

Finally, the director should keep a proctor's watchful eye on his game. He may notice some improprieties that the players themselves -- and even their opponents -- are unaware they are committing. He can then take the offending player aside to point out, in a friendly fashion, that a less tolerant opponent might at some time call a director about hesitation before the play of a singleton, or about the play of a card by dummy before his partner has called for it. By watching the field, the director can also spot habitual offenders in slow bidding and play, and can even penalize them for it, after appropriate warnings.

If a good director needs to do all these things, it means he has to spend full time directing. He cannot wander off to the bar between changes and direct well. Above all, he cannot himself play in the game and direct well.

There are two excellent reasons for this. The first, already pointed out, is that directing is a full-time job. The second is that a playing director always invites suspicion that his rulings may be self-serving.

This prohibition does not necessarily apply in a small duplicate game among friends, where the director is merely the volunteer who has taken on extra duties. The best policy in such cases is to train as many members of the group as possible in the art of directing, and let them rotate the assignment. But it is the strong recommendation of the American Contract Bridge League that a professional director not play in his own games. Indeed, his detachment is part of what is needed to make him a professional.

Starting on Time

Before a duplicate game is scheduled to begin, the director should be on hand to set up the necessary equipment. He should make sure that tables and chairs are in place, and should prepare a game registration table. Boards and guide cards should be distributed to the tables, based on his best estimate of the size of the game. He may also, if he wishes, distribute traveling score sheets, individual score cards and pencils at this time.

All this is for the purpose of being ready for the game before it starts. Later he will be busy with the players as they arrive, collecting entry fees and either registering them for the game or distributing entry blanks for them to fill out.

What is of paramount importance is to get the game started at the announced time. There is always the temptation to hold off the start of the game, while waiting for just one more pair or one more table to arrive. This not only penalizes those who have arrived on time, but gives the game a reputation for late starting -- so that more and more of the players tend to arrive later and later.

There are better ways of accommodating late pairs or late tables than to hold up the start of the game. When more players are expected, it can be sound policy to take the table or guide cards off the tables and to let the first round of play start without assigning table numbers. These cards will have to be replaced, of course, before the first round is over, but this permits a period of flexibility.

The director who expects late arrivals, and who plans to let them enter the game, should choose a movement that allows for expansion before the end of the first round of play. (This will be discussed in more detail later, in the chapters on duplicate movements.) It should also be pointed out that late entries to a game frequently entail late play, with one or more tables playing their last boards after all the other players have finished the game.

Seating Assignments

The director may assign players to their tables and seats, or he may let them pick out the seats they prefer.

In a duplicate game with a great many new players, the tendency is to seat the more experienced players in the North-South positions. This spreads the experienced players around, so that the new players can learn about the mechanics from them. Furthermore, since North is the traditional scorekeeper in duplicate games, it cuts down the hazard of improperly scored sheets.

When the players become more experienced, it is preferable not to seat one group of players in one direction, particularly if that group consists of the more experienced players. It is generally agreed that the best duplicate games, for the sake of the better as well as the poorer players, is one that has the good players well scattered about in both the North-South and East-West positions. If the director does not wish to seed his field by assigning positions to the best pairs in this manner, he can pass out seat assignments at random and hope for automatic seeding.

Game Announcements

Just before the game is to begin, the director should get the attention of all the players to make whatever announcements he deems necessary.

For an established game, with a number of experienced players, only a few announcements are needed. The director should tell what type of movement is being used, and should review the direction in which boards and players will move at the changes. It would not be out of place for him to caution even experienced players to count their cards both before and after each board is played, and he might request that post mortems be held up until the end of the round, to be indulged in then only if there is some time remaining before the change.

For a new game, with inexperienced players, the director's opening announcements should attempt to forestall some of the more common ways in which the game might be thrown off. The director may make this period a brief class session in duplicate play. If he has a blackboard, he might use it to review the method of scoring.

The following is a check list of some of the more important announcements and instructions a director might want to make at a new game, in addition to describing the movement of players and boards at the changes:

1. Keep the table cards pointed in the proper direction.
2. Check to see that the proper boards are being played.
3. Keep the arrows on the boards pointed North.
4. Count the cards both before the bidding and after the play.
5. Bid quietly, so that the bidding cannot be heard at adjacent tables.
6. Do not discuss boards in the hearing of players who may not yet have played them.
7. Remember your pair number.
8. Score on the line corresponding to the North-South pair number.
9. East-West players should check scores.
10. Hold up post mortems until the end of the round.
11. Remain seated at your table until the change is called.
12. Call the director about any questions or irregularities.

Most directors feel that the best time to make special or club announcements is just before calling the change for the last round. All the players are still in the room, and this is the time when their minds are most readily attuned to future games. Such announcements might involve special events, club activities, future games or changes in the date, time or place of some future events.

Keeping the Game Controlled

These are the two cardinal commandments for every duplicate director:

1. Keep the game moving.
2. Keep the game quiet.

Occasionally, when he tries to do one or the other, the director may get an argument from some player. He can take comfort in the fact that the player is clearly in the minority. The great majority would rather play more quickly than more slowly. And almost every duplicate player would vote in favor of a quiet room.

When two boards are played, a round should take approximately 15 minutes. For three boards, 20 minutes should be allowed; for four boards, 25 minutes.

For the sake of the majority of players who finish their rounds on time, the director should call the changes promptly. If boards are still in play at most of the tables, of course, calling for a change would be a futile gesture. The director must realize then that he has a slow game -- and either become reconciled to that fact, or find ways to speed up many of his players. But if the round has been completed at two-thirds or more of the tables, the change may be called.

Those tables still in play will continue playing after the change. Moreover, each table still in play will hold up two tables for the next round -- their own, and the table waiting for the players who are to move. But calling the change, and the stir of activity marking the start of a new round at some tables, usually spurs the slow players to finish their round faster, lest they be even further behind on the next round.

Occasionally the director will find that a table is a full board behind when the change is called, or just before a change is about to be called. In that case he should pick up the unplayed board as he calls the change and move it to its next position. The two pairs are then required to play the board at the end of the game, in a late play. This should be noted on the outside of the traveling score sheet.

Perhaps the most popular method of calling a change is with the expression, "Change, please," or "All change, please." Other accepted change calls are "All move," or "East-West move, please."

Regardless of the call used, the director should seek to have the change made as rapidly and efficiently as possible, so that the next round can get started. It would be a little too much to ask that the change also be made quietly. For it is in this short interval that some of the most memorably cutting remarks have been made regarding the bidding or play on the previous boards.

3

Types of Duplicate Games and Movements

THE PAIR CONTEST is by far the most common type of duplicate game, and much of what has appeared in this book up to this point has assumed that pair games were involved. This is only natural, since bridge is a partnership game, and the pair contest measures partnership abilities by pitting one partnership against others.

But bridge competition is by no means confined solely to pairs There are also tournaments for individuals, for teams of four (two pairs) and for teams of pairs (anywhere from three pairs on up, but usually for four or six pairs on each team).

The individual game is a test not only of the bridge skill of the individual player, but also of his adaptability. Because of the frequent changes of partnership during the tournament, it places a special premium on the ability to bid and play in a variety of systems and styles. It removes the element of familiarity with the preferences and idiosyncrasies that one often finds in long-established partnerships, and by the same token broadens the area of misunderstanding. While a great many duplicate players like to play in different tournaments with a number of different partners, this bears little resemblance to an individual tournament, in which they must play with a number of partners not of their own choosing. Because some very strange things can and do happen in individual duplicate games, players should enter them in a come-what-may spirit that puts more emphasis on socializing and fun and perhaps less on the actual results of the contest.

The duplicate director should bear this in mind in scheduling individual games, because they are so well suited to duplicate club parties and special occasions. At the same time, the director must remember that individual game movements are the most complex and difficult to arrange. To whatever extent it is possible, they should be thoroughly planned in advance, even to the point of requiring advance registration.

The team-of-four tournament is considered the most thorough test of bridge skill. Certainly this is true in the sense of measuring the ability of one team against other teams, since it eliminates two major elements of chance: the luck of the deal and the luck of drawing certain opponents for particular boards. On any single deal, members of one team-of-four will play in both directions -- North-South, as well as East-West -- against the members of one other team. Thus luck plays a very small part.

Most team-of-four tournaments are multi-session events. When there are several teams playing during any single session, the director must be specially careful that the movement is working properly, since mistakes in the movement can quickly invalidate comparisons of scores and, consequently, the contest itself.

Teams of pairs usually represent bridge clubs, country clubs, organizations or even cities. Since these are very special types of matches, most duplicate directors are never called on to conduct them. It is unwise to plan such contests for more than half a dozen large teams (e.g., teams of six pairs) in a single session, since such games can become extremely awkward and unwieldy. A new movement for conducting single session events with several teams of several pairs each can be found described in Chapter 9.

Howell Movements

The Howell movement is the one commonly used for small pair games, usually with no more than seven tables.

In a completed Howell movement, every pair in the game will meet every other pair. There is only one winning pair, of course, in a Howell game.

In order for each pair to meet every other pair, the full game must have one round less than there are pairs in the game, (since the pairs play against all the other pairs, but obviously not against themselves). But because there can be only half as many tables in play as there are pairs, some boards must lie idle each round.

Boards not in play at any given time are known as bye boards, and they can be kept on chairs, tables or in other fixed positions, called bye stands, in the game area. The boards always progress toward the next lower numbered table in the Howell movement, pausing at the bye stand for one or more rounds whenever there is a bye stand between tables. If there is more than one set of boards at a bye stand, the latest boards to arrive are placed in a position closest to the table from which they have come, and the boards already on the stand are moved one position closer to the table to which they are going next. Boards leaving Table 1 proceed toward the highest numbered table (which, in a circular movement of this kind, is deemed the table "next lower" to Table 1.)

The movement of players is slightly more complex. One pair, customarily the highest numbered pair in the game, is stationary in the North-South position at Table 1. The other pairs then play against the highest numbered pair in numerical order, moving to the East-West position at Table 1 to do so. Pair No. 1 is first in this position, followed by Pair 2, then Pair 3, etc.

Not only does Pair 2 follow Pair 1 after the first round, but continues to follow Pair 1 throughout the game, by moving to the position that Pair 1 has just vacated. Similarly, Pair 3 follows Pair 2, Pair 4 follows Pair 3, etc. Pair 1 cannot follow the highest numbered pair, which is stationary, so it follows the second highest numbered pair.

The pairs that are adjacent in number meet each other at the pivot table, customarily the highest numbered table in the game. A pair that arrives at this table sits in the East-West position for one round, then switches to the North-South position at the same table, when the pair numbered one higher than itself arrives.

Given these general rules for a Howell movement, the entire movement can be built up from the positions of all the pairs and boards during the first round. Similarly, a full Howell movement can be predicated on the movement of a single pair during the entire game, such as the following description of the progress of Pair 1 in a four-table Howell game:

Round 1: Boards 1-3 at EW-1, vs Pair 8
Round 2: Boards 19-21 at NS-3, vs Pair 3
Round 3: Boards 16-18 at NS-2, vs Pair 5
Round 4: Boards 7-9 at EW-4, vs Pair 7

Round 5: Boards 10-12 at NS-4 (after the pivot), vs Pair 2
Round 6: Boards 4-6 at EW-2, vs Pair 4
Round 7: Boards 13-15 at EW-3, vs Pair 6

The circular movement of boards, and the somewhat more erratic movements of this pair can be seen somewhat more graphically from this diagram (which traces the movements of only one member of the pair through the game):

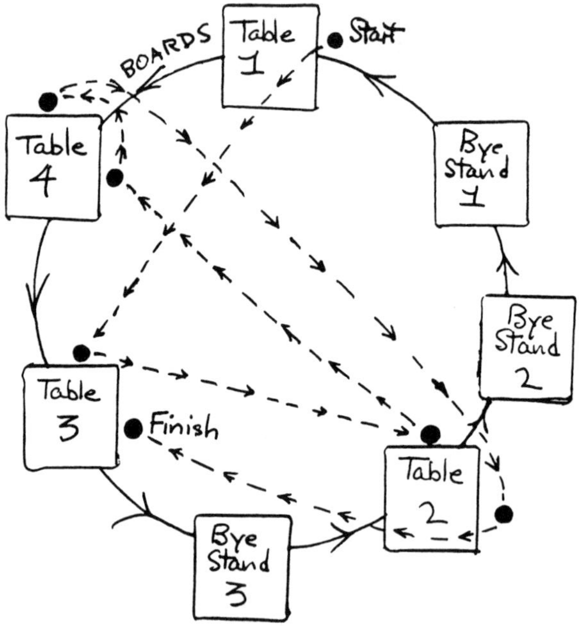

It will be recalled that a set of Howell movement guide cards was part of the equipment recommended for duplicate games. The most popular sets carry all necessary instructions for Howell movements from three to seven or eight tables. The following foreshortened illustration of a guide card shows the essential information that is included. At each position, it will be seen, are instructions for the movement of the pair at the next change. In the center of the card is a schedule showing the pair numbers and board numbers for each round played at that table.

These guide cards obviate the need for the director to know, or remember, the details of a Howell movement. It is nevertheless

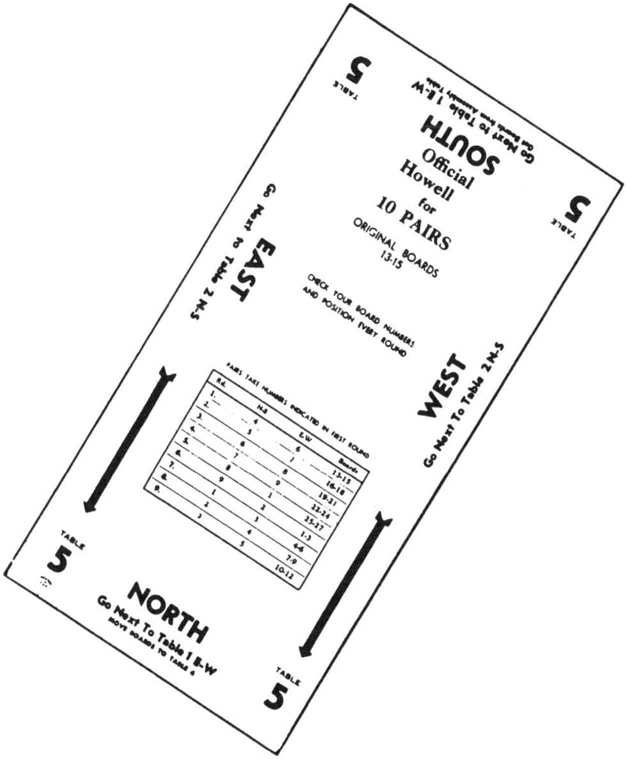

desirable for a director to understand the movement, to have a sense of its circular structure and to be familiar with the sequential movement of pairs. The director should pay special attention to the movement of boards in a Howell game, since players sometimes have a careless tendency to disregard the bye stands.

The Howell movement, incidentally, is not confined to pair games. Some individual game movements also follow the basic Howell principles.

Mitchell Movements

Most common of all bridge tournament movements is the Mitchell. It is also the most adaptable and most flexible, since it can be used with any number of tables from three on up. Ordinarily, however, the Mitchell movement is not employed unless there are at least seven tables in play.

All North-South pairs remain stationary in a Mitchell movement, and all East-West pairs move to the next higher numbered table at each change. Thus East-West pairs will have only North-South pairs as their opponents throughout the game, and North-South pairs will have only East-West pairs as their opponents. Nevertheless, the North-South pairs are competing only with the other North-South partnerships, since the comparisons of scores will be with the scores of other North-South pairs. Similarly, East-West pairs compete with the entire East-West field.

Thus, unlike the Howell movement, a Mitchell game produces two winners, one for the North-South direction and another for East-West.

The Mitchell movement is relatively easy to comprehend, and ordinarily it is fairly simple for the players to execute. Boards move, as in the Howell movement, to the next lower numbered table. East-West players move, as has already been noted, to the next higher numbered table. Normally, this progression is continued until all players have played all boards and all opponents seated in the other directions.

A schematic diagram of a seven-table Mitchell game, showing the direction of movement of boards and the movements of an East player from start to finish would look like the following:

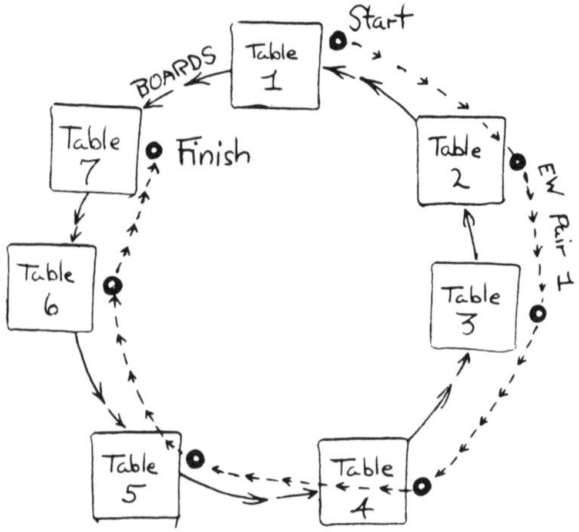

Because the player shown in the diagram started in the East seat at Table 1, he is a member of East-West Pair 1. This pair's first opponents in the game are North-South Pair 1. By contrast to the pair numbering in the Howell movements, there are two pairs designated as No. 1 in a Mitchell game, but each pair must be further identified by the direction in which it sits. All pairs take their numbers from the tables at which they start play.

With instructions that are so easy to follow, table guide cards are hardly necessary in a Mitchell game. The table cards commonly in use simply give the table numbers and compass positions, along with the reminder that boards are to be moved to the next lower numbered table.

The responsibility for moving the boards properly is generally assigned to the North-South pair (while the East-West pairs are responsible for moving themselves properly). North-South players should also keep a running check on the movement at their own tables by making sure that boards are played in regular upward sequence, and that there is the proper downward rotation of East-West pairs coming to their tables.

The relative simplicity of the Mitchell movement, however, should not lull the director into a false sense of security. He must remember that bridge players are frequently lost in a world whose outer limits consist of the hand they have just played. So preoccupied, some of the finest minds are prone to blunder over such comparatively simple concepts as the fact that five is just one higher than four.

The Mitchell movement is also the basis for progressions of players and boards in most individual, team-of-four and teams of pairs games.

The Three-Quarter Howell Movement

Frequently a duplicate director may deem it desirable to conduct a one-winner game, even though there are more than 14 pairs present. But because time is a limiting factor for most duplicate games, it is impossible for every pair to play every other pair within a reasonable time period.

The answer to this predicament is the three-quarter Howell

movement, which is quite similar to the regular Howell movement. Boards move down, and players move according to instructions on the guide cards.

As in any Howell movement, a certain number of boards stay out of play during each round. But instead of being placed at bye stands at various points in the game, all the bye boards will be on a single bye stand -- now known as an assembly table, since it is the point at which bye boards are assembled in their proper sequence. The assembly table in a three-quarter Howell movement should be positioned between Table 1 and the highest numbered table. The highest numbered table gets its new boards, after each change, from one end of the assembly table. Players from Table 1 put the boards they have just finished playing on the opposite end of the assembly table, at the same time moving all boards on the table one position closer to the highest numbered table.

The highest numbered pair is stationary throughout the game in the three-quarter Howell movement, as in the ordinary Howell. Pairs numbered from 1 through 13 follow each other in sequence throughout the game (Pair 3 taking the position Pair 2 has just vacated, Pair 2 moving to the seats Pair 1 has just left, Pair 1 moving to the position Pair 13 has vacated, etc.), again as in the ordinary Howell. But each pair numbered 14 and higher (except for the highest numbered pair in the game as noted above) remains at the same table throughout the game, but occasionally changes its position from North - South to East - West and back again, in order to produce balanced comparisons.

Guide cards for three-quarter Howell movements for six through twelve tables may be purchased. These movements are for 26 or 27 boards, generally considered ideal for a duplicate game. Guide cards for shorter, 22-board three-quarter Howells, for seven to ten tables, are also available.

The Scrambled Mitchell Movement

Just as there is a Howell movement adaptable to larger groups of players, so is it possible to arrange a Mitchell game to come up with a single winner, rather than separate winners for the North-South and East-West fields. The movement that does this is known as a scrambled Mitchell.

Actually, the scrambled Mitchell is conducted in exactly the same manner as an ordinary Mitchell. Boards progress to lower numbered tables. Players who start out in the North-South position remain stationary throughout. Players who start out in the East-West position move after each round to a higher numbered table.

The difference is that pairs starting as North-South do not remain North-South throughout the game, and pairs that start out as East-West do not remain East-West. Their transformation is accomplished, not by moving the players, but by the simple expedient of turning the direction of the guide card by 90 degrees. A North-South pair thus becomes East-West, and the East-West pair coming to the table finds that it has become instant North-South.

The effect of this is that each pair will have its scores compared with those of some pairs that started out in the North-South position and some pairs that started out in the East-West position.

A perfectly balanced comparison -- that is, a comparison of the same number of boards with every other pair in the game -- is impossible. Regardless of how many times the table cards are turned (each such turn is known as an arrow switch) during the course of the game, the director will discover that any given pair will have two or three times as many comparisons with one of the other pairs in the game as it has with a different pair. That is, Pair 5 may have played the same cards as Pair 8 on six different boards, and the same cards as Pair 13 on twelve or eighteen different boards.

Recommended "arrow switches," as developed by Dr. Lawrence Rosler, are as follows: *

Tables	Arrow North	Arrow East
9	Rounds 1, 2, 4, 8, 9	3, 5, 6, 7
10	Rounds 1, 4, 5, 7, 8, 9	2, 3, 6
11	Rounds 1, 2, 4, 10	3, 5, 6, 7, 8, 9, 11
12	Rounds 1, 2, 4, 6, 7, 8	3, 5, 9, 10, 11
13	Rounds 1, 2, 3, 5, 6, 9	4, 7, 8, 10, 11, 12, 13
14	Rounds 1, 3, 9, 13	2, 4, 5, 6, 7, 8, 10, 11, 12

In club games it is permissible to have a single arrow switch near the middle of the game.

Since all pairs will be playing some boards from the North-South position and some from the East-West position, pairs are not designated by their starting positions, such as North-South 6, or East-West 3. Instead, pairs are numbered separately, as in a Howell movement. Pairs starting in the North-South position take their

***See appendix J (page 232) for a further improvement in "arrow switches."**

own table numbers as their pair numbers. Pairs starting as East-West get their numbers by taking the number of the table at which they start, and adding to that a number equal to the total number of tables in the room.

It is the director's responsibility to see that all pairs are properly numbered. This can be done by including in the opening announcements some such statement as this:

> "There are eleven tables in the game. North-South pairs will take their table numbers as their pair numbers. East-West pairs will get their pair numbers by adding eleven to the number of the table at which they are now sitting."

Choosing the Movement

The duplicate director should decide on the type of movement he will use as soon as he can determine the approximate number of tables he will have in his game. This will enable him to select the type of equipment he will need, and even to start the disposition of the equipment around the room.

As a general rule, a game with six tables or less should use a Howell movement, and a game with seven tables or more should use a Mitchell movement. Either the three-quarter Howell or the scrambled Mitchell may be used when a one-winner movement is desired in a larger field, such as in a club championship event.

The director's initial decision should also take into account the number of boards to be played, based on the time that most of the players are willing to devote to a duplicate session.

Most players seem to prefer duplicate games that last approximately three hours, or perhaps slightly longer. On the basis of playing eight to nine boards per hour, the ideal game would then consist of anywhere from 24 to 28 boards. In areas where duplicate games are available every evening in the week, or on a number of evenings, shorter games of 20 to 24 boards have proved to be popular.

On Page 153, in Appendix B, is a tabulation that can be used as a guide to the type of movement chosen, based on the number of tables in play and the number of boards desired. The Mitchell movement variations referred to in the table are explained in detail in Chapter 6.

4

Duplicate Scoring

THERE ARE TWO phases to the scoring of the duplicate game -- the first by the players, and the second by the director.

The players score each board immediately after it has been played. Traditionally in charge of entering the score on the sheet is the player in the North seat. After scoring, North should let one of his opponents check the score.

Since each deal is treated as a separate entity in duplicate bridge, there are no carry-overs of partial scores and no accumulation of games for rubber. Instead, there are special bonuses for part scores, non-vulnerable games and vulnerable games, as follows:

Part score	50
Non-vulnerable game	300
Vulnerable game	500

These bonuses are roughly equivalent to the value of similar results at rubber bridge, if each rubber bridge deal were to be considered separately. Where duplicate and rubber bridge scoring part company completely, however, is in the matter of honors. There is no score given for the possession of honors at duplicate.

Most of the other scoring at duplicate is the same as in rubber bridge. The exceptions are that each doubled non-vulnerable undertrick after the third is 300 points, redoubled is 600, and the bonus for making a redoubled contract is 100 instead of 50.

Unlike rubber bridge scoring, in which various items are written separately for a single deal -- some above the line and some below the line -- the score for any duplicate bridge deal is expressed as a single number. This number is the total of all the elements that enter into the score. For inexperienced players, the duplicate director can obtain from most bridge supply houses charts that show the total score to be entered for any playing situation.

Traveling Scores

As already noted, the score sheets "travel" with their boards. En route, the sheets accumulate a record of the various results as the board is played at different tables.

The standard traveling score sheet can be used for either a Mitchell or a Howell movement, and is designed to accommodate 32 to 34 pairs. There are also traveling score sheets that are designed for fewer pairs. The standard sheets are completely adequate for most purposes. However, in games with a number of inexperienced players, where there is a greater likelihood of fouled boards, it is advisable to use traveling score sheets on which the full deal can be set down as a matter of record, so that corrections of misplaced cards can be made more readily.

The first time a board is played, North writes the board number in the upper right hand section, folds the sheet twice from top to bottom (printed side inside) and writes the board number on the outside of the sheet. This helps keep it with the proper board.

The double fold is for the purpose of making it easier to slip the sheet into the board (most conveniently under a few of the cards in the North pocket), and also for keeping the sheets from popping open. Should a player inadvertently see some of the previous results before he has played a board, he may not be permitted to play that board.

When a board is about to be played, North takes out the score sheet and, keeping it folded, usually secures it under some item on the table, such as the guide card or an ashtray. After the board has been played, he writes the appropriate information on the sheet, always on the line matching his own North-South pair number.

In the common types of traveling score sheets, the information to be entered includes the contract, the declarer, the number of tricks (over book) made or the number of tricks by which the contract was defeated, the North-South score, and the East-West pair number. The item that proves most troublesome for most duplicate beginners (and, occasionally, for some veteran players) is the

North-South score. This is always expressed as a single number, including all bonuses or all items pertaining to penalties. And it is always expressed from the viewpoint of North-South. Thus, either a contract made by North-South or a contract in which East-West are defeated will be represented by some number in the North-South plus column. A contract made by East-West or one in which North-South go down will always be represented by some number in the North-South minus column.

If East-West Pair 7, for example, bid 2♠ on Board 13 and East makes 3 against North-South Pair 7, the entry that North puts on the traveling score sheet will look like this:

N-S Pair	CONTRACT	BY	MADE	DOWN	Final Score North South	East West	E-W Pair	N-S Match Points
6								
7	2S	E	3			140	7	

If, on the next round, East-West Pair 5 bid to 4♠ on the same board, and East is set one trick by North-South Pair 6, North will again enter the score, and the traveling score sheet will now look like this:

N-S Pair	CONTRACT	BY	MADE	DOWN	Final Score North South	East West	E-W Pair	N-S Match Points
6	4S	E		1	100		5	
7	2S	E	3			140	7	

A double is shown by placing an "X" after the contract, in this manner: 4S X, or in this way: $4S^{X}$. A redoubled contract would be shown as $4S^{XX}$.

As play progresses, it can be seen that the traveling score sheet accumulates a record of what has taken place at the various tables where the board has been played. This provides the basis for a quick comparison of scores. When the game ends, the traveling score sheets are ready for the second part of the scoring process -- match pointing by the director.

Match Pointing

If pairs were credited with the total points scored on each hand, an unusually high score on one, two or three boards might enable them to win a tournament, even though their bidding and play might be below par on most of the remaining hands. Thus, a recklessly bid, but somehow makable, slam -- or, even worse, a foolishly bid contract, vulnerable and doubled, by opponents -- might give one pair an undeserved, but almost unassailable, advantage. As a matter of fact, total point scoring was once used exclusively in duplicate games, but because of this patent inequity it was largely abandoned and replaced by match points.

Match points are scored separately for each board, and they make the potential for each board approximately the same. A pair is awarded a match point for each pair that it beats (among those holding the same cards) and a half match point for each pair that it ties on any board.

The actual process of match pointing can be a more simple matter than making all the individual comparisons and adding up the points and half points. The simplest method is to first determine what is top and what is bottom on the board.

Bottom is always zero, since the pair that has beaten or tied no other pair in its direction has no points or half points to be added up to its credit. And top is always one less than the number of times a board has been played, since a pair that has beaten all other pairs in its direction is given one point for each of their entries on the traveling score sheet (but none for its own entry).

After awarding the top score on a board to the North-South pair that has done best, the North-South pair that has done second best gets the next higher number. 'This is continued all the way down until the North-South pair that has done worst is given its zero.

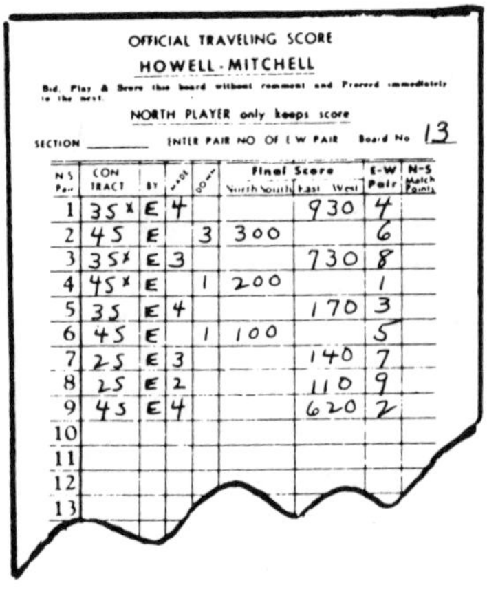
OFFICIAL TRAVELING SCORE

HOWELL-MITCHELL

Bid, Play & Score this board without comment and Proceed immediately to the next.

NORTH PLAYER only keeps score

SECTION ______ INTER PAIR NO OF E W PAIR Board No 13

N S Pair	CONTRACT	BY	Made	Down	Final Score North South	Final Score East West	E-W Pair	N-S Match Points
1	3S X	E	4			930	4	
2	4S	E		3	300		6	
3	3S X	E	3			730	8	
4	4S X	E		1	200		1	
5	3S	E	4			170	3	
6	4S	E		1	100		5	
7	2S	E	3			140	7	
8	2S	E	2			110	9	
9	4S	E	4			620	2	
10								
11								
12								
13								

Let us look, for example, at all the scores on the sheet for Board 13, mentioned in the previous section.

In match pointing the North-South pairs, the highest score in the North - South column gets top on the board -- in this case 8, since the deal was played nine times. Next, 7 and then 6 match points are awarded to the other North-South pairs with plus scores. Now match points are awarded to the North-South pairs with minus scores, beginning with those having the lowest minus scores. Thus, Pair 8, with a minus score of 110, gets 5 match points; Pair 7, with minus 140, gets 4, and so on, so that the match pointed score looks like this:

OFFICIAL TRAVELING SCORE

HOWELL-MITCHELL

Bid, Play & Score this board without comment and Proceed immediately to the next.

NORTH PLAYER only keeps score

SECTION ________ ENTER PAIR NO OF E W PAIR Board No 13

NS Pair	CON TRACT	BY	MADE	DOWN	Final Score North South	Final Score East West	E-W Pair	N-S Match Points
1	3S x	E	4			930	4	0
2	4S	E		3	300		6	8
3	3S x	E	3			730	8	1
4	4S x	E		1	200		1	7
5	3S	E	4			170	3	3
6	4S	E		1	100		5	6
7	2S	E	3			140	7	4
8	2S	E	2			110	9	5
9	4S	E	4			620	2	2
10								36
11								
12							1	1
13							2	6
14							3	5
15							4	8
16							5	2
17							6	0
18							7	4
19							8	7
20							9	3
21							10	36

Not just the North-South pairs, but also the East-West pairs have been match pointed on the traveling score sheet shown. The simplest way to match point East-West scores is by a process commonly called reciprocating, although the East-West scores are not, strictly speaking, the reciprocal of the scores of the North-South teams against which they played the board. It is rather the difference between the North-South matchpoint score and whatever is top on the board -- in this case, 8.

Thus, East-West Pair 1, which played this board against North-South Pair 4, gets the difference between their opponents' match point score of 7 and the top of 8, for a match point score of just 1. Similarly, East-West Pair 2, which played the board against North-South Pair 9, gets a match point score of 6, as the difference between the North-South score of 2 and the top of 8.

After match pointing, the director should total all match point scores as a check on accuracy of the scoring. East-West match points, of course, should total exactly the same as North-South match points on any given boards. This figure is the board check total.

For a Howell game, where each team has its own number, the match point scores should all be entered in the same area of the traveling score sheet, as in this sample of a four-table game.

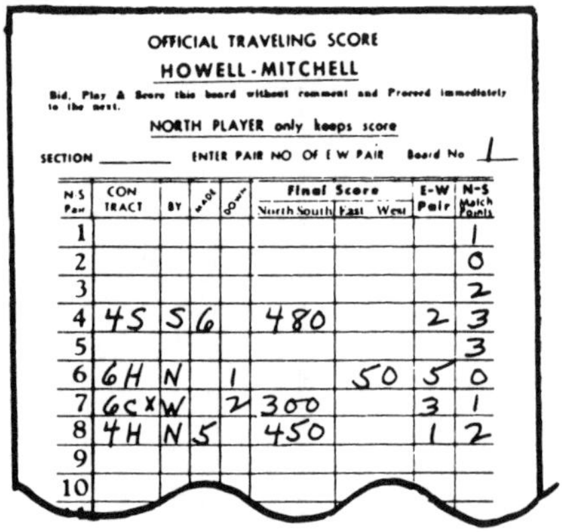
OFFICIAL TRAVELING SCORE

HOWELL-MITCHELL

Bid, Play & Score this board without comment and Proceed immediately to the next.

NORTH PLAYER only keeps score

SECTION ______ ENTER PAIR NO OF E W PAIR Board No 1

N-S Pair	CONTRACT	BY	MADE	DOWN	Final Score North South	Final Score East West	E-W Pair	N-S Match Points
1								1
2								0
3								2
4	4S	S	6		480		2	3
5								3
6	6H	N		1		50	5	0
7	6CX	W		2	300		3	1
8	4H	N	5		450		1	2
9								
10								

Passed Deals

A deal that is passed out by all four players should be so indicated on the traveling score sheet, with the notation, "Passed out," or "Passed," on the appropriate line. Some directors permit passed deals to be re-shuffled and re-dealt, if they occur on the opening round of the game. This is both improper and a poor practice. Deals passed out at one table may very well be bid by other players, using different systems and different styles. A good random test of bidding styles and play will necessarily include deals that would be passed out at some tables and bid at others. Since such hands are part of the game of bridge, they should also be a part of duplicate, when they occur.

For the purpose of match pointing, the passed deal should be regarded as having a total point score of zero -- and it is of course immaterial whether the zero is regarded as appearing in the North-South plus column or the North-South minus column.

This total point score of zero should be given its appropriate matchpoint score, which will fall just below the lowest North-South plus score, and just above the lowest North-South minus score. The match point score for a passed deal will never be zero, unless all other pairs playing in the same direction have a plus score on the board.

Another quick way to match point a passed deal is to give the North-South pair one point for each score appearing in the North-South minus column, plus a half point for each tie -- in this case, for every other passed deal.

Scoring Ties

Frequent ties in total point scores should naturally be expected. Indeed, boards in which all pairs show different results are very much the exception.

In awarding match points for such ties, the tying pairs are given consecutive positions and they divide the total match point awards for those positions. Two pairs tied for third and fourth place on a board with an 8-point top are each awarded 5 1/2 points, or the average of the 6-point award for ranking third on the board and the 5 points for being fourth.

Three pairs so tied would divide the awards for the places equally, and four tying pairs would similarly divide the awards for the four places. If all pairs show exactly the same result on a board, they split the awards for all the places, and each is given a number of match points that is exactly half of what would be top on the board. (For example, with an 8-point top, each pair in both directions is given 4 match points when the same result has been reached at all tables.)

Some directors find it simpler to think of tied pairs as earning a matchpoint total exactly half way between the highest and lowest number of match points to be awarded for their positions in the field. Thus, when three pairs are tied at a level where they should be awarded 4, 3 and 2 match points, each is awarded 3 points, or the middle figure. If four pairs are tied at the level of 9, 8, 7 and 6 match points, each is given 7 1/2, or the amount midway between the middle figures of 7 and 8.

Half match points are shown by either writing out the fraction (as in "7 1/2"), by an x (as "7x") or by a dash (as "7–"). The dash is most commonly used in major tournaments, in spite of its resemblance to a minus sign, while the x appears to be at least as popular in smaller club games.

Extra care should be exercised by the director in "reciprocating," or determining the East-West match points, when there are half-point awards on a board -- at least until the director is so familiar with subtracting fractions correctly that the process becomes virtually automatic.

Scoring Averages

For a variety of reasons within the discretion of the director, fairness can sometimes be served only by giving average scores to two competing pairs on a board. One or more people at the table may have inadvertently seen a traveling score sheet before the board was played; a player may have overheard a discussion of a board that gave him an unfair advantage, or one or more cards may have been intermingled between hands.

If the director decides that neither pair is at fault, he may award an average to both pairs, and this will be shown on the traveling score sheet in place of a score.

In match pointing a board on which averages have been given at one or more tables, the pairs involved are given average scores -- or just half of the normal top for the board. Every other pair, from highest to lowest on the board, is deemed to have tied each pair awarded an average in its own direction. The net effect of this, it will be seen, is to reduce by a half point for each average score the match point scores of those pairs that have done better than average on the board, and to similarly increase the scores of the pairs that have done worse.

The mechanics of match pointing such boards can be simplified somewhat for the director. First the pairs marked average are given their scores. Then all the other pairs are match pointed as if those given averages had not played the board at all. In effect, this reduces the top on such a board by one point for each pair marked average in the same direction. After this has been done, a half point is added to all the other scores for each average in the field.

Here is a sample match pointed traveling score sheet for a 13-

table Mitchell game in which all the situations discussed in the last three sections -- passed deals, tied and average awards -- have been encountered:

OFFICIAL TRAVELING SCORE

HOWELL-MITCHELL

Bid, Play & Score this board without comment and Proceed immediately to the next.

NORTH PLAYER only keeps score

SECTION ________ ENTER PAIR NO OF E W PAIR Board No 1

N S Pair	CONTRACT	BY	MADE	DOWN	Final Score North South	Final Score East West	E-W Pair	N-S Match Points
1	2D	S	2		90		1	6-
2	1N	N	2		120		3	10
3	1D	S	3		110		5	8-
4					average		7	6
5	average plus (NS)						9	6★
6	3N	N		1		50	11	2
7	1N	N	3		150		13	11
8					passed out		2	3-
9	2C	S	3		110		4	8-
10					passed out		6	3-
11	3D	S		2		100	8	1
12	1C	S	1		70		10	5
13	1N	N	1		90		12	6-
14								78
15								
16								
17								
18								
19								
20								
21								
22								
23								
24								
25								
26								
27								
28								
29								
30								
31								
32								
33								
34								

1	5-
2	8-
3	2
4	3-
5	3-
6	8-
7	6
8	11
9	6★
10	7
11	10
12	5-
13	1
14	78
15	
16	
17	

In match pointing this board, North-South Pairs 4 and 5 are first given their normal average scores of 6 (the "average plus" notation for Pair 5 is disregarded for the time being). Top on the board for the remaining pairs then becomes 11 -- or 10 as the normal top for the eleven remaining pairs, plus a half point for each of the two average pairs. North-South Pairs 3 and 9 tied with scores of plus 110, and therefore divide the match point scores of 8 and 9 between them; Pairs 1 and 13 tied with plus 90, and share the match point scores of 6 and 7; and Pairs 8 and 10 both had passed deals, thus tied at a zero total point score and divide the match point score of 3 and 4. It will be seen that the normal top score of 12 and the normal bottom of 0 are not awarded, even though there is one clear top result and one clear bottom. This is because some "average" awards were noted on the score sheet.

The East-West scores on this board are obtained by subtracting the corresponding North-South scores from the normal top of 12. This will work out because all the necessary number juggling has already been done in match pointing the North-South pairs.

The traveling score sheet shows an average match point score of 6 for North-South Pair 5, even though the director has noted that this pair should receive an "average plus." This will be rectified on the recapitulation sheet (see below), when the North-South pair will have 10% of the normal top added to its match point score -- in this case, 1.2 match points, for a total of 7.2 (usually rounded out to 7) -- and their opponents on the board, East-West Pair 9, will have a similar amount subtracted. Some such symbol as an asterisk on the traveling score sheet will serve as a reminder to the director.

An average plus should be awarded when a member of one pair has been clearly at fault for the circumstances leading to the average award — for such offenses as carelessly opening and examining the traveling score sheet for a board that has not yet been played. For clubs that use computer scoring, entering average or average plus scores should be simply a matter of following the computer program directions.

Fouled Boards

A board is "fouled" when one or more cards from one hand are placed in the pocket of another hand.

The problem is a relatively simple one when the initial count of the cards shows one hand to have more than 13 cards and another fewer. The director simply takes the two out-of-balance hands to pairs who have already played the boards, and lets them replace the cards properly from memory.

But when the same number of cards are exchanged between two hands, or entire hands have been placed in the wrong pockets in the tray, the error will probably not be discovered until too late, if at all.

When it is discovered, the director must restore equities in match pointing. After determining when the switch took place, the director divides the North-South pairs into two groups — one before the change, the other after. He match points the groups separately, giving each pair the number of match points it earns in its own group. At this point, the procedure varies, depending on the normal top on the board. If it is 9 or less, each pair not included in a group is deemed to have had an average for that group. Thus, every pair in the group is given a half match point for each North-South pair not in its group. So if five pairs played the board one way, and four another way, the first group will have a matchpoint top of 4, and the smaller group a top of 3. But each pair in the larger group will have 2 match points added to its score, and each pair in the smaller group will have 2 1/2 points added.

When the normal top is 10 or more, a much more complicated procedure must be followed. The appropriate scoring formula can be found in Chapter IX, Section Thirty-Three, of the A.C.B.L. Handbook of Rules and Regulations. After scoring the North-South pairs, the East-West match point scores can be made normally. Here again, a computer program should be able to handle fouled board scoring. The American Contact Bridge League's formula is embodied in the ACBL-Score program.

Recapitulation Sheets

The total score for any pair in a duplicate game is the total of all its match point scores on the traveling score sheets.

To make the process of adding these scores easier, there are inexpensive forms, known as recapitulation sheets, on which all the scores can easily be entered. As shown in the accompanying illustration, a "recap sheet" lists the names of the pairs vertically on the left and the board numbers horizontally across the sheet.

Shown here is a section of a Mitchell recap sheet, in which the North-South players are listed separately from the East-West players. Howell recap sheets are simply numbered from top to

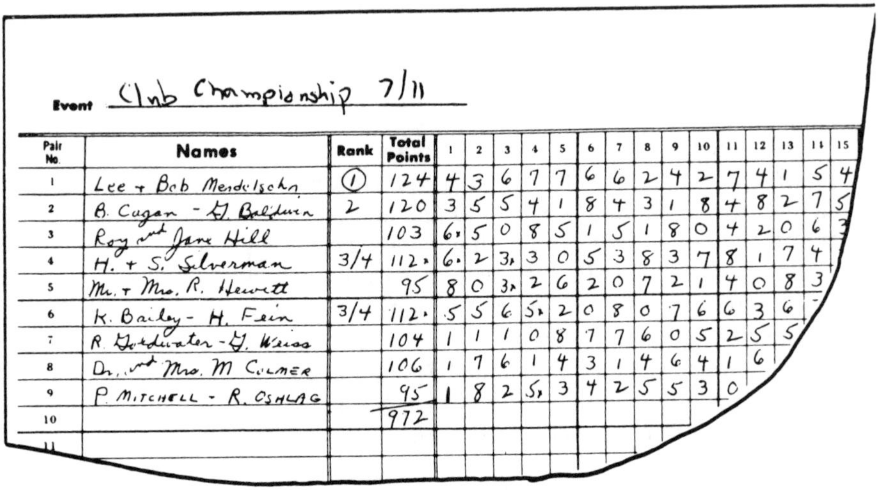

Event Club Championship 7/11

Pair No.	Names	Rank	Total Points	1	2	3	4	5	6	7	8	9	10	11	12	13	14	15
1	Lee + Bob Mendelsohn	(1)	124	4	3	6	7	7	6	6	2	4	2	7	4	1	5	4
2	B. Cugan - G. Baldwin	2	120	3	5	5	4	1	8	4	3	1	8	4	8	2	7	5
3	Roy and Jane Hill		103	6·	5	0	8	5	1	5	1	8	0	4	2	0	6	3
4	H. + S. Silverman	3/4	112·	6·	2	3·	3	0	5	3	8	3	7	8	1	7	4	
5	Mr. + Mrs. R. Hewett		95	8	0	3·	2	6	2	0	7	2	1	4	0	8	3	
6	K. Bailey - H. Fein	3/4	112·	5	5	6	5·	2	0	8	0	7	6	6	3	6		
7	R. Goldwater - G. Weiss		104	1	1	1	0	8	7	7	6	0	5	2	5	5		
8	Dr. and Mrs. M Colmer		106	1	7	6	1	4	3	1	4	6	4	1	6			
9	P. Mitchell - R. Oshlag		95	1	8	2	5·	3	4	2	5	5	3	0				
10			972															
11																		

bottom, with no directional designations. Directors can use their own ingenuity in making either type do for both kinds of games.

Pairs are listed by number at the left side of the sheet. The match points for each board are copied from the traveling score sheet onto the recap sheet, under the appropriately numbered column.

To get a pair's total score, each line is added across the sheet (whole numbers are usually totalled first, and halves added afterward), and the total is entered in the "Points" column on the left. To the left of this column is a space for designating the position in which the pair finished, e.g. "1st," "2nd," etc.

The top of the sheet has spaces for general information about the game, including one line marked "average." In this space should be entered the average score for the game, obtained by multiplying the average score for each board by the total number of boards played. (Averages are sometimes different for North-South and East-West players, or even, occasionally, for different pairs playing in the same direction; when this happens, the range of average scores should be shown, such as "132-156.")

After the totals for all pairs in one direction have been entered, these should be added to arrive at the total for the full field. As a check on accuracy of scoring, this should be equal to the average score for the field, multiplied by the number of pairs in the field. The product of this multiplication is known as the check total for the session.

Speed Scoring and the Waldman Modification

To match point the East-West pairs in a Mitchell game means a series of subtractions -- one for each pair on each board. This usually means a considerable slowing down of the scoring process.

This can be overcome by using the speedier method known as California scoring, a relatively simple technique for eliminating the subtraction step. Instead of getting East-West match point scores by subtracting the scores of their North-South opponents from top on the board, the East-West pair is given exactly the same score in match points as its opponents have been given.

So while the high match point total wins for North-South, the low total wins for East-West. If it goes against the sensitivities of a director to award first place to the lowest score, he can make just one subtraction for each East-West pair, i.e., by subtracting their California score total from the maximum score it is possible for an East-West pair to achieve (top on one board multiplied by the number of boards played).

California scoring can be used with only a straight Mitchell movement, of course, and not with Howell movements or scrambled Mitchells.

Another measure that helps speed the scoring process is known as the Waldman modification, which can be used only with an odd number of tables in a straight Mitchell movement. The East-West pairs, instead of taking the numbers of the tables at which they start, are arbitrarily assigned numbers by the director.

The result will be that East-West pairs will appear in numerical order on the top half of the traveling score sheet, instead of skipping numbers. On the sample traveling score sheet shown on P. 45, for example, it can be seen that the East-West pairs appear in this order on the top half of the sheet: 1, 3, 5, 7, 9, 11, 13, 2, 4, 6, 8, 10, 12. Using the Waldman modification, the East-West pairs would turn up in this order on top of the sheet: 1, 2, 3, 4, 5, 6, etc.

Combining the Waldman modification with California scoring makes it completely unnecessary to "reciprocate" scores, or to mark the bottom half of the score sheet at all. Instead, the match point scores are copied directly from the traveling score sheet to the recapitulation sheet, for both North-South and East-West pairs. For the East-West pairs, however, the numbering will not always start at the top of the page, but might appear in some such fashion as this: 7, 8, 9, 10, 11, 12, 13, 1, 2, 3, 4, 5, 6. But the sequence will always be the same, so that it is a simple matter to copy off the match point scores.

The following tabulation shows the East-West pair numbers that must be assigned for the Waldman modification, in each case starting at Table 1 and going up the tables in numerical order:

5 Tables: 1, 4, 2, 5, 3
7 Tables: 1, 5, 2, 6, 3, 7, 4
9 Tables: 1, 6, 2, 7, 3, 8, 4, 9, 5
11 Tables: 1, 7, 2, 8, 3, 9, 4, 10, 5, 11, 6
13 Tables: 1, 8, 2, 9, 3, 10, 4, 11, 5, 12, 6, 13, 7
15 Tables: 1, 9, 2, 10, 3, 11, 4, 12, 5, 13, 6, 14, 7, 15, 8

The pattern for any number of tables becomes obvious, once it is seen that the East-West pair at Table 2 is given a number that is one higher than the number of the middle table.

Factoring and Percentages

Up to this point there has been a tacit assumption that all the pairs in a field would play precisely the same number of boards, and that all the boards would have the same top.

In any given game, neither assumption will necessarily be true.

The combination of an odd pair in a duplicate game and a movement that is cut short before it has run its full course will almost always result in some scoring disparities The simplest problem to handle is that of different numbers of boards played by pairs in the same field. This can usually be taken care of through a process known as factoring. More bothersome is the situation in which different boards have different tops (as in non-completed Howell and scrambled Mitchell games). This can be resolved by either factoring or using percentages. With proper planning, however, all boards will have the same match point top, except in cases of emergency.

Factoring is a fairly simple process, even for those with just the mildest mathematical inclination. A pair can have its score "factored up" or "factored down." If a pair has played fewer boards than most of its field, its score can be factored up by adding to its score a fraction of the total match points it has received; the score of a pair that has played extra boards is factored down by subtracting a similar fraction. That fraction is the difference in number of boards played over the total number of boards the pair has played. The A. C.B.L. requires that factoring be done "up" only.

Thus, if one or two East-West (or North-South) pairs have played 24 boards and the rest of their field have played 26, their scores are factored up. The difference in the number of boards played is two, so the fraction becomes 2/24, or 1/12. If one pair's match point total is 159, then 1/12 of this total, or 13 1/4, is added to its score, which then becomes 172 1/4, or 172.25. The use of decimals is recommended for differentiating scores. A.C.B.L. regulations now consider a difference as small as .01 match point great enough to determine rankings.

Factoring may become rather involved in those cases where competing pairs play different numbers of boards and where boards have different match point tops. This might happen in, for example, a 6 1/2 table Howell progression that was stopped after the eleventh round (instead of being completed in thirteen rounds) because of an emergency. Assume that pair number 14 is the "phantom". (Every other pair "sits out" when they are scheduled to play pair 14.) Pairs 12 and 13 do not sit out and, as a result, play 22 boards. All other pairs sit out and play 20 boards. Boards 13-22 will have been played six times (top is 5); boards 3-6, 11-12, and 23-24 will have been played five times (top is 4) and boards 1-2, 7-10, and 25-26 will have been played four times (top is 3). The first step, after match pointing, is to factor all boards to the same top (5 in this example--the highest top in the group). Multiply each match point score on those boards with a 4 top by 5/4 and those boards with a 3 top by 5/3. After adding all of the scores, pairs 1-11 (who sat out) must have their scores factored up to conform to those of pairs 12 and 13 who did not sit out. This is done by adding 2/20, or 1/10 of the scores of each pair (1 through 11) to the pair's total score. (The same can be done by multiplying the score of each pair by 11/10.) Note: Decimals must be retained throughout these calculations.

When, however, the margin between any two positions is obviously a full point or more, it is almost always simpler to use percentages when the tops on some boards are not the same as those on others. Each pair's score can be expressed as a percentage of the total score it could have obtained by obtaining tops on all the boards it played. See Appendix A, Pages 147 - 152, for percentage tables.

Private Score Cards

Most duplicate bridge players like to be provided with score cards on which they can keep track of their game, both to assess their chances and for subsequent discussion of hands. For this purpose, directors can provide private score cards, such as the one shown here.

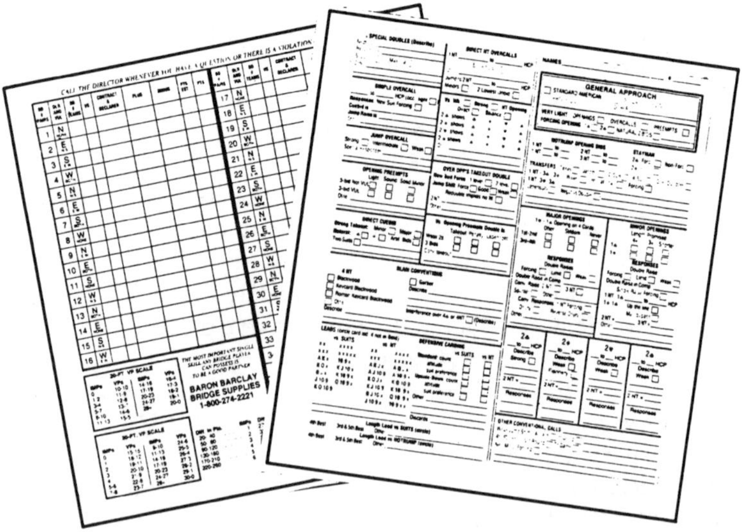

Private score cards can also help the director by providing a check on various scoring errors and discrepancies that have not been caught during the course of the game.

The card enables a pair to keep a record of every board it has played, listing the number of the opponent, the contract and result, the total point score, and an estimate of match points won. Total point scores should be listed in the plus or minus column as they apply to the team keeping the private score, and are not necessarily copied from the similar columns on the traveling score sheet.

Players should be cautioned not to let opponents see scores entered earlier on the private score cards, since the opponents may not yet have played those boards.

The reverse side of a private score card is customarily used to list the pair's bidding system and conventions. This will be discussed more fully in Chapter **11.**

Checking and Posting

When pair scores have all been totalled, then added together for the full field total, this is compared with the check total for the field. If these fail to tally, two different checks may be made: Match point totals for each board are rechecked by adding columns vertically, and the scores for each pair are rechecked by adding scores horizontally across each line on the recap sheet.

After all discrepancies have been cleared up, the recap sheet should be posted on a wall or left in a conspicuous place for the players to examine. The director should designate a specific period of time for protests before any awards may be made. Players can then use their individual score cards as a check on their own scores and on the accuracy of their estimates. The traveling score sheets should also be made available for examination during the protest period. It is also a good idea to post the recap sheet at the next game.

Finally, when the boards are being gathered up, one card should be turned face up in each board, usually in the North pocket, to indicate that the board has already been played in a duplicate game.

Tournament Scoring

Scoring in large tournaments differs in some details from that of the smaller club duplicate games.

Traveling score sheets, for example, are not used. Instead, the scores are all entered on individual pick-up slips, like those shown here, each time a board is played. North, as usual, does the scoring -- on the left side of the slip when North-South has a plus score, on the right side if East-West has a plus score. There are two types of pick-up slips in use, one which has space for scoring one board and a second which has space for three boards. Space is provided for all the information normally found on the traveling score sheet, plus a breakdown of the total score -- the slip on the left is shown scored for East-West bidding 2♠ and making an over-trick.

Once North has entered the score, he hands the slip to a member of the East-West team, who checks and initials it, and one of the players indicates that the slip is completed by marking a large "X" on the back. After each round of the tournament the slips are collected by caddies and taken to the scoring table.

N-S No. 1	Board No. 19	E-W No. 5
N S — Contract	Made 3 — Down	(E) W — Contract 2S
PLEASE CIRCLE POSITION OF DECLARER		
	Trick Score	60
	Extra Tricks	30
	Part Score, Game and Doubled Bonus	50
	Slam Bonus	
	Premium for Defeating Contract	
N-S Total	Do Not O.K. Erasures or Corrections. Make Out a New Score O.K. RBC	E-W Total 140

N – S PAIR	ALL DEALS PLAYED THIS ROUND WILL BE SCORED ON THIS CARD. CIRCLE DIRECTION OF DECLARER.				E–W OK			E – W PAIR
N - S SCORE	MADE	DOWN	N - S CONTRACT	BOARD NUMBER	E - W CONTRACT	MADE	DOWN	E - W SCORE
			N S		E W			
			N S		E W			
			N S		E W			

Tournament recapitulation sheets also carry more information than the recap sheets for smaller games. Since many tournament events are held in more than one session, the recap sheets usually have columns for scores carried over from earlier sessions, and for the total of all sessions. The match pointing columns are wider, allowing space for both the total point scores and the match point awards.

In the section for scoring North-South, the plus total point scores for North-South are placed on the left side of the space, and the minus scores on the right side. The match point awards are on the opposite side of the space, usually entered in red or blue pencil, to distinguish them quickly from the total point scores. The placement of total point scores is reversed on the East-West section of the recap sheet, so that any pair examining the sheet will always find its own plus scores on the left side of its own line.

Total point scores can be posted to the recap sheets as the pick-up slips come in to the scoring room. This permits the scorers to begin match pointing almost as soon as the last boards of the tournament have been played.

Carry-Over Formula

In many major tournament events, some pairs are eliminated during the early sessions of the event and the remaining pairs qualify to compete in the final rounds. Generally, approximately half of the pairs entered are eliminated, and the rest qualify.

The match point scores earned during the qualifying sessions are actually part of the tournament, but since they were won against a larger and presumably weaker field, only a fraction of these points are added to the scores of the final sessions.

In working out the carry-over formula, let

C equal the score to be carried over,
M equal the match point score in the qualifying rounds,
Q equal the number of qualifiers,
E equal the number of entries in the entire field,
A equal the final round average match point score per board,
B equal the number of boards played in qualifying rounds, and
S equal the sum of all scores made by all qualifying pairs.

Then, $C = M \times Q/E \times ABQ/S$

This formula is abandoned when the spread between the highest and lowest carry-over scores is too great, and it is replaced by a simpler formula that tends to narrow the spread. The spread may never be greater than the top match point score on two boards in the finals when there is one qualifying round and one final round; not more than the top on three boards when there are two qualifying rounds and one final round, and not more than the top on four boards when there are two qualifying and two final rounds. When the spread is too wide, the qualifying scores are simply multiplied by a fraction whose numerator is the maximum spread allowed and whose denominator is the difference between the highest and lowest qualifying scores. See Chapter IX, Section Twenty-Nine, of the A.C.B.L. Handbook of Rules and Regulations for more details.*

*See appendix I (page 231) for discussion of computer scoring.

5

Howell Movements

AS POINTED OUT in Chapter 3, the Howell movement is best suited to small duplicate games, usually with no more than seven tables.

The progression of boards and players is somewhat more complex than in a Mitchell game, and therefore it requires greater watchfulness on the part of the director. The movement is considerably simplified, however, through the use of Howell table guide cards, readily available from bridge supply houses. These guide cards enable the players to cooperate with the director in helping to run the movement properly.

Even with the guide cards, however, it is helpful for the director to know the positions of bye stands and bye boards, relative to the tables in play. The following guide shows the position of bye boards for Howell games of three to seven tables:

3 Tables -- one set of boards on a bye stand between Tables 2 and 3, and another between Tables 3 and 1.

4 Tables -- two sets of boards on a bye stand between Tables 1 and 2, and one set between Tables 2 and 3.

5 Tables -- four sets of boards on an assembly table between Tables 1 and 5.

6 Tables -- two sets of boards on a bye stand between Tables 1 and 2, one set between Tables 2 and 3, one set between Tables 3 and 4, and one between Tables 5 and 6.

7 Tables -- six sets of boards on an assembly table between Tables 1 and 7.

The director should take extra care to see that boards are moved onto bye stands and assembly tables, and should watch out for players who innocently or absent-mindedly try to follow the rule of moving the boards to the "next lower table." As an additional safeguard it is wise to place the bye stands and assembly tables squarely in the path between the two tables that they are connecting. This is virtually imperative in the absence of Howell table guide cards.

With or without guide cards, however, the director should learn how to use schedules and master sheets, such as those appearing in the appendices at the back of this book. These provide a continuous check on a duplicate game, whether Howell or Mitchell, and can be used as a check on the pattern of the movement.

How to Read a Schedule

A schedule is a complete diagram of a duplicate movement, arranged by tables, which is usually the simplest way for a director to visualize and follow the movement.

Here, for example, is what might be regarded as the simplest of all Howell schedules -- that for a two-table game:

	Table 1			Table 2		
Round	Boards	N-S	E-W	Boards	N-S	E-W
1	1-6	4	1	1-6	2	3
2	7-12	4	2	7-12	3	1
3	13-18	4	3	13-18	1	2

The schedule, it will be noted, can be segmented into separate schedules for each of the tables. Since a schedule is arranged so that table information is dominant, only the table numbers appear on the top line.

The column to the extreme left designates the number of the round. This is also where the round number appears on most Howell guide cards. The next three columns give complete information for the first table -- the boards to be played, the North-South pair number and the East-West pair number. This is followed by three columns with the same information for the second table.

In this schedule, it can be seen that the board numbers for both tables are exactly the same. In a two-table game, it is obviously necessary for both tables to play the same boards on the same round. (In any other arrangement, some of the players will have to play some boards more than once -- a clearly impossible procedure.) When the same boards are played at more than one table in the same round, this is known as a relay.

In any two-table relay, half the boards to be played are given to one of the tables, and the other half to the other table. As the boards are played, they are moved to a position between the tables (a chair will do), where they can be picked up by the other players.

While a schedule is relatively easy to follow, it grows more unwieldy as tables are added, eventually carrying far too much information to be taken in at a glance. For larger games, therefore, a master sheet can be used to compress the same information into less space.

How to Read a Master Sheet

A master sheet takes the form of a matrix to describe a duplicate bridge movement.

In the left hand column (or what is sometimes known as the vertical coordinate) are the numbers of the rounds, just as they appear on a schedule. But across the top (the horizontal coordinate) are the board numbers, rather than the table numbers. To find which pairs are playing a particular set of boards on any given round, one merely finds the column for the board numbers and the row for the round number. Where these two meet are the numbers of the two pairs playing that set of boards on that round. The North-South pair number is conventionally given first, then the East-West pair, in this fashion: 4-5 (meaning North-South Pair 4 is playing against East-West Pair 5.)

Here is an example of a master sheet for a four-table Howell game:

Rd.	Bds. 1-3	4-6	7-9	10-12	13-15	16-18	19-21
1	8-1			6-3		7-2	4-5
2	5-6	8-2			7-4		1-3
3	2-4	6-7	8-3			1-5	
4		3-5	7-1	8-4			2-6
5	3-7		4-6	1-2	8-5		
6		4-1		5-7	2-3	8-6	
7			5-2		6-1	3-4	8-7

The master sheet can show very quickly which pairs play against each other on any round. It also shows just as quickly which boards are played by these pairs, and which are bye boards on any given round (the blank spaces on the matrix). What it does not show as readily are the tables at which this should take place -- key information, from the standpoint of the director.

A study of the master sheet will show that diagonals, from the upper left to lower right, will show both tables and bye stands, from the beginning of the movement to the end. To simplify the process of following diagonals, and thus of getting table information as well as information about round and board numbers, a combined master sheet and schedule has been developed. The above master sheet would thus appear in this form:

Rd.	Bds. 1-3	4-6	7-9	10-12	13-15	16-18	19-21	Table
1	8-1			6-3		7-2	4-5	
2	5-6	8-2			7-4		1-3	4
3	2-4	6-7	8-3			1-5		3
4		3-5	7-1	8-4			2-6	Bye
5	3-7		4-6	1-2	8-5			2
6		4-1		5-7	2-3	8-6		Bye
7			5-2		6-1	3-4	8-7	Bye
	Table	Bye	Bye	2	Bye	3	4	1

On this combined master sheet and schedule, the rounds appear from top to bottom, in order; the boards appear from left to right in order; and the play at each table can be followed from upper **left** to lower right.

Howell Movements for 3-7 Tables

Schedules and master sheets for Howell movements for three, four, five, six and seven tables appear on Pages **157 through 165 in** Appendix C.

None of these has irregularities of any kind, except for the three-table movement.

With each pair playing against only five other pairs, the three-table game presents some rigorous limitations to the movement designer. The movement on the Howell table guide cards gets around the difficulty by having a three-table relay on the final round.

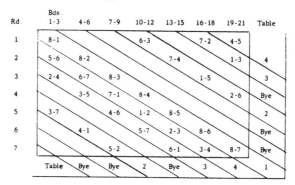

In such a relay, the boards are divided as evenly as possible among the tables. With three boards to a round, each table will get one board; with four boards to a round, the extra board is left available for the first table to complete its first board, etc.

With an even number of boards per round (four or six), it is possible to work out a three-table movement in which there is no relay, but in which the movement of boards to the various tables is considerably different from that in the normal Howell movement. A schedule for this movement is shown on Page 157, Appendix C.

Foreshortened Howell Movements

Whenever a Howell movement is ended short of completion, there will be some extra work for the scorer, as noted in Chapter 4. This happens because some boards will be played more times than other boards, thus making for different tops on the boards.

Let us see how this works out.

In the four-table Howell movement, for example, nine boards stay on the bye stands during each round of play, and the remaining twelve boards are in play. Since there are seven rounds in the movement, the total number of times that boards are played (counting each time each board is played as one) during the entire game will be seven times twelve, or 84. Because the number of boards in play -- 21 -- is evenly divisible into 84, the movement is balanced. If each board is played four times (84 divided by 21), all boards will have the same top.

Now let us suppose that a four-table Howell game has been started, and that the play is slower than anticipated. As the hour grows late, the director decides to end the game after six rounds. Twelve boards have been in play in each of six rounds, for a grand total of 72 boards played during the game. But since 72 is not evenly divisible by 21, some boards will necessarily have been in play more times than others. Thus the boards have different tops, and the director has scoring problems.

Once a Howell movement gets under way, then, it must be completed, in order to avoid these scoring difficulties.

If the time pinch can be anticipated, however, there are ways to foreshorten some Howell games by setting up special movements with fewer boards, in which all pairs do not get to play each other. Or, by increasing the number of boards per round, these special movements can be used to provide games with different numbers of boards than the normal Howells do.

Thus it is possible to cut a four-table game down to six rounds by putting just 18 boards into play. With three boards to a set, a total of twelve boards will be played in each round, and a grand total of 72 boards in the six rounds. Since 72 is evenly divisible by 18 (the number of boards in play), all the boards are played a similar number of times and have similar tops. Using four boards per set, the same movement provides a 24-board game. The schedule for this movement, which requires a constant relay between two tables, appears on Page **158**, Appendix C.

A full five-table Howell movement will normally comprise either 18 boards, which some directors consider too few, or 27 boards, which under some circumstances are too many. Two special five-table Howell movements can be used to vary the length of the game. In one, all pairs play 21 boards in seven rounds, missing two other pairs; in the other, all pairs play 24 boards in eight rounds, missing one other pair. The second involves a two-table relay. Both are based on the three-quarter Howell principle, to an extent. Master sheets for these movements appear on Pages **159-161**, Appendix C.

A full six-table Howell runs to 22 boards, usually deemed adequate, or it may be extended to 33 boards, which is far too many for the ordinary duplicate game. Applying the three-quarter principle to the six-table Howell provides an eight-round game of 24 boards, or a nine-round movement of either 18 or 27 boards. Master sheets for these movements are on Pages **162-164.**

The normal seven-table Howell game consists of 26 boards, and this can be cut to 22 boards by using the short (eleven-round) three-quarter movement. Master sheets are on Pages **165 and 171.**

All three-quarter Howells, of course, are shortened movements. They provide one-winner games over a reasonable time span, at the cost of not having each pair play every other pair. Master sheets for 26-board three-quarter Howell movements for eight to twelve tables appear on Pages **166-170** of Appendix C, and master sheets for the shorter 22-board movements for seven to ten tables are on Pages **171-174.**

Half Tables in Howell Games

An odd number of pairs should offer no problems in most duplicate games.

The odd pair creates what is known as a half table. In the Howell movement, a half table is treated just as though it were a full table. The odd pair is seated at one of the tables in the game. The table has a normal guide card. The usual set of boards is placed on the table. The only difference is that there are no opponents, and therefore, no cards are played at that table.

This situation is known as a sit-out, i.e., the pair at that table "sits out" one round of play. And the non-existent opponents for that round are known as a phantom pair.

The most convenient phantom in a Howell game is the stationary, normally the highest numbered, pair. Since this pair customarily sits at Table 1, this becomes the sit-out table. The director should announce the number of the phantom pair and the number of the sit-out table, so that the players will know when they reach the sit-out round. Since all the other pairs play the highest numbered pairs in rotation, this round will correspond to their own pair numbers. If any pair other than the highest numbered becomes the phantom, there can be no sit-out table, since the point at which the sit-out occurs moves from table to table (just as the phantom pair, if it were real, would move from table to table).

There is no change in the scoring for a half table Howell game, except that each board will have been played one time less than if the half table were a full table, and the top is therefore a point lower. The recapitulation sheet will show a regular pattern of blank spaces, representing the boards skipped by each pair.

The half table is handled in precisely the same way in a three-quarter Howell movement. Since there are more pairs than rounds in the three-quarter Howell, however, not all pairs will sit out. As a result, some pairs will play more boards than others.

If the highest-numbered pair is treated as the phantom in the three-quarter movement, then all other stationary pairs (that is, all those pairs that remain at the same table throughout the game) will play one more round than the other pairs. In such a case, it will be necessary to factor scores.

There will be no problem with board values, however, if the

three-quarter movement is completed, because all boards will have been played the same number of times.

Adding Late Pairs

When there is a half table in a Howell game, adding a late pair to the movement is no problem at all. The late arrivals are simply given the number of the phantom pair, and they then complete the movement, whether it is a regular Howell or a three-quarter Howell.

The late pair can be added at any time during the first round of play, or even after the second round has begun. They will then play their first round boards against the appropriate opponents after the rest of the game has ended, and while the other traveling score sheets are being scored. With this contingency in mind, the director should choose for the first sit-out a pair that will be willing to stay on to play a late round, if necessary.

Adding a late pair to a Howell game with full tables is trickier, but possible.

Although a half table in the normal Howell game is usually given boards and a table guide card, this will not now be the case. Instead, a second stationary pair is created, so that the movement will have some similarity to a three-quarter Howell.*

The second stationary pair will not be the pair that arrived late, but one of the moving pairs in the original movement. The simplest procedure is to make the original Pair 2 stationary, assigning it a new number just above the highest numbered pair in the original movement.

It is immaterial whether this pair is stationary in an East-West or a North-South position. Actually, it would be preferable to change the direction of their boards occasionally, so that about half the boards are played in each direction. The re-numbered pair should also make the appropriate pair number corrections on the traveling score sheets of any boards it has already played.

The late pair is then designated Pair 2, and it takes the normal positions of Pair 2 for the rest of the game. This pair, in effect, has had a sit-out for the first round. Other pairs arriving at the

*Since the movement of the boards is irregular, this method is not applicable to a six-pair Howell movement. It is necessary to rearrange the game into an eight-pair movement with a sit-out, if adding the late pair is necessary.

position of the new stationary pair will have a sit-out for that round, then will resume their normal movement, following the pair with the next lower number. If the new stationary pair has switched directions from their original position, they should advise any pairs arriving at their table of that fact.

In this movement the moving pairs will play one round less than the stationary pairs, and their scores should be factored up accordingly.

The same procedure can be followed in adding a late pair to a three-quarter Howell movement. The new stationary pair, however, should be the lowest numbered pair that is not already sitting at a table with another stationary pair.

The steps required for adding late pairs to various movements are shown in Appendix B, Pages **154-166**.

Adding Late Tables

Not only pairs, but full tables, can be added to a Howell game already in progress.

As in the case of adding a late pair, the new table is added without adding any boards to the movement. Instead, the new table relays boards with one of the tables already at play.

Since this new table is tacked on, or appended, to another table in the game, it is known as an appendix table.

The appendix table must set up its relay with a table that originally had two moving pairs. This is known as the transfer table of the appendix movement.

In setting up an appendix table, it is necessary to assign numbers and progressions to the pairs at the transfer and appendix tables as follows:

1. The East-West pair at the transfer table keeps its original number and maintains its original progression in the movement.
2. The North-South pair at the transfer table is assigned the next number above the highest pair number in the original game, and remains stationary at its table.
3. The North-South pair at the appendix table is given the original pair number of the North-South pair at the transfer table, and assumes the progression for that number.

4. The East - West pair at the appendix table is assigned the next number higher than the new number for the North-South pair at the transfer table, and remains stationary at its table.

With only full tables in play, there will be no sit-out and therefore no necessity to factor scores.

More than one appendix table can be added to a Howell movement, as long as there are tables with only moving pairs available, onto which the new relay tables can be tacked.

When a late pair has been added to a Howell movement at the end of the first round, and another late pair arrives early in the second round, an appendix table can be made up of the second late pair and the pair that is sitting out.

The transfer table in this case will be the table that had been given a new stationary pair. The pair sitting in the opposite direction at the appendix table will also be stationary. All the pairs that would have sat out in the late pair movement will now go to the appendix table, instead. The movement can be completed at the end of the game, when appropriate pairs play the boards missed earlier. Factoring will no longer be necessary.

The director may wish to work out a non-duplicating series of arrow switches for the new stationary pairs.

6

Mitchell Movements

THE MITCHELL MOVEMENT is the one that the duplicate director will encounter most frequently.

For the most part, he will find Mitchell movements to be trouble-free. But the true test of a director lies not in the simple situations, but in the difficult ones. A good director learns to handle troublesome situations with the confidence and grace that make them seem routine.

In setting up a Mitchell game, the director should try to arrange the tables in the shape of a U, or horseshoe. The lowest numbered table should be at one of the points of the U and the highest at the other end, with the others arranged in numerical sequence between them.

That arrangement will simplify changes, since players and boards need move only to the adjacent tables.

As already noted in Chapter 3, the best Mitchell games are those at which the stronger pairs are seeded, or scattered, through both the North-South and the East-West fields. This can be done by placing them at every second, third or fourth table, depending on the number of good pairs in the game.

Odd and Even Number of Tables

The Mitchell movement that all but runs itself is the one in which there is an odd number of tables. The boards and players in motion during the game move smoothly around each other. As a case in point, consider a seven-table Mitchell game, with three boards per round.

In the first round, East-West Team 1 plays Boards 1-3 at Table 1. For the next round, East-West 1 moves up to Table 2, and Boards 1-3 move "down" to Table 7. In the third round, the pair moves up to Table 3, the boards down to Table 6. In the fourth round, East-West Pair 1 moves to Table 4, and Boards 1-3 go to Table 5. Then, in the fifth round, the pair and the boards pass each other in opposite directions, East-West 1 moving from Table 4 to Table 5, and Boards 1-3 moving down from Table 5 to Table 4.

On each round after that, East-West Pair 1 will similarly bypass boards it has already played, and will find boards it has not yet played at the new table. The same thing will be true of every other East-West pair in the game.

But now let us consider an eight-table Mitchell movement of three boards per round, and assume that it is played in the same manner. East-West Pair 1 plays Boards 1-3 at Table 1 in the first round. Then Pair 1 moves to Table 2, and Boards 1-3 go to Table 8. Next the pair moves to Table 3, the boards to Table 7. For the fourth round, the pair moves to Table 4, the boards to Table 6.

So far, so good. But Round 5 brings trouble. Both East-West Pair 1 and Boards 1-3 move to Table 5 together. At the same time, every other East-West pair in the game moves to a table to find boards it has already played. The movement grinds to a halt.

This will always happen in a Mitchell movement with an even number of tables. So the first problem the director needs to learn how to avoid with an even number of tables in a Mitchell movement is that of having the East-West pairs meet the boards they have played before.

There are two ways to do this: The Mitchell movement with a skip, and the Mitchell movement with a bye stand and relay.

Mitchell with Skip

Let us again consider East-West Pair 1 in an eight-table Mitchell movement of three boards to a round.

On Round 1 they play Boards 1-3. On the second round, they move to Table 2 and play Boards 7-9, which were passed down from Table 3. They play Boards 13-15 on the third round at Table 3. On the fourth round, their boards are 19-21.

The fifth round was the one where they previously had trouble, running into boards they had played before (Boards 1-3). But suppose they pass by Table 5 for this round, and proceed on to Table

6. There they will find Boards 4-6, which they have not yet played. And every other East-West pair will similarly find boards they have not yet played, if they skip one table in their regular progression at this point.

If the normal movement is then resumed, East-West 1 will again encounter new boards -- 10-12 -- at Table 7. And at Table 8 they will meet Boards 16-18, which they have not yet played. Every other East-West team will have a similar experience. The movement is over, and the troubles noted for an even number of tables in a Mitchell game have been avoided.

But East-West Pair 1, in skipping Table 5, has not played against North-South Pair 5. And it has not played Boards 21-24. It would be nice if East-West 1 could now proceed to Table 5 and play Boards 21-24. But it wouldn't work. North-South Pair 5 has already played those boards. And North-South Pair 1, which has not played Boards 21-24, has played against East-West Pair 1.

So the skip by East-West pairs has in effect cut one full round out of the movement. Instead of playing all 24 boards in the game, all pairs will play 21 boards, and all will miss playing one pair in the opposite field. The recapitulation sheet will show a regular pattern of blank spaces for the missed boards.

The skip should be called after half the number of rounds that would complete the full Mitchell movement have been played. This will also be half the number of tables in the game.

Thus, in a six-table Mitchell game, the skip should come at the end of the third round; in an eight-table game, after the fourth round; in a ten-table game, after the fifth round; in a twelve-table game, after the sixth round, and in a 14-table Mitchell, after the seventh round. In each case, this is just before the players would have encountered boards they had played before, if the normal Mitchell movement would be followed.

It is up to the director to keep track of the rounds played, and to call, "All East-West pairs will skip one table, please," or "All East-West pairs will move up two tables for this round only." As a reminder, the director can list the number of rounds to be played on a sheet of paper, with a red line or asterisk at the point of the skip. As each change is called, he should cross off the appropriate round number on the sheet, in order to be aware of the skip when the time comes.

Mitchell With Bye Stand

Sometimes a director is faced with an even number of tables in a Mitchell movement, but does not wish to cut a full round out of the game with a skip. He (or the players) may, for example, want to play the full 24 boards in an eight-table or a twelve-table Mitchell game.

It is possible to do this by using a bye stand and relay, in place of the skip in the movement.

Let us see how this will work out, again using an eight-table game. The director will first place the appropriate boards at the first four tables. He will place the next set -- Boards 13-15 -- at a bye stand between Tables 4 and 5. The remaining boards will be distributed in order to Tables 5, 6 and 7.

Because one set of boards has gone to the bye stand, there will be no boards for Table 8. Table 8 will play the same boards as Table 1, by means of a relay, in each round of the game.

As in any Mitchell movement, the boards will always move to the next lower table, except that each set of boards will be short-stopped for one round when it reaches the bye stand, remaining out of play for that round. The boards shared by Tables 1 and 8 will move to Table 7. East-West pairs will move to the next higher table, and will participate in the relay when they play at Table 8 and at Table 1.

This schematic diagram shows the movement of Boards 1-3, the first set, and of the East player from East-West Pair 1 for the first five rounds of such a movement:

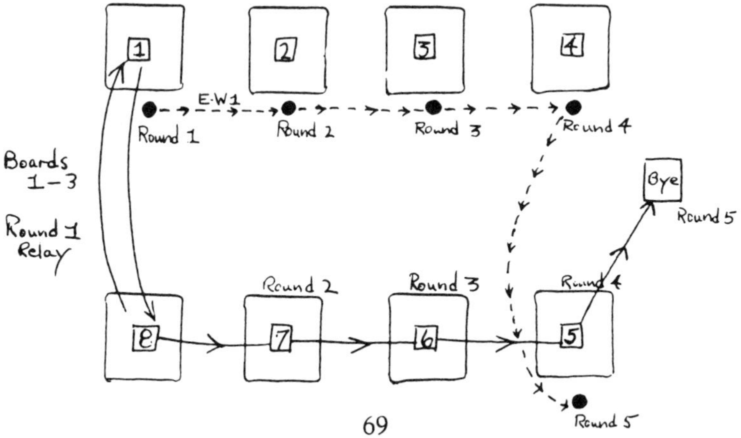

In this movement, East-West Pair 1 plays Boards 1-3 in the relay at Table 1; Boards 7-9 at Table 2; Boards 13-15 at Table 3; 19-21 at Table 4; 4-6 at Table 5; 10-12 at Table 6; 16-18 at Table 7, and 22-24 in the relay at Table 8. Thus East-West Pair 1 will play all the boards and will play against all North-South pairs, as will all the other East-West pairs.

In a ten-table Mitchell movement, boards should be relayed between Tables 1 and 10, and the bye boards should be played between Tables 5 and 6. In a twelve-table game, Tables 1 and 12 relay, and the bye stand is placed between Tables 6 and 7. And in a 14-table movement, Tables 1 and 14 relay, and the bye stand is positioned between Tables 7 and 8. (With 14 tables, however, the bye stand and relay procedure is somewhat redundant, since all pairs can play up to 26 boards with an ordinary skip movement.)

These tables are chosen as a matter of convenience in explaining the movement, and not because they must be the ones chosen for the purpose. As a matter of fact, the relay may be between any two adjacent tables -- as long as the bye stand is equidistant from those two tables. Thus, if Tables 8 and 9 are chosen for the relay in a 12-table game, the bye stand must be placed between Tables 2 and 3. In that way there will be five tables between the bye stand and Table 8, moving in an upward direction, and also five tables between the stand and Table 9, moving in the lower numbered direction.

Whenever there are relays in a movement, the relaying tables should be close to each other, preferably in adjacent positions, in order to facilitate the exchange of boards between them.

Sometimes it will be necessary for the director to adjust to the shape of the room in which the game is played, in order to keep relaying tables close to each other. Some juggling is certainly required in the extreme case when all the tables are strung out in a line.

In an eight-table game of this kind, for example, the director might decide to place the relay between Tables 1 and 2, with the bye stand between Tables 5 and 6. Or he might place Table 8 at one end of the room, next to Table 1, and Table 7 at the far end. Then there could be the more traditional relay between Tables 1 and 8, and the bye boards can be placed between Tables 4 and 5.

Relays are shown on master sheets by placing one of the relaying sets of pairs above the other for the round in which the relay takes place.

While master sheets are not really necessary for normal Mitchell movements, there are sample master sheets for an odd table Mitchell game, for an even table game with a skip, and for an even table game with relay and bye stand on Pages **175-177** in Appendix D.

Corrections for Misplaced Bye Stands

If the director, in the confusion that often surrounds the start of a game, places the bye boards in the wrong position, steps can still be taken to salvage the movement -- provided the bye stand was placed just one table too high or one table too low.

If the bye stand was placed one table too low (e.g., between Tables 3 and 4 in an eight-table game in which the relay was between Tables 1 and 8) trouble will develop just after the halfway mark of the game. The East-West pairs at two tables -- the highest-numbered table and at the table whose number is just half that of the highest-numbered table -- will meet boards that they played before. Thus, in the fifth round of an eight-table game with 24 boards, East-West Pair 4 (now at the relay table) will encounter Boards 13-15, which it played in the first round, and East-West Pair 8 will meet Boards 1-3, which it played in the first round.

At this point, the movement can be almost fully corrected, by following these procedures:

1. Start the round just after the halfway point with the normal downward movement of all boards, and upward movement of all East-West pairs.
2. Move the bye stand to its proper position.
3. Exchange sets of boards between the bye stand and the table that is now directly below the bye stand (but which has been directly above the bye stand until this round).
4. Have the North-South pair at this same table change places with the North-South pair at the highest-numbered table, for this round only. For scoring purposes, these two North-South pairs must retain their original numbers. (This exchange will result in the only flaw in the movement, since these North-

South pairs will play against East-West pairs they have met before, and will therefore miss playing with one of the East-West pairs.)

5. For this round and for the remainder of the game, boards will be relayed between the highest-numbered table and the second highest-numbered table -- no longer between the highest-numbered table and Table 1.

The round when these changes are made is known as the correction round. Following the correction round, all North-South pairs return to their original position, and stay for the rest of the game.

When the bye stand has been placed one table too high (e.g., between Tables 5 and 6 in an eight-table movement which has had a relay between Tables 1 and 8) trouble will again develop just after the halfway mark. This time it will be East-West Pair 1 and the East-West pair whose number is just above the mid-point that will meet boards they have played before.

The correction procedure is somewhat simpler, at least until the final round. These steps must be taken:

1. Start the round just after the halfway point with the normal downward movement of all boards and upward movement of all East-West pairs.

2. Move the bye stand to its proper position.

3. Exchange sets of boards between the bye stand and the table that is now directly above the bye stand (but which has been directly below the bye stand until this round).

4. For this round and for the remainder of the game, Table 1 will relay boards with Table 2, and the boards that would normally have been relayed between Table 1 and the highest-numbered table will be played at the highest-numbered table without a relay.

5. The last round is an adjustment round. North-South Pair 1 plays against the same East-West opponents they played in the round before the relay was changed, and they play the set of boards that North-South pair would have played if there had not been a change in the relay (the only boards these two pairs have not played to this point). East-West Pair 2 plays against the same North-South opponents they played in the

round before the relay was changed, and they relay their boards with North-South Pair 2.

All in all, the cure is almost worse than the ailment when a bye stand has been misplaced. Having once gone through such correction procedures, the director will probably thereafter exercise extraordinary care in seeing that the bye stands are always equidistant from the two relay tables.

Half Tables in Mitchell Games

Just as in a Howell movement, a half table in a Mitchell game may be treated as though it were a full table.

The extra pair is usually put in the East-West field, and started out at the highest-numbered table. That automatically makes the correspondingly highest-numbered North-South pair a phantom, and all East-West pairs will have a sit-out round when they come to that table.

If there is an odd number of tables in the game (counting the half table), a simple Mitchell movement can be used. A set of boards will be placed at the half table. All North-South pairs will get to play all the boards in this movement, while East-West pairs will miss one round. This means, of course, that average scores will be lower for the East-West field.

If there is an even number of tables, counting the half table, the bye stand and relay movement is advisable. As a matter of practice, there will be a bye stand, but no relay, in this case. Since the relay table is also the sit-out table, and therefore East-West have no opponents in this round, the boards can be played at their original table without being relayed. The East-West pair sitting out may even kibitz at the table with which they would otherwise be relaying boards.

Not recommended for an even number of tables, including the half table, is the skip movement. With a skip, an East-West pair would miss playing not only the set of boards in their sit-out round, but an additional set because of the skip movement. Furthermore, one East-West pair will skip its sit-out table, and will, as a result, play more boards than the other East-West pairs. As if this weren't already bad enough, one set of boards will miss the sit-out table, and thereby have a higher top than the others. Factoring becomes very involved, and this movement should be avoided.

The One-and-a-Half Table Appendix

Sometimes, when there is a half table in a game, the director may find that the standard movement he plans to use will result in either too few or too many boards.

With 9 1/2 tables, for example, a bye stand movement would mean that all North-South pairs would play either 20 or 30 boards, depending on whether there were two or three boards to a round. East-West pairs, meanwhile, would play either 18 or 27 boards. Both the director and players might feel that this would be either too few or too many boards for a satisfactory game.

Similarly, with 10 1/2 tables, the normal Mitchell movement would mean either 22 or 33 boards played by the North-South pairs, while the East-West pairs would play either 20 or 30. Something in between might well be preferred.

One way to get around this difficulty is to foreshorten a movement that calls for the larger number of boards by stopping the game one or two rounds short of completion. This is often satisfactory. But it is subject to the possibly trivial complaint that comparisons are unfair, because pairs in the same field play different groupings of boards. North-South Pair 1 in an 11 1/2-table game, for example, might play Boards 1 through 27, while Pair 3 would play Boards 7 through 33 -- so that almost a fourth of the boards played by these two pairs would be different ones. This may be bridge, the critics say, but hardly duplicate bridge.

A solution that has been worked out for this problem goes by the rather unwieldy name of "one-and-a-half table appendix Mitchell." The movement is slightly more complex to set up than most, but once it has been started it should move smoothly.

An appendix table always involves a relay, whether the movement is Mitchell or Howell, since such a table is added, or appended, to the basic movement.

In setting up a one-and-a-half table appendix Mitchell, the director should first subtract 1 1/2 from the total number of tables in the game. The difference he gets is known as the base, and this determines the basic movement. If it is an odd number, the game will be run much the way a straight Mitchell is run. If it is an even number, there will be a skip in the movement. The skip must come after the round that is equal to half the base number.

In this movement, all tables, including the half table, are numbered. Boards are distributed to all but the two highest-numbered tables. Table 1 will then relay its boards with the highest-numbered full table. And the lone East-West pair at the highest-numbered table has a sit-out round.

As in any Mitchell movement, the boards move to the next lower table (skipping the two highest tables, of course), and the players move to the next higher table whenever a change is called.

The one-and-a-half table appendix Mitchell can be used to some purpose with the following numbers of tables:

- 8 1/2 tables, to shorten the straight Mitchell from 27 boards (for North-South pairs) to a 21-board game.
- 9 1/2 tables, to lengthen the bye stand movement from 20 boards to a 24-board game.
- 10 1/2 tables, to lengthen the straight Mitchell from 22 boards to a 27-board game.
- 11 1/2 tables, to lengthen the bye stand movement from 24 boards to a 27-board game.

For any other number of tables, the movement has little real utility.

A master sheet for a 9 1/2-table game using this movement is included in Appendix D, on Page 178.

Adding Late Pairs and Rovers

To the possibly confusing assortment of Mitchell movements already discussed -- straight Mitchell, skip, bye stand and one-and-a-half table appendix -- still another must be added to make the director's repertory complete. That is the Rover, or "bump," movement.

The Rover can be used at any time as a distinct and separate Mitchell movement in any half table game. But its chief utility comes in the ease with which late pairs can be added to Mitchell movements without disrupting the game.

The principle is simple. The extra pair is designated as the Rover, and it becomes a moving North-South pair in either a straight Mitchell or a skip movement. The Rover moves to designated tables during the game, and "bumps" the North-South pairs sitting at those tables, replacing them for one round. When bumped by the Rover, the North-South pair has a sit-out round.

The Rover movement is based on the number of full tables in play, and the half pair is not counted as an additional table. Thus, with 11 1/2 pairs, there will be a straight Mitchell; with 12 1/2, the movement will be a skip Mitchell. The Rover pair is given the North-South number just above that of the highest North-South pair.

The Rover always starts to play in the North-South seats at Table 2. Thereafter it generally moves to the North-South position at higher-numbered tables, usually skipping one table on each round. There are enough exceptions and variations in this procedure so that the use of guide cards is advisable in a Rover movement. Or the director can merely copy the appropriate Rover movement on a slip of paper, and give it to the roving pair. Movements for Rover pairs in games ranging from 7 1/2 to 18 1/2 tables appear in Appendix E on Pages **186-187.**

What makes the Rover movement especially useful for accommodating late pairs is the fact that the Rover pair itself has a sit-out for the first round of play. That means that a pair can be put into the game as a Rover at any time until the start of the second round of play.

Late pairs can also be handled in a number of other ways in Mitchell games.

If there is already a half table in the game, the late pair merely fills out the table. In a straight or a skip Mitchell game, this will make no difference at all, other than to require late play of a board or two at the end of the game. Filling a half table in a bye stand Mitchell means introducing a relay between Table 1 and the newly-filled table. With a one-and-a-half table appendix movement, the late pair fills the half table, and the movement is changed to a straight or a skip Mitchell, depending on the number of tables, by giving sets of boards to the tables that have none. Or the one-and-a-half table appendix may be converted to an appendix Mitchell (see next section, below), if there is an appropriate number of tables.

If the Mitchell game already has full tables, the director has a wide number of options in treating a late pair, depending on the type of movement that was started and the number of tables in play. The chart on Pages **154-156** in Appendix B lists these options by order of preference in each case.

The same general principles may be followed if two, three or more late pairs are to be brought into a game. In such cases, the director must use his own ingenuity and judgment, since the combinations and permutations of options are too numerous to tabulate handily.

The Appendix Mitchell and Multiple Relays

One aspect of any relay movement is that it permits pairs to play a higher proportion of the boards in a game in fewer rounds of play.

This can be shown in a rather extreme form by picturing two 13-table sections side by side, with Table 1 of Section A alongside Table 1 of Section B, Table 2 of A alongside Table 2 of B, etc. In each round of a Mitchell game, each table of Section A relays its set of two boards with its corresponding table in Section B. At the end of the round, both boards are given to the Section A tables, for passing to the next lower table. Then all East-West pairs in both sections move to the next higher tables for the next round of relayed boards.

At the end of 13 rounds of play, each of the pairs will have played all 26 boards and each of the boards will have been played 26 times. More time will be taken than is normal for a 26-board game, since relays slow a movement. It is possible to score the game as though the two sections were one, with a top of 25 for each board, but this, of course, means that match pointing will be considerably more difficult.

Multiple relays can also be used for smaller sections. With five tables opposite five tables, all pairs can play ten or fifteen boards (depending on whether there are two or three boards to a round) in five rounds. Then the East-West pairs can change places, each moving to the corresponding table in the adjoining section. While the first group of boards are being scored, all pairs can play another ten or fifteen boards. A total of 20, 25 or 30 boards can thus be played by all pairs. The net result would be similar to a ten-table Mitchell game, without a skip in the movement. All East-West pairs would play all North-South pairs.

The same thing could be done with seven tables opposite seven tables, with 28 boards played and with no skip. With six tables opposite six tables, two skips would be necessary, so only ten rounds would be played. These multiple relays are sometimes called a twinned Mitchell movement.

Multiple relays can also be used within a single section Mitchell game. This is known as the appendix Mitchell. It is more complex than most movements, and it differs considerably from the one-and-a-half table appendix Mitchell.

But the appendix Mitchell does have the advantage of limiting the number of boards played in a large section (14 or more tables playing a 26-board game), and of permitting all the players to play the same boards. As in the multiple relays described above, tops on the boards go up one point for each relay that takes place. And the movement can be used to accommodate late tables.

The appendix Mitchell is built around a base comprising any prime number of tables. (A prime number is any number than cannot be divided evenly by any number other than one and itself. Sample primes: 5, 7, 11, 13, 17, 19.)

The movement can be used with any number of tables, but it needs to be based on a smaller prime number. The difference between that base prime and the number of tables in the game represents the number of relays that are required.

All this can be simplified with an example. Let us assume a game of ten tables. The highest prime number that can be used is seven, since eight, nine and ten are not primes. So the game will be set up with three relays, since seven from ten leaves three.

Here is the procedure the director would follow in running a ten-table appendix Mitchell game:

1. He would distribute three boards to each of the first seven tables.
2. Table 8 would be placed near Table 1 for a relay; Table 9 near Table 2, and Table 10 near Table 3.
3. East-West players at Table 1 through 3 would be instructed to remain stationary throughout the game; so would North-South players at Tables 8 through 10.
4. East-West players at Tables 4 through 10 would be instructed to move to the next higher table, but skipping Tables 1 through 3, at each change; North-South players at Tables 1-7 would be instructed to move up two tables, but skipping Tables 8 through 10, at each change.
5. All boards would move to the next lower table at each change.

This movement would permit a 21-board game for ten tables, which would otherwise have to be restricted to either 18 or 27 boards in a skip Mitchell.

It hardly seems worth the trouble.

But suppose the director has a nine-table game, but thinks another full table may arrive before the second round has started. He can set up an appendix Mitchell movement with two relays. If two other pairs arrive before the second round starts, he can put them at Table 10, slipping them easily into the movement, and requiring them to stay for a late play of one set of boards.

Scrambled Mitchell Considerations

The scrambled Mitchell movement described in Chapter 3, it will be remembered, is used for the purpose of getting a single winner in a Mitchell game. This is done by means of one or more arrow switches, or of moving the table cards around 90 degrees, in any ordinary Mitchell game, without varying the movement of boards or players.

Since arrow switches themselves do not affect any elements of a duplicate movement, it follows that they can be made with any kind of Mitchell movement. Therefore any kind of Mitchell movement can be converted into a scrambled Mitchell.

With certain types of movements, however, the director needs to take some extra precautions.

There is no problem at all with any Mitchell movement involving full tables, whether there is an odd or an even number of tables, or whether a skip movement or a bye stand and relay are used with an even number. The director need only make sure, as he must in any scrambled Mitchell game, that when he calls for an arrow switch the guide cards and boards are turned at all tables, including both tables involved in a relay.

The scrambled Mitchell will also work in games with half tables, whether the number of tables is odd or even, and whether a bye stand or skip movement is used (remembering that a skip movement is not recommended for any half table Mitchell game). The extra precaution that the director must take is in numbering the pairs. It will be remembered that North-South pairs in a scrambled Mitchell movement take their table numbers, while an East-

West pair takes the number equal to its table number plus the number of tables in play. So in order to keep the pair numbering consecutive, the director should count only full tables when announcing the number of tables as the base for East-West pairs to use in computing their pair numbers. The same thing is true in a one-and-a-half table appendix Mitchell movement, where the appendix table is counted as one of the full tables, but the half table is not counted at all.

The scrambled Mitchell can similarly be used with a Rover movement. But the Rover pair must be careful always to take the position that was originally North-South, regardless of the position in which the boards are to be placed in any round. With a Rover, the director should make extra sure that all the guide cards in the room have the same North-South orientation.

Other changes made to accommodate late pairs will have no effect on the scrambled Mitchell. Even if the addition of a late pair means changing from one kind of movement to another, this will not matter, since any Mitchell movement can be scrambled with arrow switches. But when there is a late play, it should be from the seats which the late pair would have taken on the first round in the game, and not necessarily the direction in which they find themselves at the end.

While arrow switches do not affect any Mitchell movement, they do add an additional complicating factor. If the movement is already a complicated one, the new director may find the situation bordering on total confusion. So it would be the better part of wisdom, in such cases, not to use a scramble with some of the more complex movements, such as multiple relays and appendix Mitchells. And unless a director has complete confidence in his ability to handle the problem, he should not permit late pairs in a scrambled Mitchell game if it means that the movement will have to be changed drastically.

Games of More than One Session

Sometimes a director may want to schedule a game that runs for two -- or possibly even more than two -- sessions. This will almost invariably be a championship event, and therefore it will seek to determine a single winner.

The simplest and least troublesome way to do this is to run the game as either two scrambled Mitchell or two three-quarter Howell movements, or, even better, one straight Mitchell game and one three-quarter Howell. As long as all pairs play the same number of boards, and all boards have the same top, the pair with the highest total score for the two sessions can be declared the winners

To make comparisons as fair as possible, every effort should be made to balance out any conceivable advantage that some pairs may have. With two scrambled Mitchell movements, for example, the pairs that originally had even numbers should take North-South seats, and the originally odd-numbered pairs should sit East-West. Each pair will then face approximately three-fourths of the other pairs as opponents at least once.

To minimize confusion, all pairs should be given new numbers for the second session, based on their new positions. Different recap sheets should be used for the two sessions, and the second session score should be added to the first according to names, rather than numbers.

If the director decides on using the three-quarter Howell movement for the two sessions, no pair should be permitted to take a stationary position (i.e., one in which they remain at the same table throughout a session) for both sessions of the game.

A minor problem the director may encounter with events that go on for more than one session is that the same players may not come back. If two sessions are held in the same day -- with one, say, in the afternoon and the other in the evening -- the chances are usually good that the same players will show up for both. But while this is a common arrangement for major tournaments, it is rare for local and club games. So the director who schedules multiple sessions several days or a week apart should be prepared to find some of his original players missing at subsequent sessions.

If new players show up for a second session, it is still possible to get them into the game. They will not be eligible for championship awards, of course, just as players who dropped out after the early session are ineligible. The simplest arrangement is to accept just enough new pairs to substitute for pairs that have dropped out. If one member of a pair drops out, and another is substituted, the pair should be permitted to take its normal position in the second session, but should be ineligible for championship awards.

What the director should try to do is make the second session as much like the first as possible, in terms of the type of movement and the number of tables.

When the director is quite certain that all the pairs that came to the first session will appear for the second, he can run an interwoven movement, to give his game greater symmetry. That is, final comparisons will be quite balanced, and all pairs will face all other pairs -- or almost all other pairs.

An interwoven movement consists of one Mitchell movement, preferably scrambled, and one interwoven Howell movement.

The interwoven Howell consists of two Howell movements combined into one. There are two separate groups of players in the game, just as there are two fields in a Mitchell movement. The members of one group in an interwoven Howell, however, play only against each other, whereas the members of one field in a Mitchell movement never play against each other. By combining the two, therefore, it is possible to have a two-session game in which virtually all pairs get to play against each other.

The principle on which an interwoven Howell is based is that of keeping all boards in play. One group plays the boards it would normally play in a Howell movement, while the second group plays the bye boards for that round. But since the normal Howell has one more set of boards in play than it has sets of bye boards, it is necessary to have one set of boards relayed in an interwoven Howell. The relay, of course, is between one table from each of the two groups.

When there is an even number of tables in an interwoven movement, the Mitchell game should have a bye stand and relay, and it will necessarily have one more round of boards than the interwoven Howell. When there is an odd number of tables, the first round of the Mitchell movement is omitted, and the pairs that would have met in this round will meet at Table 1 of the interwoven Howell, instead. In this case, the Howell has one more set of boards than the Mitchell.

If a full bye stand and relay Mitchell movement would take too long (as when there are ten tables, three boards to a round, thus a total of 30 boards), a skip Mitchell can be used instead. This would mean that each pair in the game would not meet one other pair in either of the two sessions.

Mitchell Movements

Master sheets for interwoven movements for seven, eight, nine and ten tables are included in Appendix D, on Pages **179-185**.

Games of More than One Section

When more players turn up than can conveniently be placed in a single game, the director can split the game into two or more sections. In effect, he will be creating two or more separate games.

Dividing a large group gives the director considerable flexibility about the kinds of Mitchell games he can set up. If 22 tables turn up, for example, he can divide them into two 11-table sections and run a straight Mitchell. If he has 24 tables, he can split them into sections of eleven and thirteen tables, in order to run straight Mitchell games in both sections, thus avoiding the need for either a skip or a bye stand and relay.

What should be avoided, however, are separate sections in which there are different numbers of boards per round, particularly if both sections are seated in the same room. With 20 tables, for instance, the director may be tempted to split the group into sections of eleven tables and nine tables. The larger section would naturally play eleven rounds of two boards each, for a total of 22 boards. Playing two boards per round, the smaller group would get to play an unsatisfactory total of 18 boards. So the director might decide to have them play three boards per round; curtailing the movement by one round would then give a total of 24 boards.

But then the players in each group would be disturbed by the changes called for the other group. The bridge player concentrating on a hand does not like to shift his concentration to other matters, such as whether he is in Section A or Section B, even though he feels obligated to heed any announcement by the director.

A much better arrangement for 20 tables, then, would be two sections of ten tables each. With a bye stand and relay movement, each section could play two boards per round, for a total of 20 boards; with a skip movement, each section could play three boards per round for a total of 27 boards (or 24 boards in a curtailed movement).

When the sections are of different sizes, the players may have to put up with some minor inconveniences. If the two games do not end at the same time, those still playing may be disturbed by the chair-shuffling and milling about of those who have completed their game. To alleviate this, the director should ask players who have finished their game to be considerate of others who have not. Or the director may decide on the more extreme measure of curtailing the longer movement by a round or two, in order to have the sections end their games simultaneously.

With one section of an odd number of tables and another of an even number, a skip might have to be called for just one of the sections, if that is the movement chosen. When the director announces, "All East-West players in Section B will skip one table for this change only," the players will have to listen carefully, and then decide whether it applies to them. Since such an announcement would normally come between rounds for both sections, this amount of thinking (extraneous to the real thinking about the bridge) should not be an excessive burden.

The same situation occurs when there are two sections of different sizes, both with even numbers of tables, if a skip movement has been chosen. The players will have to listen carefully to both skip announcements to see whether they are affected. (North-South players should listen, too, because it is their duty to ask the newly-arriving East-West pair whether they have just skipped a table).

This difficulty can be surmounted easily in larger tournaments where there are sections of varying sizes, but all with even numbers of tables. When the sections are large enough, the skip can be called before half the rounds have been played, without adversely affecting the movement. In an 18-table section, with 13 rounds to be played, for instance, the skip can be called at any time after the fourth round. In a 16-table section, with 13 rounds, the skip can be called as early as the fifth round. And in a 14-table section, with 13 rounds, the skip may be called after the sixth round. Thus, with three sections of 14, 16 and 18 tables, respectively, one skip can be called after the sixth round, to apply to all three. To determine the earliest round at which the skip can be called for any section, it is merely necessary to subtract half the number of tables in the section from the number of rounds to be played.

Twinning Boards

The description of the twinned Mitchell movement earlier in this chapter showed how two sections, with corresponding tables side by side, could relay boards throughout a game and thus make for a much higher top on each board.

The same result can be achieved without relays. Instead, the cards in all the boards for one section are matched, or twinned, in the other.

The procedure is quite simple. If Boards 1 and 2 are to be played at Table 1 in each of two sections, for example, the players in one section get two boards numbered 1 and the players in the other section get two boards numbered 2. They shuffle, deal and play the cards in one of the boards. After they have finished, they reconstruct the identical hands from the cards in the second board. The two tables then exchange the twinned boards, and they play the second board in the round. The identical thing is done at all the other tables for their corresponding boards in the first round. Thus each section plays the identical deals that the other section does.

If there are three sections, one section waits while the first hand is played in the other two sections. Then each of the tables that has played one board makes two twins of that board, one to be played by each of the other sections. If there are four sections, two sections wait during the play of the first hand, and those who have played will twin three other boards.

Twinning can be used to provide higher tops on each board, or simply to make the challenge more uniform for all sections of a multi-section tournament, by having all pairs play all the same boards.

The procedure for twinning can take various forms. Perhaps the simplest is one in which each player picks up the hand he has just played and arranges it by suits. The cards in the corresponding board are then placed face up on top of their tray, in either two, three or four fairly even piles. Each player then picks up cards that match those in his hand, until he has all 13. The hands are then checked against each other, and then carefully placed in the proper tray of the proper board.

In larger tournaments, hands are frequently pre-dealt and printed on sheets that are distributed to all tables, along with sets of boards. The players at each table make up the boards to match the printed sheets. (The cards are usually separated by suits in advance, to make the twinning easier.) The movement then starts, with the boards going to their next table.

Sections must be large enough, of course, so that the players can play the required number of boards without encountering those they have helped twin from the printed sheets. Thus, with a 15-table section, the twinned boards move to the next lower table, and the East-West pairs to the next higher table -- all before actual play begins. Each East-West pair will play the normal 26 boards before it encounters the boards it has helped twin. In a 14-table section, the boards could move to the next lower table, and the East-West pairs could stay put for the start of play. With a normal skip after the seventh round, the East-West pairs would play 26 boards without encountering the boards they helped twin.

Events with Qualifying Sessions

When a large field enters a tournament event that is scheduled for more than one session, it is a common practice to qualify finalists in the early session or sessions.

The number that will qualify in each section (usually about half of the number entered) is normally announced during the opening session. Qualification is customarily determined by position within the section -- and within the North-South or East-West field -- even though some non-qualifiers in other sections may have much higher match point scores.

Those who qualify are privileged to enter the final session or sessions. Sometimes the entire scores from the qualifying session are carried over into the final, although in major tournaments it is the rule to carry over only part of the score, as determined by the carry-over formula discussed in Chapter 4. A consolation tournament is usually held for those who fail to qualify. There is no carry-over to the consolation tournament, which often accepts additional pairs that were not entered in the original elimination event.

In most events in major tournaments, which always have enough entries to make large sections possible, straight Mitchell movements are the rule.

Mitchell-Howell Combination Games

When it is desired to get one winner from a field of 20 or 21 tables, an effective way of creating two sections is to set up two separate movements, one a scrambled Mitchell and the other a Howell. The scrambled Mitchell will have 13 or 14 tables, and the Howell will have seven.

In that way, each pair will be able to play 13 rounds against 13 different opponents, for a total of 26 boards. If boards are twinned, identical boards can be played in both sections when the Mitchell section has 13 tables. With a 14-table Mitchell section, an appendix Mitchell movement can bring about the same result.

If both sections are treated as a single field for scoring, there can be a 19-point top on each board, since each deal will be played 20 different times. If the two sections are scored separately, the Mitchell game will have a 12-point top for each board and the Howell game a 6-point top. Scores for the pairs in the Howell game will need to be doubled, in order to bring both sections to parity.

Each table in the Howell game twins one of its first round boards, and the correspondingly numbered table in the Mitchell game twins the other board for those rounds. Tables 8 through 13 will have to twin both of their first round boards, since these will be bye boards in the first round of the Howell movement.

The combined Mitchell-Howell movement can also be used with 22 or 23 tables, by enlarging the Mitchell section and using an appendix Mitchell movement. When the boards are twinned, however, all relay tables in the Mitchell section will have to wait until one board has been played and twinned by the other tables before starting play on the first round.

7

Individual Movements

THE SPIRIT OF FUN can readily enter an individual duplicate game, and the director should try to keep it there.

As players encounter unfamiliar styles and systems of bidding and play, misunderstandings are rife and results are frequently outlandish. At the same time, for those players who like to learn more about bridge -- as most good players do -- the individual game can be a learning laboratory. A sense of adventure and a sense of humor help make it a more effective one.

For the director, sadly, an individual movement can be anything but fun. Most of the movements are complex, and it is impossible for the director to keep a thorough check on the movement of players at the changes. Players are milling all around the room just at the time the director must move the boards. Because of the strangeness of systems and conventions, players seem more inclined toward post mortem discussions, making for more noise and delay. And a single mistake in player movements can throw the game badly out of kilter.

For this reason, the director should elicit maximum cooperation from the players in an individual contest. He should ask that discussions be curbed, particularly those involving conventions and styles that the players may never again encounter -- a prospect that they may find most pleasant.

While some player progressions in individual movements are as regular and uniform as those in a straight Mitchell game, they still vary from player to player. Because of this, it is always sound practice to distribute guide cards or guide slips to all players. The illustration on the next page shows a sample individual guide card. It should be noted that each player has his own number.

The participants have a strong temptation to check off on their personal guide cards the rounds they have completed -- and indeed this helps keep the game moving more smoothly. But it doesn't help the director, who then has to try to erase the circles, checks and crosses, including some in indelible ink. Nor does it help to have players absent-mindedly put the guide cards in pockets and purses, only to discover their inadvertent petty larceny several weeks later.

So it is a good idea to copy the guide card information onto slips of paper that the players can deal with as they wish. Or, better yet, distribute slips with the guide cards, so that the players can do their own copying.

24-PLAYER INDIVIDUAL

Player 1

Round	Position	With	Boards
1	1N	5	1-3
2	4E	21	13-15
3	1E	18	7-9
4	1S	4	10-12
5	5S	24	4-6
6	2S	17	19-21
7	6W	10	16-18

For small individual games, table guide cards can serve the purpose adequately, and individual cards are unnecessary. In either event, however, players should be asked to check the numbers of their partners and opponents on each round, as extra insurance that the movement will not be fouled.

Individuals for Eight Players

The simplest individual movement to construct is one for eight players, or two tables.

The two-table game lends itself to the ideal movement, in which all the players play all of the boards and in which each player has every other player for a partner once and for an opponent twice.

This can be worked out by using the Howell principle. The highest numbered player is stationary. He plays with player No. 1 as his partner for the first round, player No. 2 next, and the others in sequence. Similarly, as in Howell movements, each of the players numbered from 1 through 7 takes the position just vacated by the next lower numbered player, with No. 7 following No. 1. The game comprises either 21 or 28 boards, depending on whether there are three or four boards to a round.

The simple schedule on the next page shows the entire movement. It is also shown on Page **188**, Appendix F.

No boards are shown for Table 2, since all boards are relayed between the two tables throughout, always a necessity in a two-table game.

		Table 1				Table 2			
Rd.	Boards	N	S	E	W	N	S	E	W
1	1-3 (1-4)	8	1	6	2	5	7	3	4
2	4-6 (5-8)	8	2	7	3	6	1	4	5
3	7-9 (9-12)	8	3	1	4	7	2	5	6
4	10-12 (13-16)	8	4	2	5	1	3	6	7
5	13-15 (17-20)	8	5	3	6	2	4	7	1
6	16-18 (21-24)	8	6	4	7	3	5	1	2
7	19-21 (25-28)	8	7	5	1	4	6	2	3

This movement can be expanded up to 14 tables, or 56 players, by adding on more two-table sections. This will give as many different comparisons for each board as there are tables in the game. The limitation, however, is that each player can play only within his own section, and therefore has only seven different partners and faces only seven different opponents. A schedule for this movement will be found on Page 203.

In adding two-table sections, the sets of three or four boards are distributed to the sections in numerical sequence. If there are seven sections, each gets one set of boards. If there are fewer than seven sections, the highest-numbered boards go onto an assembly table between Table 1 and the highest-numbered table.

Each two-table section relays its boards within the section until it has played the full set. The boards are then moved to the next lower section, with the first section moving its boards to the assembly table, and the highest section getting its boards, in numerical order, from the assembly table.

The sections may be numbered or designated by letters. The players would be designated correspondingly. If sections are numbered, players in the second section may start with 11, in the third section with 21, etc. -- omitting numbers 9, 10, 19, 20, etc. If sections are lettered, players would be designated by a combination of numbers and their section letters (e.g., 1A, 3B, 7C, etc.).

Individuals for Nine or Ten Players

With nine players, it is clearly impossible to have a stationary player throughout, since each of the players must sit out for one round. Instead, all players move for all rounds. The schedule on Page 189 of Appendix F shows the movement, which follows the Howell pattern. Each player plays 24 of the 27 boards in the movement, and sits out for one set of three boards.

In a ten-player individual, the same situation holds, but with two players sitting out each round, so that each player will miss two rounds of the movement. Each player will necessarily miss having one other player as a partner (playing eight rounds, each can have only eight partners, although there are nine other players), and two of the players will be an opponent only once. A schedule for a well-balanced movement, created by Prof. Olof Hanner, appears in Appendix F, Page 189.

Individuals for Twelve to Fourteen Players

When only two tables are in play, it is a simple matter to relay either two, three or four boards between the tables. This lends a high degree of flexibility to the number of boards played and thus the length of the game.

But when there are three tables, at least three boards are needed for a full relay, so that a game that calls for a relay requires three boards to a round. That means that a complete individual movement for 12 players -- filling three tables -- calls for the play of 33 boards, which is too many for most duplicate games.

A schedule for a twelve-player game, showing the full eleven rounds, appears on Page 190 of Appendix F. But it is not necessary to complete the movement. It can be cut off after eight rounds for a 24-board game, or after nine rounds for a 27-board game. All boards will have been played the same number of times, and all players will have played the same number of boards. This curtailment has the disadvantage of limiting the number of partners each player has, but it also cuts the game time down to a more reasonable period.

It is also possible to run a 12-player individual without relays, as a Howell movement of eleven rounds of two boards each, for a total of 22 boards. This means that in each round there will be three sets of boards in play and eight sets of bye boards. The schedule appears on Page 190 of Appendix F.

A somewhat similar individual movement for 13 players, but with no stationary player, is shown in the schedule on Page 191 of Appendix F. There are 26 boards in play in this movement, but each player gets to play only 24, since he sits out one round.

A 14-player individual movement was worked out by James N. Kavanagh, of Fort Wayne, Ind., but a better balanced movement for 14 players was developed by Prof. Hanner. The schedule for the latter appears in Appendix F, Page 191.

The Individual for 16 Players

There are two individual movements for 16 players, one of them a movement of 15 rounds and the other for a 12-round game.

The 15-round movement is an elegant one in which each player gets to play with every other player for one round. With two boards per round, this means a total of 30 boards -- or a game that would last almost four hours, which most duplicate clubs feel is too long. But it is such a nice, well-balanced movement that it seems a shame not to use it when there are just 16 players. It would be worth rushing the game a bit, in order to get the 15 rounds played in reasonable time. Another possibility is a technique popular in England, where a board is eliminated from one or more of the rounds (in both pair games and individuals), in order to cut the game down to a more appropriate length.

The 12-round movement has a more convenient 24 boards. In this movement, four players are stationary, one at each table and each in a different compass position. The other players follow the familiar Howell progression, moving in numerical sequence. Only six boards are in play at any one time, and one set of boards is relayed between two of the tables.

Schedules for both movements are on Page **192** of Appendix F.

The Rainbow Movement

Up to this point, most of the individual movements considered have borne some resemblance to the basic Howell progression. That is, the players follow each other in numerical order, and there is frequently one stationary player.

The Rainbow movement for individual duplicate games bears a much closer resemblance to the Mitchell movement. In the Mitchell, it will be recalled, there was one stationary group (the North-South pairs) and two moving units (the boards and the East-West pairs). With the proper number of tables, or the proper modifications, the Mitchell movement can always be worked out so that pairs will encounter neither the pairs nor the boards they have met before.

In an individual game, however, there are five units that must be considered -- boards, North players, South players, West players and East players -- instead of the three units of a pair game. One of the five may remain stationary, of course, but the other four must move -- either in different directions, or to different positions in the same direction.

This is precisely what happens in the Rainbow movement. North players remain stationary. Boards move to the next lower table. South players move to the next higher table. East players skip one table and move to the next higher table after that. West players skip one table on the way down, moving in the same direction that the boards do. The three moving fields of players were once designated by colors -- red, white and blue -- and this is how the Rainbow movement got its name.

While the progression described above is traditional for the Rainbow, it is not mandatory. Any pattern will do, as long as each of the five units -- boards, North, South, East, West -- moves in a manner different from all the others.

Thus, if the director wished, he could have the boards reverse their traditional direction and move up one table, North move up two tables, South up three tables, East up four tables and West up five tables. The movement would work just as well, as long as the players were competent in counting tables. (Note that in a five-table game there are only five positions to which the units may move, so that any change in the pattern merely changes the field that moves to a particular table. Thus, whichever field is told to move up five tables will in fact be asked to remain stationary; whichever moves up four tables will actually be doing the same as moving down one table, etc.)

In the Rainbow movement, it can be seen, a player starting in one compass position will never encounter any other player who began in the same compass position, either as a partner or as an opponent. No East player, for example, will ever be at the same table with another East player. But, as in the Mitchell movement, his scores will be compared with those of other East players.

The Rainbow movement will not work for games of certain sizes. Suppose, for instance, there were six tables. The East player who played the first set of boards at Table 1 would next move to Table 3, where he would play the fourth set. His next move would be to Table 5 -- and there he would meet the first set of boards again.

So the Rainbow movement will not work for six tables. Nor for eight tables, nine tables nor ten tables. But it will work for five tables, for seven tables, for eleven tables, or for any other prime number of tables. So here prime numbers again assume importance, as they did in the Appendix Mitchell movement.

Thus the Rainbow movement can be used for 20 players (five tables), 28 players, 44 players, 52 players, 68 players, or 76 players.

The players are not limited to a single partnership at each table. They may play three boards with three different partners at a table. This is done quite simply by having North remain stationary, while all the other players move in a clockwise direction around North after each board is played. Or two boards may be played with different partners at one table by the simple expedient of having South and East change seats after the first board has been played.

But all players must be careful to take their original compass positions when they move to a new table, after a change has been called.

This chapter will continue to discuss individual duplicate movements in upward sequence of size, to correspond to the schedules and master sheets in Appendix F. When Rainbow movements are appropriate for a game of any particular size, it will be mentioned along with possible alternate movements.

Individuals for 20 Players

The five-table individual is perfectly adapted to the Rainbow movement. The trouble is that the full game provides for 15 different partnerships. At one board per round, that is generally deemed too few, and at two boards per round, too many.

A curtailed Rainbow would work, but this would cut down the number of partnerships -- already reduced to a certain extent by the nature of the Rainbow movement itself -- or, using the English system, it would cut down the number of boards played with some of the partners. Nevertheless, a schedule for a five-table Rainbow movement appears on Page 193 of Appendix F, for those who might like to use it. This is a schematic schedule, which helps visualize the positions of the players at the start of each round.

There is, however, another movement for 20 players in which each player gets to play with each of the other 19 as partners. This is a movement that is divided into four separate segments, or stanzas.

A game divided into stanzas differs from other duplicate games in that separate groups of boards are introduced into the game for each stanza, played by all the players (with occasional exceptions), and then withdrawn from the game as new boards are introduced for the next stanza. The boards that have been played at all tables can be scored while subsequent stanzas are in progress.

The players follow guide cards for their somewhat random movement in the 20-player individual, and need not be especially concerned about which boards are being played, except that they move the boards to the next lower table after each round. But the director needs to be concerned about the fairly intricate pattern of play, and should keep a close watch on where boards are being played, especially in the final stanza.

In a one-session game, this movement can reasonably accommodate only one board per table per round. In a two-session game, either two or three boards can be used in each set. (The full movement, with three boards per round, would call for the play of 57 boards, or 27 in one session and 30 in the second.)

The director distributes one set to each of the five tables. When a change is called, the boards are to move to the next lower table, and the players to the positions assigned on their guide cards. But the first stanza, although it has five tables and five sets of boards, has only four rounds. Thus the boards have not been completely played, so the director sets them aside for play later in the game. He then distributes the next set of boards for the second stanza.

All sets are played at all tables in the second and third stanzas. But in the fourth stanza, after distributing the new boards, the director re-introduces the boards that were not fully played in the first round. These he places at the appropriate table, at the rate of one per round, to substitute for the boards that would normally be played at these tables in the fourth stanza. In the master sheet for this 20-player movement on Page 194 in Appendix F, the numbers of the boards to be substituted and the numbers of the players to get those boards are indicated in parentheses.

This is not a simple movement, but it is one that a director can take pride in handling smoothly, once he has reached the point where he feels he can master it.

Individuals for 24 and 25 Players

A 24-player individual movement, for which guide cards are needed, permits all players to play 21 boards in 21 different partnerships.

The game is played in seven rounds, of three boards per round. With just 24 players, there will be six tables in play, so that there will be one set of bye boards on each round. The North player remains stationary during each round, and the other players move clockwise around him after each hand is played.

The movement is somewhat reminiscent of a three-quarter Howell, with the three highest-numbered players remaining at the same tables throughout the game. The other players follow each other in the Howell sequence, within their own groups of seven. A master sheet for the movement is on Page 195 of Appendix F.

The 25-player movement consists of five stanzas, each of five rounds. Every player in the game will sit out one round and play 24, and will have every other player as a partner for one round. Guide cards or guide slips are absolutely necessary for this movement.

The movement works better as a two-session game than in one session. As a one-session game, it is played with one board per round. Boards move to the next lower table in the group of tables from 1 through 5, until they have been played at all of the tables and the stanza is over. Then a new set of boards is distributed for the second stanza. Table 6 is given an additional set of five boards, and these remain at the table throughout all five stanzas. This means that there will be a total of 30 boards in play in this movement, although each player gets to play only 24 of the boards.

As a two-session game, two boards can be played in each round.

This permits Table 6 to relay boards with Table 1, and thus eliminates the need for an additional set of boards at Table 6. Each player has every other player as a partner for one set of two boards, and gets to play 48 of the 50 boards used in the game. Scoring can take place at the end of each stanza.

The neatest division would be 26 boards for one session and 24 for the other. But this opens up the possibility that some players may discuss boards they have played with others who have not, since one stanza will be only partially completed. If the director wishes to avoid this situation, he should schedule one session of 30 boards and another of only 20.

A master sheet for this movement appears on Pages 196-197, in Appendix F.

Individuals for 28 Players

Since seven is a prime number, a seven-table individual game can be run as a Rainbow movement. Seven rounds of three boards per round are played. There are three separate partnerships in each round, as the West, South and East players pivot around North after each board. Each player thus plays 21 boards with 21 different partners. The master sheet appears on Page 200 of Appendix F.

A second 28-player individual movement permits a complete cycle of individual play, in which each player has 27 different partnerships, and thus has every other player in the game as a partner for one round. Although this is based on the principle of the Rainbow movement, it is divided into four stanzas -- the first two consisting of seven rounds, the third of six rounds and the fourth of seven rounds.

As in the normal Rainbow movement, boards move to the next lower table after each round. In the fourth stanza, however, the director must replace one set of boards at one table in each round with a set of boards from the incomplete third stanza. In the master sheet on Pages 198-199, Appendix F, the substitute board number and the players who get that board are shown in parentheses. Sets of boards put in play in the fourth stanza will be played only six times, compared with seven times for all other boards.

This movement is quite adaptable to multi-session events. As a single session game, it runs for 27 boards. Distributing two boards per set for a two session game gives a total of 54 boards, nicely divisible at stanza's end into 28 and 26. Three or four boards per round can provide a four-session game of 81 or 108 boards, with the breaks coming at the end of stanzas.

Individuals for 32 Players

There are three different ways to run an individual game for 32 players. Master sheets for two of the three appear on Pages 201-202 of Appendix F.

Perhaps the most interesting of the three is an appendix Rainbow movement, in which an extra table is grafted onto a seven-table Rainbow. Four players -- one seated in each compass position -- remain stationary in this movement. The boards and all other players move between rounds, but they move only among the basic seven tables, and act as though Table 8 did not exist.

The boards move down a table, West moves down two tables, East moves up a table, South moves up two tables and North moves up three tables. This is an illustration of the complete flexibility of the Rainbow movement, noted earlier in this chapter.

But any player who moves to a position where a stationary player is already seated loses out in this game of non-musical chairs, and must go instead to Table 8. North takes his normal position at Table 8, but all the others move one position around the table in a clockwise direction, with West moving around North to the East position. There is a similar clockwise swing around North after each board is played, so that each player has three different partners in a round. The players at Table 8 thus play the third board in their normal positions. They then resume their regular places in the seven-table Rainbow movement, just as though they had not interrupted their normal progression.

The boards at Table 8 remain stationary there throughout the game. With 24 boards in play, this movement provides 21 different partnerships for each player.

For a 32-player individual in which each player plays all 24 boards with 24 different partners, there is a movement that requires guide cards. There are three boards to a round, and three different partnerships are created in the usual manner of a clockwise pivot around North after each hand. Players take their original compass positions for four rounds, then all shift (including North) to the next counterclockwise position for the last four rounds.

The third individual movement for 32 players involves two different groups of 16 players each, and is in fact two distinct 16-player movements. Each player plays only with the others in his own group, both as partners and opponents. But the same boards are played by both groups, so that there are eight comparisons -- and a match point top of 7 -- for each board. This movement, if completed, provides 15 different partnerships for each player, and a game of either 15 or 30 boards. After each round, the North player is responsible for returning the boards to an assembly table, and the North player for the next round should pick up his new boards, as indicated on the guide cards. There is no master sheet for this movement in the appendix, but the 15-round individual movement for 16 players provides a reasonably accurate facsimile, if boards are twinned and if players in the second section add 16 to their numbers.

Individuals for 36 Players

A guide card movement for 36 players is designed for nine rounds, and can be played with either two or three boards per round. With two boards per round, there are a total of 18 boards played and 18 different partnerships for each player; three boards per round permits 27 boards and 27 separate partnerships per player.

All players retain their compass positions for six rounds, then shift one position counterclockwise for the last three rounds. With two boards per round, South and East exchange seats after the first board. With three boards, East, South and West move clockwise around North after each board.

Another 36-player individual movement weds a seven-table Rainbow to a two-table individual. Boards are relayed among Tables 1, 8 and 9. This three-table relay requires either the use of three boards per round or twinning two full sets of additional boards.

This amount of twinning, of course, is extremely laborious and time-consuming, and is not recommended for the normal duplicate game. Without twinning, however, three boards must be played with each partner, since players do not pivot around North in this movement, but go on to their next change at the end of each round. Since the full game provides 35 different partnerships for each player, this would mean 105 different boards played in five stanzas. At the rate of one stanza per session, a five-session game is required, which makes it far too cumbersome for most duplicate games, including major tournaments.

Individuals for 40 Players

Two individual movements for 40 players can be used.

The first is a movement divided into three stanzas, with five different partnerships and two boards per round in each stanza. This provides a total of 30 boards for the three stanzas, and of 15 partnerships for each player. At the end of the second stanza, ten of the boards will have been fully played and can be match pointed.

The other 40-player individual movement also calls for 30 boards for the full game, but it can be cut short after eight or nine rounds, if a game of 24 boards or one of 27 boards is desired. This is a guide card movement, with three boards per round, in which players pivot clockwise around North after each board.

Individual for 44 Players

Since this is an eleven-table game, and eleven is a prime number, the Rainbow movement can be used. Using two boards per round, the full movement calls for 22 boards in eleven rounds, with 22 different partnerships for each player. South and East should exchange positions after the first board in the round, then resume their normal positions when the change is called.

Individuals for 48 Players

The appendix Rainbow movement can be used for the twelve-table game, just as it can for the eight-table game.

Again, the movement is constructed around a base of eleven tables. Also again, four players -- one in each compass position -- are stationary. In the eleven-table base, boards move down one table, North moves down two tables, East moves up one table, South moves up two tables, and West moves up three tables. A player coming to a position where there is a stationary player moves instead to Table 12, then resumes his normal movement on the next round. Table 12 keeps the same set of boards throughout the game.

There is also a guide card movement for 48 players.

Either of these movements can be conducted as a one-session or as a two-session game. In each case, there will be two boards per round. For the one-session game, East and South should exchange positions after the first board of each round, then resume their normal positions after a change is called. In the two-session version, all players maintain their normal compass positions for the first session, playing two boards per round with the same partner; then South and East should exchange positions for the second session. The one-session game consists of 24 boards, and the two-session game of 48 boards, with the guide card movement; both provide 24 partnerships per player. The appendix Rainbow movement has only eleven rounds per session, so that in the one-session game each player gets to play 22 boards, and in the two-session game 44 boards, with 22 partnerships per player in either case.

Individual for 52 Players

With 52 players filling just 13 tables, we have a prime number, which lends itself to the Rainbow movement. The movement runs for 13 rounds; with two boards per round, a total of 26 boards are played. To provide 26 different partnerships for each player, South and East should exchange positions after the first board of each round.

A two-session game for 52 players is somewhat more complicated, but a mixture of movements can permit each player to have every other player in the game as a partner for one board.

The first session is precisely the same as the one-session game described above.

For the second session, players take their original seats. Next, South and West must exchange seats. Now, the first board in the movement must not be played. Instead, the first change is called, with boards moving down, and South, East and West players making their normal progression for the Rainbow movement. From here on, the movement proceeds normally for twelve rounds of one board per round. At this point, each player will have played every player outside his own field save one, and no one within his own field. The game must now be changed from a Rainbow to an interwoven movement, similar to the interwoven Howells described in the last chapter.

The interwoven movement actually consists of four separate 13-player individual games, using the same group of 13 boards. Each player stays within his own field, except during what would be his sit-out round in the 13-player individual. The four players who would be sitting out will now play together at Table 13. They will be the same players who skipped a board in the previous Rainbow movement, and the board they will play will be the one they had skipped.

The interwoven movement in this two-session game requires guide cards.

Provisions for Odd Players

The individual movements described thus far have been able to accommodate 8, 9, 10, 12, 13, 14, 16, 20, 24, 25, 28, 32, 36, 40, 44, 48 and 52 players. Rainbow movements can also be used for 68 or 76 or even more players, but it is usually more feasible to split such large groups into more than one section.

Any game whose players fill out the tables evenly can also be reduced by one. That is, any movement for a game with, say, 28 players can also be used for 27 players. Player No. 28 is a phantom in such a movement, and the three players who would normally have played with him in any one round will have a sit-out for that round. In this way, provision can be made for games with 11, 15, 19, 23, 27, 31, 35, 39, 43, 47 and 51 players.

There are still some missing numbers, but all of these can be handled by splitting the group of players into two or more sections. With 17 players, for instance, the director could divide them into one section of eight and one of nine players. With 30 there could be two sections of 15 each (with six players sitting out each round), or three sections of eight, nine and 13 players (with only two sitting out each round).

It would be difficult in most cases to have the sections play the same boards, unless they were of the same size or, at worst, unless they played the same number of boards. But it would be one way of accommodating odd-sized groups.

There are better ways. One is to require advance registrations for an individual duplicate game. In this way a director can also know how big a group to plan for, especially if he does not have a full stock of guide cards for games of various sizes. Then, if players who have not registered appear, they can get into the game only to the extent that players who have registered fail to show up

Another method, which virtually guarantees a game of feasible size, is to have two volunteer stand-by players. For some suitable consideration, such as one or more free entries, or assuring a happy marital relationship with the director, the stand-by comes to the game without any assurance of playing in it. Clubs can rotate the stand-by role, with two stand-bys required for an individual game and only one for a pair game in which partnerships are guaranteed.

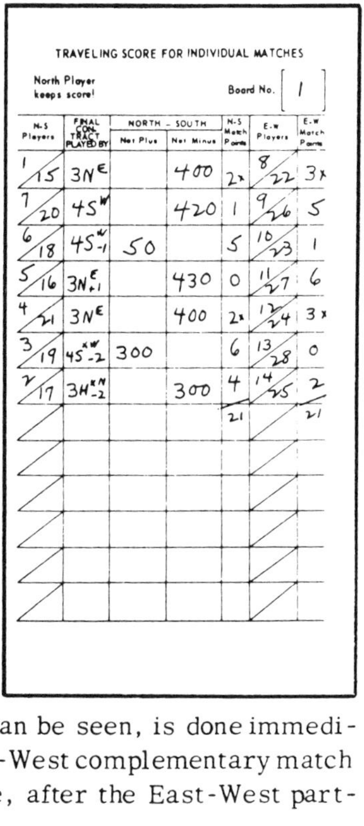
TRAVELING SCORE FOR INDIVIDUAL MATCHES

North Player keeps score!

Board No. 1

N-S Players	FINAL CONTRACT PLAYED BY	NORTH - SOUTH		N-S Match Points	E-W Players	E-W Match Points
		Net Plus	Net Minus			
1/15	3N E		400	2½	8/22	3½
7/20	4S W		420	1	9/26	5
6/18	4S W -1	50		5	10/23	1
5/16	3N E +1		430	0	11/27	6
4/21	3N E		400	2½	12/24	3½
3/19	4S XW -2	300		6	13/28	0
2/17	3H XN -2		300	4	14/25	2
				21		21

Scoring Individuals

The traveling score sheet for an individual duplicate game is necessarily different from the pair game traveler, since it must allow for entering scores for four different players each time a board is played. The standard score sheet used for individuals is shown at the right.

The example shown is from a seven-table game. Players are asked to place the lower number above the slash line for each partnership and the larger number below. This simplifies the entries from the traveling scores to the recapitulation sheet, where the players are entered in numerical order.

The North-South match pointing, it can be seen, is done immediately after the total score, and the East-West complementary match point score is entered on the same line, after the East-West partnership numbers.

Because the player numbers rarely appear in order, extra care must be exercised in entering the match point scores on the recapitulation sheet.

8

Team-of-Four Movements

MOST TYPES of team-of-four competition permit five, or as many as six, players to a team. This allows for substitutions of pairs or individuals during a match, usually between sessions. The advantages of this system become especially obvious during the long drawn out and exhausting play of major tournaments.

A club team-of-four contest, however, can do very well with just four players on each team, particularly if the game is to be completed in a single session. Play in such a game is no more trying than that of the ordinary duplicate pair contest.

In team-of-four play, each full team gets a number, and the two pairs that make up the team are designated by that number and by their compass positions at the start of the match. Thus, one pair will be known, for example, as North-South 5, and their teammates will be East-West 5 throughout the contest.

All team-of-four movements are designed so that each board is played team against team. That is, the two pairs of one team will play the same boards against the two pairs of one other team. If North-South 1, for example, plays Boards 7-9 against East-West 5, then East-West 1 will play those three boards against North-South 5. This is the standard way of comparing team strength, and it is the rule for team-of-four play in all situations, whether there are two or twenty teams in a game.

Team-of-Four Scoring

Four different types of scoring are used in team-of-four games:

1. Board-a-match
2. Total points
3. International Match Points (IMPs)
4. Victory Points

Board-a-match scoring is the same as match point scoring, but with only two tables in play. Either the same result will be achieved at both tables, or there will be a North-South winner at one table (the North-South pair that does better than the other) and an East-West winner at the second table. But both these winning pairs are on the same team-of-four, so their team wins the point. The only match point scores awarded in board-a-match scoring are one, one-half or zero.

These team-against-team comparisons are the only ones made at board-a-match scoring, regardless of how many other pairs play the same board and what results they have achieved. North-South 3 may bid 4♠ on a board and make six against East - West 8, while North-South 8 may bid 7♠ on the same deal against East - West 3 and go down one. Team 3 gets one match point, even though every other North-South team in the room bids and makes 6♠. The winner of the game, of course, is the team with the highest match point score.

In total point scoring, the actual points scored by one of the teams are compared to the points scored by the other, in order to determine the winner. Since vulnerability is predetermined by the boards, this differs from rubber bridge scoring in that a vulnerable game is worth 500, a non-vulnerable game 300, and a part score 50. But, as in rubber bridge, honors are usually included as part of the score. In total point scoring, a large swing on a single deal can make a substantial difference in the final results.

To modify the effects of such swings, while still maintaining some of the characteristics of rubber bridge scoring, the system of International Match Points was devised in Europe, and quickly won widespread acceptance around the world.

International Match Points, more familiarly called IMPs in the duplicate bridge world, are based on the differences between the scores of two teams. A very small difference, such as that between making a contract of 2♡ and a contract of 2NT, is worth nothing at all. A very sizable difference, amounting to 4,000 total points or more, is worth 24 IMPs. Generally, a difference of 10 to 12 IMPs is considered a fairly substantial swing on one board, and this can represent anything from 430 to 740 total points. A total point difference that is about twice as great, or from 900 to 1490 points, however, is worth only 14 to 16 IMPs, or very little more.

Thus the big swings are rewarded in IMP scoring, but not so substantially that such disasters on one or two hands are fatal for the unfortunate team.

Here is the IMP scoring table that became effective in 1962:

Difference	IMPs	Difference	IMPs
0 to 10	0	750 to 890	13
20 to 40	1	900 to 1090	14
50 to 80	2	1100 to 1290	15
90 to 120	3	1300 to 1490	16
130 to 160	4	1500 to 1740	17
170 to 210	5	1750 to 1990	18
220 to 260	6	2000 to 2240	19
270 to 310	7	2250 to 2490	20
320 to 360	8	2500 to 2990	21
370 to 420	9	3000 to 3490	22
430 to 490	10	3500 to 3990	23
500 to 590	11	4000 or more	24
600 to 740	12		

If both pairs on a team-of-four make plus scores on the same board, their IMPs are awarded on the basis of their total positive scores. If one pair on a team has a plus and the other a minus, but the plus is larger, the IMPs will be based on the difference between those scores. Only one team may get an IMP score on any board. The team that has a net minus score simply gets no score at all.

Normal Mitchell-Howell traveling score sheets will do quite well for all three scoring methods. All official scoring should be done by the North players. An East-West pair may, if it wishes, keep a separate score sheet as a check, but care should be taken not to mingle these with the official tallies.

Victory point scoring is used principally in large tournaments, but may be used to score club team-of-four games as well. The use of Victory Points is treated in the next chapter.

Types of Team-of-Four Contests

Most team-of-four events are just like any other duplicate game -- one-session contests in which a number of teams enter, and the top scoring team comes away the winner. This will almost always be an event with board-a-match scoring. With a possible top of only 1 on each board, such competitions are likely to end with a number of teams closely bunched near the head of the list.

In these games, as in normal pair games, each team gets to play from two to five boards against every other team, or against most of the other teams, depending on the size of the field. A larger field ordinarily requires two sessions to get comparisons among all teams.

Other team-of-four games consist of a series of head-to-head matches; these are prevalent in major tournaments, or in continuing competitions over a long period of time, even up to a year in duration.

In these head-to-head matches, one team plays for an entire session, usually lasting anywhere from 24 to 32 boards (invariably a number divisible by four) against one other team, with one of the two teams emerging as the winner of that match. In later sessions these teams take on still other teams, and the winner of the most matches ultimately becomes the winner of the contest.

These sessions may be held on succeeding days, or sometimes two a day, as in major national tournaments, or they may be held over longer intervals, such as one every two or three weeks or a month. Those that are spaced out in this fashion may be run by having all teams meet in a central playing room, or individual matches may be arranged between the teams and held in their homes.

For all these methods of play, the outcome should be the same. But the manner of conducting the game differs substantially. When the players all meet in a single game area, all the teams can use the same boards. The larger number of comparisons that can be made usually adds interest to the game, although these do not affect the scoring. The movement, which is quite simple, is described below.

Head-to-head matches may take one of two forms: round robin or knockout. In a round robin event, every team entered gets to play at least one match with every other team in the contest. But if two matches are played with one other team, then two matches must be played with all other teams. The winner is simply the team that wins more matches than any other. In the event of ties, if there is no time allotted for a playoff, then the winner is the team that won the match between the two contending teams.

A knockout event is a multiple elimination contest. A team that loses a fixed number of its head-to-head matches (usually one or two) is knocked out of the contest. In a double knockout event there will eventually be only two teams left in the contest. They play each other until one team has lost two matches.

Head-to-Head Match Movements

When two teams meet in the privacy of their homes, the play should be in separate rooms. One pair from a team sits North-South at one table; the other pair sits East-West at the second table. One-fourth of the boards to be played go to each table, and the cards are shuffled, dealt and played, and the boards scored. The scores are kept at the tables, and do not travel with the boards. The two tables then exchange boards and play them.

When half the boards in the match have been played in this manner, scores may be compared, by common consent of the two teams and the local regulations. They are then ready to start the second half of the match.

For the second half, the North-South pair from one team moves into the other room and exchanges places with its teammates. Both pairs of the other team, however, remain stationary. In this way, each pair from each team has an opportunity to play against both pairs of the other team. The remaining boards are then distributed, half to each table, and shuffled, dealt, played and exchanged. If 28 boards are to be played in all, seven boards will be distributed to a table for each of the four segments of the match.

The procedure is considerably different when all the teams meet in the same playing area.

Here the tables are arranged as at any duplicate game. At the start, all the members of a team sit at the same table. Then the director instructs the East-West pairs to move to the table of their opponents for the session. This should be as far distant from their home table as possible, in part so that the pairs on any one team may not hear each other's shouts of triumph or cries of anguish.

Then half the total number of boards to be played are distributed among the tables. After each round the boards are moved in their customary direction -- to the next lower table -- but the players remain where they are. The entire movement must be completed, i.e., all tables must play all boards.

Next the two pairs on one of the two competing teams in each match exchange places. (As a rule of convenience, the director should ask the lower-numbered team in each match to remain stationary.) Then the remaining boards are distributed to the tables, played and moved in the same manner.

If pick-up slips are not used for scoring, it is customary to permit the teams to do their own score-keeping (usually using IMP scoring in this type of contest). After agreeing on the outcome, they report to the director only who won the match and the margin of victory.

Movement for Odd Number of Tables

In a game of one or two sessions in which each team competes with the whole field, players as well as boards must move, so that more complicated progressions are necessary.

When there is an odd number of tables in the game, however, the movement is hardly more difficult than that of a straight Mitchell game. It is known as the American Whist League movement, and is sometimes called the skip progression.

All members of each team sit at the same table at the start of the game, and the teams take the numbers of the tables at which they first sit. Boards are distributed to tables in their normal sequence, with the lowest-numbered set going to Table 1.

Before the cards are shuffled and dealt, however, the first change is called. This will separate the pairs on the same team, and thus get the game ready for play.

At each change, the boards move to the next lower table. The East-West pairs move in the same direction, but they skip a table at each change. Thus, East-West Pair 9 starts at Table 9 in a 13-table game, but plays its first boards at Table 7, after the first change is called. At the succeeding changes, this pair will move, in order, to Table 5, then Table 3, Table 1, Table 12, Table 10, Table 8, Table 6, Table 4, Table 2, Table 13 and Table 11. With twelve rounds played, the movement will be complete.

As another feature of this movement, both the North-South and East-West pairs play all their sets of boards in sequence--North-South in the normal upward sequence and East-West in downward sequence. The East-West pair whose movement was described above will start out playing Boards 15-16, then 13-14, then 11-12, etc.

It is a simple and elegant movement, and it has very little chance of going astray, with reasonably intelligent and attentive players. All teams should get to play all boards and all opposing teams, and all North-South pairs play each set of boards against the same team that their East-West teammates meet on those boards. The field must therefore be limited to the number of teams that can complete the movement in a single session.

A master sheet is hardly needed, but a sample master sheet for a 13-table game appears on Page 204, Appendix G.

Split Movement for Even Number of Tables

The American Whist League movement obviously will not work with an even number of tables. For the East-West pairs, moving two tables at a time, will arrive back at the table (and the North-South pair) where they started.

A number of methods have been devised to get around this difficulty. Probably the most adaptable and easiest to use is the split movement, in which the game is split into two segments, insofar as the distribution of boards is concerned.

There are two irregularities in this movement, but they are different from the many irregular features encountered thus far, and they are perhaps a trifle more difficult to execute. They are, in order:

1. The cross-over: The East-West pairs pick up the boards they have just finished playing and take them to their home tables, at which their partners are sitting in the North-South seats.
2. The split: The boards are redistributed by the director in a pattern that resumes their movement just before the cross-over took place -- just as though there had been no rounds of play between the cross-over and the split.

And if the semantics of defining those terms are not difficult enough, there is this additional complication: the cross-over and the split take place after different rounds, depending on the number of tables in play.

To help simplify these movements, there are master sheets for 8, 10, 12, 14, 16, 18 and 20 tables, based on the split movement, on Pages 205-211 of Appendix G.

The split movement begins in the same way as the American Whist League movement, with all teams seated together at their tables, and all boards distributed in normal sequence. The first change is called, again in the same manner, before any boards have been played. Boards move down one table, and East-West players move down two tables.

The game proceeds in this manner until the cross-over. Then the East-West pairs take the boards they have just played to their home tables, and make a special move to the table of the team-mates of the pair that their partners have just played.

From this point, they move down two tables at each change -- until the split, or break. Here there are two irregularities in the movement. The East-West pairs make another special move, as indicated in the chart on Page 113, and the director must take the boards and redistribute them. If the last set of boards played at Table 1 before the cross-over consisted of Boards 4-6, then Boards 7-9 must now go to Table 1; if they were Boards 11-12, then Boards 13-14 now go to Table 1. All the other boards are distributed in normal upward sequence. The director need only keep in mind the boards that Table 1 played just before the cross-over.

From here on the progression will be the same as in a game with an odd number of tables. Boards continue moving to the next lower table, and East-West pairs move down two tables.

For the final round, new boards must be introduced, and shuffled and dealt. These boards must be relayed between pairs on the same teams. These relays are all shown on the master sheets. As a general guide, however, the teams simply play with the only teams they have not yet met in the game.

If the game has already run long enough, the final round can easily be omitted. This will mean that each team will miss meeting one other team in the game, hardly a major problem.

The chart below gives the following information for games from eight through twenty tables:

The round after which the cross-over is made.

The set of boards at Table 1 for the round <u>after</u> the cross-over.

(Sets of boards are designated by letters of the alphabet in this chart. In a ten-table game, for example, the sets are shown as "A" through "J". But it should be noted that the first set of boards played at Table 1 is "B", not "A", since boards are moved to the next lower table before the first round is played.)

The East-West pair at Table 1 for the round after the cross-over.

The table at which East-West Pair 1 will play in the round after the cross-over.

The round after which the split (and redistribution of boards) takes place.

The set of boards at Table 1 for the round after the split.

The East-West pair at Table 1 for the round after the split.

The table at which East-West Pair 1 will play in the round after the split.

The relay round.

Tables	Cross-over	Bds. at Table 1	E-W at Table 1	E-W 1 at Table	Split	Bds. at Table 1	E-W at Table 1	E-W 1 at Table	Relay
8	1	H	7	3	2	C	6	4	7
10	2	I	7	5	4	D	8	4	9
12	2	K	9	5	4	D	8	6	11
14	3	L	9	7	6	E	10	6	13
16	3	N	11	7	6	E	10	8	15
18	4	O	11	9	8	F	12	8	17
20	4	Q	13	9	8	F	12	10	19

The larger team-of-four games are usually played in two sessions. The split is often a convenient point at which to break after the first session.

The Double Skip Movement

There is another, perhaps simpler, method of handling even numbers of teams -- a method that eliminates the need for having East-West players take boards to their teammates, as well as the need for the director to make a special move of the boards.

This might be called the double skip movement, and it works in this way:

There are two points of irregularity in the East-West player movement and one in the board progression. The number of the round just preceding the first irregularity is indicated as "special first" in the chart below. The East-West players skip an extra table after this round has been played (from Table 6 to Table 3, for example) and the boards move normally. The number of the round just preceding the second irregularity is indicated as "special second" in the chart. The East-West pairs skip an extra table after this round, as well, and the boards skip a table on the way down, instead of moving to the next lower numbered table. The last, or relay, round is the same as in the split movement.

Tables	Special First	E-W at Table 1	E-W 1 at Table	Special Second	Bds. at Table 1	E-W at Table 1	E-W 1 at Table	Relay
8	1	6	4	5	H	7	3	7
10	2	8	4	6	I	7	5	9
12	2	8	6	8	K	9	5	11
14	3	10	6	9	L	9	7	13
16	3	10	8	11	N	11	7	15
18	4	12	8	12	O	11	9	17
20	4	12	10	14	Q	13	9	19

Stagger Movement for Even Number of Tables

In the Stagger movement, there are constant relays among all tables and during all rounds.

The even-numbered field is divided in two, and the first table in the first half relays with the first table in the second half, the second table in the first half relays with the second table in the second half, etc. Thus, with a ten-table movement, Table 1 would relay with Table 6 and Table 2 would relay with Table 7.

The boards are also divided between the two stanzas, half of them to be played in the first stanza and half in the second.

There are as many rounds as there are teams entered, but the first round of play is skipped entirely. As in most other team-of-four movements, this is the round in which members of the same team are seated at the same table. Boards then move down one table, and East-West pairs move down two tables.

Since the first round is skipped, each team will miss playing one set of boards in the first stanza. In the second stanza, however, all boards will be played by all teams. To start the second stanza,

East-West pairs move down three tables from the point at which they finished the previous round. Otherwise, skipping down the usual two, they would meet their own teammates.

A master sheet for a ten-table game, using the Stagger movement, appears on Page 212, Appendix G.

New England Relay Movement for Even Number of Tables

This is another movement with a constant relay involving all the tables in the game.

This time, however, instead of splitting the game into two stanzas, bye stands with bye boards are used.

Again, the field is split into two sections, and the relays are conducted in the same manner, with the lowest-numbered tables in one section relaying with the lowest-numbered table in the other.

Teams start by sitting together at their tables. Then the boards are distributed in sequence, starting with Table 1 -- but then alternating between bye stands and tables. The higher-numbered group of tables get no boards at all at the start of the game.

For the first round of play, boards make one move toward Table 1, going from tables to adjacent bye stands and from bye stands to the next table. All East-West pairs move down one table. Then the boards are played in relays among all the paired tables. At the end of a round, the boards are re-assembled for movement from the lower-numbered table in each relay.

Master sheets of games of six teams and ten teams, using the New England Relay, appear on Pages 213-214 of Appendix G.

Mirror Mitchell Movement for Even Number of Tables

Still another full game relay for an even number of tables in team-of-four games is the Mirror Mitchell movement, sometimes called the Barclay movement.

In this movement, too, the field is split into two sections, and the boards are all relayed between corresponding tables in the two sections. Instead of assembling teams at the same table, however, the East-West pairs take their initial positions at the table with which their partners will relay the first set of boards. Thus, in a ten-table game, Table 1 will relay with Table 6, so North-South 1 will play against East-West 6, and East-West 1 will play against North-South 6. In this way, both parts of each team-of-four duel take place simultaneously.

When the change is called, boards and East-West pairs in the first half make the standard Mitchell moves, the boards going down one table and the players going up one table. In the second group, the boards also move down one table, but the East-West players remain stationary while the North-South pairs move up one table. In this way, both pairs in each team will continually be relaying boards with their partners.

The disadvantage of this movement is that relay tables should be near each other, while it is imprudent to place members of the same team close together when they are playing the same set of boards. This can be largely circumvented by having each pair of relay tables twin their boards during the first round. With twinned boards for the full movement, it is no longer necessary to relay -- nor, by the same token, to keep the tables close together.

When each of the sections has an odd number of tables, the movement can be run as a straight Mitchell. But when each section has an even number of tables, it is necessary to use one of the standard Mitchell movement modifications, such as a skip movement or a bye stand and relay movement.

Team-of-Two-Pairs

Another type of game that clubs may use is known as the team-of-two-pairs. This is differentiated from the team-of-four contest in that the two pairs of a team sit in the same direction (either North-South or East-West) against two pairs of an opposing team. The teams play a set number of boards against each other, as in team-of-four play.

In scoring, the higher score of each team's pairs becomes the team's score, either in IMPs or total points. Thus each team may end up with a plus score at the end of the match.

Players have quickly found ways to capitalize on this type of scoring. One pair, for example, might bid boldly and the other conservatively; one might take all finesses to the left, and the other to the right.

As a countermove, some clubs change the scoring to make the worst result, rather than the best, the team's score.

Occasional games of this sort may act to perk up the interest of club members.

9

The Swiss Movement

THE BEST WAY TO RANK a group of bridge teams is by means of a round robin, in which each team gets to play a match against every other team. But because this is extremely time-consuming, a type of elimination contest known as the Swiss movement has gained increasing popularity for team play.

The Swiss movement, simply described, is one in which winners play winners and losers play losers in a series of short team-of-four matches. This continues for as many rounds as are needed to produce one winner, provided one team has won all of its matches. Binary arithmetic fans will see that the number of rounds that must be played is that power of two which is equal to or higher than the number of teams in the field, but less than double that number.

The movement is borrowed from the Swiss system of conducting chess tournaments. Because it is readily adaptable to team play in bridge, but not to pairs or individuals, the Swiss movement suggests that the natural unit in bridge play is a team of four, just as the individual player is the natural unit in chess.

The director has two principal responsibilities in conducting a Swiss team contest. The first is to provide appropriate and expeditious matching of teams for each round. The second is to keep the game from becoming an all-night affair.

Setting Up the Movement

In large tournaments it is preferable to seed the entire field into two groups, with the stronger players placed in alternate sections and matched initially against teams in the adjacent section. For a club game, it is better to avoid the extra complication of seeding teams.

For easiest management, the game should be set up into two sections, designated A and B, each having an equal number of tables. Teams should be numbered consecutively. One pair from each team sits North-South in its home section, that is, the section containing the table to which the team is originally assigned. The team's East-West pair moves to the corresponding table in the other section. For example, in a 16-team field, either Team 9 or Team 16 is assigned to Table B-1; its East-West pair goes to Table A-1 for the first round.

The size of the field will determine the number of rounds to be played. The time available for the game should determine the number of boards per round.

With eight or fewer teams, it is preferable to play a round robin, rather than a three-round Swiss movement. More than eight and up to 16 teams will require four rounds to produce a winner, more than 16 and up to 32 require five; more than 32 and up to 64 require six, and more than 64 and up to 128 will require seven. A two-session contest should be mandatory if there are more than 128 teams.

In large fields, with two-session tournaments, seven-, eight- or nine-board matches are usually played. For club games, six-board matches are usual, and five-board matches are common. Many club Swiss team events will run five matches of five boards each, which works well with a field of more than 16 and up to 32 teams.

The time allowance should be seven minutes per board for actual play, or 28 minutes per round for four-board matches, 35 minutes for five-board matches and 42 minutes for six. In addition, the director must allow five to ten minutes between rounds for scoring and for making out team assignments for the next round. In a well-run game, 3 1/2 hours should be adequate for five rounds of five boards each and just over 3 hours for four rounds of six boards each.

Odd Numbers of Teams

An odd number of teams in a Swiss movement, while not a complete disaster, is the bane of a director's existence. There are two basic methods of playing with an odd number, neither of them wholly satisfactory.

Each method involves setting up a separate three-team match and maintaining three-team matches during the entire course of the game. Thus, if there are 15 teams in a Swiss game, Teams 13, 14 and 15 are assigned to play a three-team match for the first round. The North-South pair of Team 13 will first play East-West 14; North-South 14 will play East-West 15, and North-South 15 will play East-West 13. In the next segment, North-South 13 will play East-West 15; North-South 14 will play East-West 13, and North-South 15 will play East-West 14 -- in each case playing the same boards played by their teammates in the first segment. After this, these three teams will join the main stream of the game, and three other teams go through the same procedure.

The two methods are:

1. Half Matches -- In order to have the three-way match completed at the same time as all the other matches in the first round, each of the two segments must consist of half a match. To accomplish this equitably, it is necessary to have an even number of boards per match. Six boards per match is probably the ideal number in most club games, so that the half-matches will consist of three boards each.
2. Full Matches -- If full matches are desired, then each three-way match will take two full rounds to complete. In this case, it is necessary to have an even number of rounds in the event.

There are problems inherent in either method. When half matches are used, the club director has a harder time pairing teams that have not played each other before, since some teams will have played against more opponents than others. As a last resort, the director might pair up teams that have played each other in a half match earlier, but this is an undesirable solution.

The chief problem with taking two full rounds to play a three-team match is that it may bring about a fundamental violation of the Swiss movement principle, in that some teams are given opponents without regard to their standing. A superior team in a three-way match could virtually get a gift of two automatic victories, while other superior teams in the field encounter a stronger challenge in their second matches.

To a lesser extent, the same problem exists with half matches. So when there must be three-way matches, it is best to put three middle rated teams in the group for the opening round or rounds, and to group teams with similar records into the three-way matches thereafter.

Because of these drawbacks, other solutions have been tried for the odd team problem. One club, in a college area, has a stand-by team available if an odd number of teams shows up. The stand-by team, if called on, gets to play free. Another method, more feasible for most clubs, would be to split up the members of the last team to arrive and make them fifth members of other teams, with a requirement that a different member of the five-man teams sit out in each round. Or, if there are already enough extra people present as fifth or sixth members of teams (not likely in most club games) an additional team might be formed. Best results are obtained by requiring a prior reservation for a guaranteed entry.

Directing the Swiss Event

Ideally, all teams should end their play and turn in the results at the same time, so that the director will have all the information he needs to make assignments for the next round. But nothing ever happens ideally in running bridge tournaments. To come as close to the ideal as possible, the director should make extra efforts to keep all rounds on time.

The best device is to announce, about three to five minutes before a round should come to an end, that no new boards may be started in that round if the cards have not yet been removed from the board. This means that such matches must be foreshortened, since the unplayed board or boards cannot be counted.

Because timing is so critical to the Swiss movement, a team that fails to complete its full complement of boards for a second time should be penalized and then penalized more severely for successive failures, unless it can be reasonably shown that the team was the victim of slow opponents in all such rounds. Further, a team that deliberately slows down play after having achieved a clear scoring advantage in early boards should be subject to very severe penalties.

In order to cut down on post mortems, the director should call for all score slips after allowing an appropriate interval for comparisons and scoring -- about two minutes. Teams not turning in their scores on time may be penalized if this slows down the matching of teams for the next round. Teams who turn in their score slips early should be asked to assemble away from still-running matches, for quiet discussions, or preferably to adjourn to another room or hallway if one is available.

The time between matches, when the director is making new assignments, should be adequate for all but the most drawn-out post mortems. The director should use as little time as possible for this chore, but speed and skill in matching teams is developed only with experience, and the use of the director's own tricks of the trade.

The objectives in pairing up teams are to bring together teams that have not played each other before and have the same or very similar scores at that point. As a practical matter, however, the director will first seek to match up scores, and then determine that the teams have not previously opposed each other.

The director need not wait for a round to end before making assignments for the next round. He may assign teams with similar records to play each other on vacated tables. But unless these teams have perfect records -- of either the blemished or unblemished variety -- it is preferable not to assign teams for the next round until three identical or virtually identical scores have been turned in. Even if two teams have precisely identical scores, the director may eventually find it necessary to assign one to play against a team with a better or worse record (usually when there is only one team in the field with a better or worse record).

To expedite team assignments, the director may find it helpful to place the slips bearing team records into different slots, using some type of holder to keep teams with identical records together. Within any slot, he should separate the slips of teams that have already played together.

Just as round robin team events can be carried through full playing seasons, so can Swiss team events be arranged to continue through several sessions. As in the ordinary round robin, each team would be matched against only one opponent in a session, playing a full complement of perhaps 24 to 32 boards. New pairings would be made between sessions.

A director can schedule such a running Swiss team event to be played once a month or once every four or six weeks over a playing season that might run five, six, nine or twelve months. In order to assure attendance of all teams each team should have at least five and preferably six members, with some provision made for substitutions.

Scoring

Any method of scoring can be employed for Swiss movements, but the most common are those usually used in international team play: total IMPs, IMPs converted to Victory Points, or matches won (determined by IMPs).

In the last case, after arriving at the net IMP score for the match, each team is customarily given a win, a tie or a loss, and both the pairings for subsequent rounds and the winners of the entire event are determined on the basis of the total number of wins.

A win may be given 1 point, a tie 1/2 point and a loss 0 -- or the director may decide that a specific margin, such as 1 or 2 IMPs, should be required for a win, and that any margin under that would constitute a tie. Some directors predicate the margin on the number of boards per round, and may require a winning edge of, say, 1/2 IMP per board. Actually, the reasoning behind this is faulty; the more boards played in a team match, the better the test, and a longer match should therefore need a narrower margin to win.

Another scoring method that has gained some popularity is the use of quarter points. Thus there might be five possible match scores: 1 point, 3/4, 1/2, 1/4 or 0. In a seven-board match, for example, a margin of 3 or more IMPs might be regarded as a win, an advantage of 1 or 2 IMPs might give the leading team 3/4 and the other team 1/4, while a dead tie would give each 1/2. Most clubs will find scoring and matching made much easier, however, if a margin of as little as 1 IMP is regarded as a win.

When some teams have played half matches in a Swiss team event, the score for those rounds should be in half points. So a team that has won a half match scored at IMPs should get 1/2 point for its win, and the losing team 0; in the event of a tie, each would get 1/4 point. If quarter points are normally used in the scoring, these would have to be adjusted to eighth points for half matches, after designating the appropriate margins for what should constitute a full win in a shorter match.

Directors might find it much simpler to award as many as 8 points per match won, in order to eliminate the use of fractions. Thus a clear win would be worth 8 points, a tie 4 and a clear loss 0. If the director wanted to differentiate close matches, a narrow win might be worth 6 points and a narrow loss 2. Half these numbers of points would be awarded for all half matches.

The use of Victory Point scoring also eliminates the need for fractional points, and at the same time provides a wide spectrum of scores to recognize different margins of victory. The total number of Victory Points awarded is the same for each full match, e.g., in a six-board match the winning and losing teams could be given a total of 20 Victory Points, divided between them according to the margin of the win. Thus the team that wins by 1 IMP will get 11 Victory Points, vs. 9 for its opponents; a team winning by 10 IMPs will get 16, and its opponents 4, and a team winning by 20 or more IMPs will get 20 Victory Points to none for its opponents. A table for converting from IMPs to Victory Points, suggested for use in club games, is shown on the next page.

When half matches are used in a game, adjustments may have to be made in the Victory Point scale to assure that the total for the half match will be exactly half the total for the full match. Thus the scale calls for a total of 14 Victory Points for four-board matches, while the total for an eight-board match is 26. It would be necessary in this case to revise the eight-board Victory Point scale to a total of 28 VPs.

There are a number of ways to break ties, either for the purpose of team pairing or for determining the winner of an event. One might be a run-off match, and another the use of total IMPs scored. Probably better than either of these is the use of what is known as "Swiss points." A team's Swiss points are simply the total number of points won by all its opponents. The theory, of course, is that a team that has done well against good opponents is probably superior to a team that has done equally well against mediocre opposition. Ties are not broken for master point awards in ACBL-sponsored events; tied teams must split these awards.

VICTORY POINT SCALE

Result in IMPs	Win-Lose V.P.	Result in IMPs	Win-Lose V.P.	Result in IMPs	Win-Lose V.P.	Result in IMPs	Win-Lose V.P.
3 Board Match		**4 Board Match**		**5 Board Match**		**6 Board Match**	
0	= 5-5	0	= 7-7	0	= 8-8	0	= 10-10
1	= 6-4	1	= 8-6	1	= 9-7	1	= 11-9
2-3	= 7-3	2	= 9-5	2	= 10-6	2	= 12-8
4-6	= 8-2	3-4	= 10-4	3-4	= 11-5	3	= 13-7
7-9	= 9-1	5-6	= 11-3	5-6	= 12-4	4-5	= 14-6
10+	= 10-0	7-9	= 12-2	7-9	= 13-3	6-7	= 15-5
		10-12	= 13-1	10-12	= 14-2	8-10	= 16-4
		13+	= 14-0	13-15	= 15-1	11-13	= 17-3
				16+	= 16-0	14-16	= 18-2
						17-19	= 19-1
						20+	= 20-0

Result	Win-Lose	Result	Win-Lose	Result	Win-Lose	Result	Win-Lose
7 Board Match		**8 Board Match**		**9 Board Match**		**10 Board Match**	
0	= 12-12	0	= 13-13	0	= 15-15	0	= 17-17
1	= 13-11	1	= 14-12	1	= 16-14	1	= 18-16
2	= 14-10	2	= 15-11	2	= 17-13	2	= 19-15
3	= 15-9	3	= 16-10	3	= 18-12	3	= 20-14
4	= 16-8	4	= 17-9	4	= 19-11	4	= 21-13
5-6	= 17-7	5-6	= 18-8	5	= 20-10	5	= 22-12
7-8	= 18-6	7-8	= 19-7	6-7	= 21-9	6	= 23-11
9-10	= 19-5	9-10	= 20-6	8-9	= 22-8	7-8	= 24-10
11-13	= 20-4	11-13	= 21-5	10-11	= 23-7	9-10	= 25-9
14-16	= 21-3	14-16	= 22-4	12-14	= 24-6	11-12	= 26-8
17-19	= 22-2	17-19	= 23-3	15-17	= 25-5	13-14	= 27-7
20-22	= 23-1	20-22	= 24-2	18-20	= 26-4	15-17	= 28-6
23+	= 24-0	23-25	= 25-1	21-23	= 27-3	18-20	= 29-5
		26+	= 26-0	24-26	= 28-2	21-23	= 30-4
				27-29	= 29-1	24-26	= 31-3
				30+	= 30-0	27-29	= 32-2
						30-32	= 33-1
						33+	= 34-0

Scoring Equipment

Various types of scoring forms have been devised and are in use for Swiss team events. The three that are most often used include slips for recording the results of each match, like that shown here.

TEAM NUMBER 11C	ROUND 5	You are playing against team 4
You sit N-S at Table 4G	& E-W at Table 4H	
RESULTS (circle one) WON (LOST) TIED	MATCHES WON 3	
	MATCHES TIED 1	
NET IMPS (±) -21	If result is close, verify with opponents.	

The first form on Page 126 is used for maintaining a running record of a team's performance. Alternately, a team recapitulation sheet which has spaces to show the results for each round and such information as the number of the opposing team, cumulative scores, etc. can be used.

It would be possible to combine two of these items of scoring equipment into one, if the director trusted his players to fill in and keep their own team records. The team captain would fill in the results of each round, total the results for all rounds up to that point, and turn his card in to the director after he had made his entries for the round. Such a team record card is shown on the bottom of Page 126.

At the end of a match, both winning and losing captains would be required to turn in their cards together, to give the director an opportunity to check. He would then copy the information from the team records onto his summary sheet, and place the record cards in their appropriate slots for pairing the next round. When the pairings were made up, the director would fill in the new assignments on the team records and return them to the captains. If desired, additional columns could be added to the record card for Swiss points and for team members sitting out.

TEAM RECORD CARD KEPT BY THE DIRECTOR

SWISS TEAMS WORKSHEET — TEAM NO. 11 C

TEAM CAPTAIN D. STRASBERG

RD.	VS.	MATCH RESULT	CUM. MATCHES	SWISS POINTS	SAT OUT
1.	11D	+1	1		G. BOEHM
2.	8D	+1	2	1	L. HARMON
3.	1D	+1	3	3	W. PASSELL
4.	7C	+1	4	5 3/4	D. STRASBERG
5.	4H	0	4	5 3/4	A. BOEHM
6.	10L	+1	5	10 1/4	G. BOEHM
7.	3J	+1	6	15 1/4	L. HARMON
8.	9F	+1	7	20 3/4	W. PASSELL

TEAM RECORD CARD KEPT BY THE TEAM CAPTAIN

SWISS TEAM RECORD CARD

Team Captain D. Strasberg Team No. 11C

Round	Vs.	N-S Table	Scores IMPs	Scores VPs	Cum. Results	Opp. OK
1	11D	11C	+10	16	16	LT
2	8D	8C	-3	7	23	RM
3	1D	8C	+25	20	43	JR
4	7C	6D	+13	17	60	TZ
5	4H	4G	-4	6	66	AB
6	10L	10K	+22	20	86	MP
7	3J	5I	+1	11	97	LJ
8	9F	9E	-32	0	97	TNB

Swiss Pairs

While the Swiss movement has already proved its popularity for team play, it has thus far appeared much less satisfactory for pair or individual events. There have been some efforts to develop methods of having pairs play in a Swiss type of elimination movement, mainly by converting actual duplicate scores into something resembling IMP scores through the determination of a "par" score for the full field in a normal pair movement. Although this permits the division of the field into a top and bottom half, which is a desirable first step in an elimination contest, it tends to be slow and unwieldy and has found little favor with players.

A relatively fast and simple Swiss tournament for pairs* creates temporary teams in such a way that no pair is unduly helped or penalized by the quality of its teammates.

1. Divide the entire field into two sections, designated A and B, just as in a club Swiss team event.
2. The first round (and each subsequent round) is conducted in two stanzas. In the first stanza, the North-South pair at each table has as teammates the East-West pair at the corresponding table in the other section. In the second stanza, the players in Section B change their positions at the table (by means of an arrow switch), so that the North-South pair at each table has as teammates the original North-South pair at the corresponding table in the other section.
3. Score each round by matches, IMPs or Victory Points.
4. Reseat the players in two-table groupings according to scores (i.e., highest-ranking pairs should be placed at Table 1 in Sections A and B, or, if there are more than four top-ranked pairs, at as many tables as needed in the two Sections).
5. Repeat play as in 2, above.
6. Score and repeat the movement, until there is only one winning pair.

What takes place in the two stanzas of each round is this: Each pair gets a fully-balanced team-type of comparision with the other pair at its table, and a normal pair game type of comparison with each of the two pairs at the corresponding table in the other section. Barring ties, one pair in each two-table grouping should win

*Publisher's Footnote: This is known as the Groner Movement.

two matches, two pairs should win one match apiece, and one pair should win no matches. At the end of the first round, one-fourth of the field should be in the top group, one half in the median group and the other fourth in the bottom group.

A game with 16 or fewer pairs can be finished in just two rounds, preferably with twelve boards to a round, or six to a stanza. For more than 16 and up to 32 pairs, the movement would require at least three rounds, with eight boards to a round, four per stanza. More than 32 and up to 64 pairs can be accommodated in a four-round movement, with six boards per round, three per stanza. Since the two-round movement means that each pair plays against only two opponents, the director will find it far more interesting to conduct a three-round event, with eight boards per round.

Odd tables can be handled even more easily than in a Swiss team event. Simply make the odd table an appendix to one of the two-table groupings, and have all boards played at the two other tables relayed to the third table. The two pairs at the appendix table will remain stationary throughout the round, and will make score comparisons with the table at which the arrow switch takes place (normally Section B). This comparison will determine the scores of the two pairs at the appendix table; the pairs at the arrow switch table will get their scores only from comparison with the results at the corresponding table in the other section.

For better differentiation of results, the use of Victory Points or IMPs is strongly recommended for this movement.

10

Larger Teams of Pairs

ON OCCASION, the duplicate director may be called on to conduct contests for teams of more than four players -- that is, teams with three, four, six or even more pairs. Generally, such large teams will represent bridge clubs, country clubs, or even cities. The club games are often conducted in several sessions, usually extending over a season of nine months to a year.

Traditionally, most contests involving large teams of pairs are head-to-head matches, in which one team plays against one other team at a time. There may be more than two teams in the entire league, in which case the teams face each other on a round robin basis.

However, matches among a number of large teams, all meeting at one place at the same time or times, have been gaining in popularity recently. A simple way to conduct such contests is to divide each team into teams of four, and then conduct a regular team-of-four movement, taking precautions to avoid having teammates meet each other during the contest.

There is an even better method, however. A new movement in which several large teams of pairs can meet each other in the course of a single game is described later in this chapter.

Most directors will never encounter the need for running a game for large teams of pairs. The movements are not difficult to master, however, and some knowledge of them may come in handy. And directors who frequently have good attendance may enjoy splitting the game up into several large teams of pairs, to add an extra competitive fillip. With twelve tables, for example, the director might split the entire group into six teams of four pairs to a team; with 18 tables, the group could be divided into six teams of six pairs each.

The special advantage of such an arrangement is that it need not disturb the pair game at all. The game works out so that there can be the normal winning pairs, as well as winning teams.

This movement for more than two large teams will be described later in this chapter. First, various methods of conducting head-to-head team matches will be discussed.

Gruenther Relay

A relay between two sets of tables, known as a Gruenther movement, can be used to accommodate teams with virtually any number of pairs.

Half the pairs from one team sit North-South in one row of tables, and half the pairs from the second team sit North-South in the other row. The remaining pairs take East-West positions at tables with members of the opposing teams. The game proceeds as two separate Mitchell movements, with all boards relaying between the two rows.

With an odd number of tables in each row, a straight Mitchell can be used. With an even number of tables in a row, a skip Mitchell may be used. It is also possible to use a bye stand and relay Mitchell for an even number of tables, but this can prove awkward, since one relay is imposed upon another. For that reason, it is necessary to have at least three boards per round, and to place the Mitchell relays at different positions in the two rows. (This will also necessitate the placement of the bye stands in different positions in the two rows. Since the bye stands will be included in the overall relays between rows, these can just be vacant tables; the boards that would ordinarily stay on the bye stand will be retained by the opposite table for that round.)

When it is desired that all or most of the pairs on one of the teams play all or most of the pairs on the other, it is a simple matter to have one of the teams change positions at the halfway mark.

If there are 16 pairs on each of the teams, for example, the tables will be arranged in two rows of eight. Team A will sit North-South in one row, and East-West in the other, and Team B will take the reverse arrangement. Using a skip movement, seven rounds will be played in each row. At this point, the Team B pairs change positions, with the East-West pairs in the first row moving to the North-South seats in the second row, and the North-South pairs in the second row moving to the East-West seats in the first. Fresh boards are distributed to all tables, and another skip Mitchell movement of seven rounds is played. The game will thus have 14 rounds, and every pair will get to play against 14 of the 16 pairs on the opposing team.

A contest of that kind can be conducted in either one or two sessions. As a one-session game, it would have two boards per round, for a total of 28 boards; in two sessions, it could have either three boards per round, for a total of 42 boards, or four boards per round for a total of 56.

Since the Gruenther relay is simply two simultaneous Mitchell movements, guide cards are unnecessary. To illustrate the full movement, however, a master sheet of a two-session contest for teams of 16 pairs appears on Pages 215-216 of Appendix H.

As in any large-scale relay movement, this one has the disadvantage of having the same sets of boards played simultaneously at adjacent tables. To get around this, it is advisable to twin all boards during the first round of play. After this is done, Table 1 should shift to a point half way down its row (by moving players, boards and guide cards, but not necessarily the tables themselves), and other tables should move correspondingly. Then the change is made, as East-West players move to the next higher table and boards move to the next lower table for the second round of play.

With twinned boards, it is also much simpler to conduct bye stand and relay movements in each of the two rows, when the number of tables in a row is even.

When the number of tables in each row is odd, it is possible to run an American Whist League movement, in which boards move down one table and players move down two tables in each of the rows. This hardly seems worth while, however, since the American Whist League movement is designed for team-of-four games, in which the same boards are played by corresponding pairs of the two teams involved. There would appear to be no point in doing this for larger teams of pairs.

Baldwin Schedule, with Modifications

For teams with as few as six pairs, the Gruenther relay offers one clear advantage. All the boards played up to the mid-point, when one of the teams changes positions, are completely played at that point, and they can be scored during the second half.

But with only four pairs on a team, the Mitchell principle can no longer work, since there are only two tables in each row. The Baldwin schedule for two teams of four pairs gets around this difficulty by imposing the Howell principle on the movement of one of the teams.

Pairs from Team A sit North-South at the first two tables, and East-West at Tables 3 and 4. Pairs from Team B take the opposing positions at all tables. All pairs from Team A remain stationary, regardless of whether they sit North-South or East-West. And all Team B pairs move, regardless of their compass positions. Their movement is in the Howell pattern, following each other in numerical sequence.

With anywhere from six to eight boards per round, all boards are relayed among all four tables. The following schedule shows the full movement:

		Table 1		Table 2		Table 3		Table 4	
Rd.	Bds.	N-S	E-W	N-S	E-W	N-S	E-W	N-S	E-W
1	1-6	1A	1B	2A	2B	3B	3A	4B	4A
2	7-12	1A	2B	2A	3B	4B	3A	1B	4A
3	13-18	1A	3B	2A	4B	1B	3A	2B	4A
4	19-24	1A	4B	2A	1B	2B	3A	3B	4A

Players on the B team, it can be seen, move to the next lower table after each round, and take the vacant positions at those tables.

Because the four-table relay can be extremely awkward, here is a modification of the Baldwin schedule, using the bye stand and relay principle.

	Table 1			Bye	Table 2			Table 3			Table 4		
Rd.	Bds.	N-S	E-W	Bds.	Bds.	N-S	E-W	Bds.	N-S	E-W	Bds.	N-S	E-W
1	1-6	1A	1B	19-24	13-18	2A	2B	7-12	3B	3A	7-12	4B	4A
2	7-12	1A	2B	1-6	19-24	2A	3B	13-18	4B	3A	13-18	1B	4A
3	13-18	1A	3B	7-12	1-6	2A	4B	19-24	1B	3A	19-24	2B	4A
4	19-24	1A	4B	13-18	7-12	2A	1B	1-6	2B	3A	1-6	3B	4A

The positions and movement of players is exactly the same as on the normal Baldwin schedule, with Team B players moving to the next lower table after each round. But the boards are distributed to the various tables, with a bye stand between Tables 1 and 2, and a relay only between Tables 3 and 4. Contrary to their normal motion, boards move to the next higher table or bye stand.

A similar Howell type of movement for two teams of six pairs can also be worked out, with three relay and three bye stands. A schedule and master sheet for this movement, along with the two schedules shown here, appear on Pages 217-219 of Appendix H.

Multiple Team Movements

When there are more than two large teams playing together at one time, it is possible to place them so that a quite symmetrical movement results, using the Mitchell principle. (This is the new movement mentioned earlier in this chapter.)

As long as there are even numbers of pairs on each of the teams, the movement will be well balanced, with each team playing every other team the same number of times. With odd numbers of pairs, the movement becomes not only unbalanced, but almost too cumbersome to use effectively, so that an even number of pairs on each team is highly desirable.

At the start, the director assigns letters to each of the teams. The teams themselves then assign numbers to each of the pairs, so that the full designation of any pair will be something like 1C or 3G. When the number of pairs is even, half the pairs (those with the lower numbers) will sit North-South and the other half will sit East-West.

The director then assigns starting positions to all pairs, according to the first line of the master sheet for the game that is being conducted. With three teams of four pairs, for example, the first line (Round 1) would be as follows:

1A - 3C   1B - 3A   1C - 3B   2A - 4C   2B - 4A   2C - 4B

As is true in every case, table numbers and sets of boards follow in normal sequence across the first line of the master sheet. Thus, Team 1A will play North-South against Team 3C on the first round, playing the first set of boards at Table 1; Team 1B will play North-South against Team 3A, playing the second set of boards at Table 2, etc.

At the end of the first round, boards move to the next lower table, and East-West players move to the next higher table. The same shift is made after each round, except that East-West players must skip a table at one or more times in the movement. The skip takes place at a frequency (in rounds) that is one less than the number of teams competing. Thus, if there are three teams competing, an East-West skip is necessary after every two rounds; with four teams, East-West will skip a table after every three rounds, etc.

When there are as many as eight different teams competing, and if the game is to last only seven rounds, it is possible to have a movement in which East-West will not have to skip at all. But this is not necessarily the best movement for such a group. Two master sheets are shown in Appendix H for eight teams of four pairs, for example. In the first, there is no skip, but there is a built-in imbalance, in that each team plays six sets of boards three times and ten other sets just once. The second master sheet calls for a skip in the movement, but it is balanced better, with each team playing twelve sets of boards twice and four sets just once.

Because the total movement follows the Mitchell pattern, it is possible to have pair winners -- both North-South and East-West -- as well as team winners. The movement can therefore be used for a group of pre-set teams, or a duplicate game can be divided up into groups of teams to add extra spice to the session.

With an odd number of pairs on each team, as already noted, the game becomes extremely irregular.

Just three pairs on a team is not too bad. For a game with four teams of three pairs, a total of 24 boards can be played, with four boards in each of six rounds. Each team plays every other team six times, and each team plays every board three times. But the movement needs to be somewhat uneven. East-West pairs move up one table after the first and second rounds, up two tables after the third, and up three tables after the fourth and fifth.

But with five pairs, troubles multiply. Teams do not play each other the same number of times (although they play all the boards the same number of times). The movement, however, has to be described as wild. East-West pairs move up anywhere from one to four tables -- and occasionally move down three tables.

Because four pairs seems to be the most popular number for most teams (with substitutions of other pairs permitted), most of the master sheets and schedules in Appendix H are for four-pair teams.

Larger Teams of Pairs

These are on Pages 221-227. On Page 220 is a three-pair team game master sheet, and master sheets for a five-pair team game, a six-pair team game andan eight-pair team game appear on Pages 228-230.

Teams of Pairs Scoring

Where just two teams are involved in a game, any type of scoring may be used. Board-a-match scoring can be used, with each board considered a win, loss or a tie; total points can be used, with honors counted or not counted; or the increasingly popular International Match Points may be used.

In multiple team movements, there are frequently no direct comparisons between teams on the same board. But since each board is played a number of times, it is a fairly simple matter to merely match point each board, and to rank the teams according to the match point totals for all their pairs.

For this purpose, the director might find it helpful to have his players modify the traveling score sheets at the start of the game. In place of the North - South numbers, the number of team designations should be written in, with all pairs on one team grouped together. For a game with four teams of six pairs, for example, the North-South pair column should be changed to read: 1A, 2A, 3A, 1B, 2B, 3B, 1C, 2C, 3C, 1D, 2D, 3D. The East - West pair designations can be filled in as they turn up in the game.

To make it easier to total team scores, all the North-South pairs on a team should appear together on the recapitulation sheet, and East-West pairs on the same team should similarly appear together on their side of the recap sheet. The team's overall score would be the total of its North-South match points added to the total of its East-West match points.

11

The American Contract Bridge League

AS FAR AS duplicate bridge in the United States is concerned, the American Contract Bridge League is the hub of the universe. It is a nonprofit organization to which any North American resident or U.S. citizen living abroad may belong. Its area of coverage includes Canada, Mexico and various nearby islands, as well as the United States and all U.S. government and military stations.

The League is affiliated with the World Bridge Federation, through which it takes part in international bridge championship events.

Through its committees and staff, the A.C.B.L. plays a key role in a wide variety of activities concerned with duplicate bridge. It represents North America on the International Commission that writes laws of duplicate (as well as rubber) bridge, and is the recognized arbiter of these rules and their interpretations for its area, as well as of the ethical principles to be followed.

The League's national tournament directors are recognized authorities in the field of conducting duplicate games and tournaments. The A.C.B.L. also has a program for training duplicate directors at various locations around the country, often in conjunction with North American Bridge Championships.

The A.C.B.L. publishes a monthly magazine, *The Contract Bridge Bulletin*, with comprehensive coverage of news of interest to duplicate bridge players, including a calendar of forthcoming major tournaments held around the country.

A.C.B.L. Tournaments

The American Contract Bridge League conducts three kinds of major tournaments — NABC, regional and sectional.

There are three North American Bridge Championships held each year — Spring, Summer and Fall — usually in various U.S. cities, or occasionally in Canada. An NABC tournament goes on for approximately ten days, and some of the major events are spaced out over most of the ten-day period. There is almost always a major event for teams of four and one for pairs, and these are sometimes open only to players who have achieved a recognized status in duplicate play. Winning such events can be part of the qualification for representing the United States in international competition.

Regional tournaments cover a number of states — or, as in the case of Canada or Mexico — an entire country. Some 85 to 90 regional tournaments are held annually. Most of them extend over three- to five-day periods, but some regionals are scheduled for as long as ten days.

Finally, there are sectional tournaments, usually covering cities or parts of states. A sectional is almost always held over a long weekend (Friday, Saturday and Sunday), and anywhere from ten to twenty sectionals will be going on around the country on any given weekend. Sectional tournaments are also sometimes held at groups of clubs, when they are called Sectional Tournaments at Clubs (STaCs). These may go on for a full week.

Club Games and Sanctions

Although the major tournaments and their stars get most of the publicity, the great bulk of duplicate bridge is played at local clubs — bridge clubs, industrial clubs, school clubs, country clubs, etc. More than 4,000 clubs are sanctioned as affiliates of the American Contract Bridge League.

Clubs run duplicate games on varying schedules. Some meet as infrequently as once a month, while others have as many as two games a day — one in the afternoon and another in the evening. Some clubs even schedule a sandwich break for lunch. (But most duplicate players seem to have an aversion to playing in the morning, perhaps because they like to use their mornings to sleep off the catastrophes of the previous evening's game.)

An established director may direct a game for any sanctioned club. But a new director, desirous of running a club duplicate for the first time, must pass a Qualified Director's examination given under the auspices of the A.C.B.L. This examination covers general knowledge of directing, scoring and laws.

The American Contract Bridge League has several special publications designed specifically for clubs. One of these, *Duplicate Bridge for Small Clubs*, describes the essentials of duplicate play and equipment, as well as Mitchell movements and scoring. Another is a pamphlet called *Adventures in Duplicate*, for beginning duplicate players. The A.C.B.L.

(2990 Airways Boulevard, Memphis, TN 38116) will send a supply of these to clubs on request. Most useful to the director, however, is the *A.C.B.L. Handbook of Rules and Regulations,* one copy of which is supplied free to a club manager. The Handbook covers a wide variety of subjects concerning club games and activites. As changes are made, corrections are sent out.

Masterpoints

A major service to duplicate bridge players was the institution by the American Contract Bridge League of a system of recognizing bridge achievement. This is done through awards of masterpoints and fractional masterpoints, sometimes known as rating points (100 rating points equal one masterpoint.)

Masterpoints may be awarded by an sanctioned club for regularly scheduled games of three or more tables, and are awarded at all larger tournaments sanctioned by the League. The difference is in the size of the awards, which are scaled to reflect the size and character of the event.

Two types of clubs are sanctioned by the A.C.B.L.: Proprietary and Sponsored. A Proprietary club is one organized by an individual, partnership or corporation for the purpose of conducting sanctioned duplicate games. A Sponsored club may be operated for the employees of a company, the members of a social club or country club, or any similar group.

A game held by a club (unless it is a Class 1, or Bridge Plus+, game, described below) must be scheduled at regular intervals — that is, once a week, once every three weeks, once a month, etc. Games may be scheduled throughout the year, or for only certain parts of the year. A single club may hold a number of regularly scheduled games, e.g., Monday evening, Tuesday afternoon, Tuesday evening, etc.

Every club game is placed in one of four classes by the A.C.B.L. Masterpoints are awarded according to the classification of the game, with the winners receiving awards based on the number of competitors and level of skill. Second place is awarded 70% as much as first, third place 50%, fourth, place 35%, fifth place a fifth of the first place award, sixth place, a sixth, etc. Awards are given to approximately 40% of all players in each field, e.g., North-South, East-West.

A Class 1 game is deemed a transition from the bridge class to duplicate play, and must be run by a teacher accredited by the A.C.B.L. Class 2 games are limited to players below a certain rank, based on masterpoint holdings, and are generally conducted for the purpose of encouraging inexperienced players to take part in duplicate games; no player with an A.C.B.L. rating of Club Master (20 or more masterpoints) or higher may take part in a Class 2 game. Class 3 games, by and large, are those conducted by invitational clubs; various competitive limitations may be enforced in Class 3 games. Class 4 games are designed for serious duplicate bridge competition and must be open to all A.C.B.L. members in good standing.

Clubs may accommodate players at varied levels of skill by holding so-called "stratified" games. Players are divided into two or three levels, based on the largest number of masterpoints held by any member of a pair or team. Awards are then made based on how well each player does within his own stratum, although lower-ranked players who do better than those in the higher strata are eligible for the higher awards.

For each regularly scheduled weekly game held by a club, as many as four club championship games may be held per year, but not more than one in each calendar quarter. Higher awards are given for these games (in direct proportion to the class of the game), in accordance with a masterpoint plan available from the A.C.B.L.

The American Contract Bridge League keeps masterpoint records for all its members. It is not sufficient, however, for an individual to be a member of a sanctioned club. He or she must be a member of the A.C.B.L., as well; such a membership may be taken out at the local club.

All awards at major tournaments are sent directly to the records section at the League. Clubs may also make monthly reports of masterpoints won in their games to the League, or they may issue certificates to the players, who in turn send them to the A.C.B.L.

Pigmented Points

Gold points are awarded for section tops and overall awards in regional or higher-rated events.

Red points are awarded for all placings in regional or higher-rated events that do not qualify for a gold point award.

Silver points are awarded for all events at sectional tournaments.

Title	Total Master Point Requirements	Pigmented Point Requirements
Life Master	300	100 pigmented points, of which 25 must be gold, 25 must be red or gold, and 50 must be silver
NABC Master	200	50 pigmented points, of which 5 must be gold, 15 must be red or gold, and 25 must be silver
Regional Master	100	15 silver plus 5 red or gold
Sectional Master	50	5 silver
Club Master	20	None
Junior Master	5	None
Rookie	0-4.99	None

The League Charity Program

Each year the trustees of the A.C.B.L. Charity Foundation select one or more beneficiaries of the League charity program. Considerable effort is expended to promote and publicize the program and substantial amounts of money are raised.

Charity games are conducted at all levels — national, regional, sectional, unit and club. Some A.C.B.L.-wide events are held simultaneously at a great many locations throughout the country, usually with the same hands played everywhere.

Clubs may participate in the program by holding two sessions of charity games per year per sanctioned session — or more, if it wishes to substitute charity games for its allowable club tournament sessions. Charity game awards are made on the basis of 70% of sectional.

Common Violations and Rulings

The duplicate director is urged to obtain, study and keep handy a copy of Laws of Duplicate Contract Bridge, mentioned in Chapter I. While he should be prepared to make all kinds of rulings in accordance with those laws, he will ordinarily find that most of his rulings will relate to no more than four or five situations. He should be especially familiar with the following laws:

Call Out of Turn -- Laws 28, 29, 30, 31, 32, 33 (and also Law 25)
Insufficient Bid -- Law 27 (and also Law 26)
Dummy's Rights and Limitations-- Laws 42, 43 (and also Law 9)
Leads Out ofTurn -- Laws 53, 54, 55, 56, 57, 58
Revoke -- Laws 61, 62, 63, 64

Conventions, Proprieties and Ethics

It is always incumbent on duplicate bridge players (as it should be on rubber bridge players) to explain any bid to the opponents on request. A player may request an explanation of a bid during the auction, at his turn to call. He may also ask for explanations when the auction has ended, if he is to make the opening lead. Further, declarer or either defender may ask for explanations of the bidding during the play, when it is their turn to play.*

To streamline and simplify the explanation of bidding systems and conventions, duplicate directors should provide their players with convention cards on which such special bidding practices can be noted. These cards come with spaces for private score records on the back side, as noted in Chapter 4. The convention card is frequently the only explanation that a seasoned duplicate player will need.

Some 15 different bidding conventions are listed by the American Contract Bridge League as Class 1 Conventions, and their use must

*As regular tournament procedure, the A.C.B.L. requires that opponents be alerted by the partner of the bidder (simply by using the word "Alert") when any "conventional" bid -- that is, a bid having some special meaning -- is used.

be permitted at all tournaments sanctioned by the A.C.B.L. or conducted by franchised clubs. In addition, a club director or governing body may permit or prohibit the use of any or all other conventions, including a long list known as Class 2 Conventions of the A.C.B.L.

Club directors are generally inclined to permit, rather than prohibit, the use of various conventions and systems. Club games can thus give players wider experience with a variety of bidding practices, and at the same time they can be testing grounds for new bidding methods and techniques. A new bidding idea, if it turns out to be a superior method of partnership communication, will probably win its way eventually into the realm of widely accepted bidding practice.

Playing signals and bidding, of course, are the only proper means of partnership communication in bridge. But there are also, sad to say, a host of improper methods of partnership communication. Sooner or later, many of these will be called to the attention of the director, and therefore they fall within his province.

The director must therefore familiarize himself, not just with the laws, but also the ethics and proprieties of the game. He will soon discover that virtually all of them deal with giving unauthorized information by means of words, gestures or expressions, and thus constitute improper communication.

While the laws have explicit penalties, any penalties or adjustments that should be made because of improprieties are left largely to the discretion of the director. In making his rulings, he not only wants to see justice done among the parties involved, but he also wants them to work for the best interests of his game. He needs to be enough of a psychologist to differentiate between real and imagined infractions, enough of a realist to know whether a violation was intentional or inadvertent, and enough of a diplomat to keep anyone from feeling he was unfairly dealt with.

A studious director can get to know all the laws, and can rigidly follow the accepted interpretations of the laws. He can also learn and memorize all the proprieties and ethical principles. But if he is looking for a workable rule of thumb, it might well be this:

Let the punishment fit the crime; let the penalties restore the equities.

Even in cases where the penalties are spelled out by the laws, and the offended party is given a choice of remedies, the director should urge him to select the one that most closely restores him to his position before the offense was committed -- rather than the one that gives him the greatest advantage. If he can get most of his players to do this consistently, and if his own discretionary rulings are of the same nature, he will be conducting a truly superior game, because it will be one that comes much closer to being a true test of skill.

And that, after all, is what duplicate bridge is all about.

Appendix A

SCORING DATA AND PERCENTAGE TABLES

Part I: Howell Games

Tables	Type of Game	Boards in Play	Boards Played	Board Check Total	Grand Check Total	Average
3		20	20	6	120	20
3		25	25	6	150	25
3 1/2		21	21	6	126	18
3 1/2		28	28	6	168	24
4		21	21	12	252	31 1/2
4		28	28	12	336	42
4 1/2		18	18	12	216	24
		27	27	12	324	36
5		18	18	20	360	36
		27	27	20	540	54
5 1/2		22	22	20	440	40
6		22	22	30	660	55
		24	24	30	720	60
		27	27	30	810	67 1/2
6 1/2		26	26	30	780	60
7		26	26	42	1,092	78
7	Short 3/4	22	22	42	924	66
8	Short 3/4	22	22	56	1,232	77
	3/4	26	26	56	1,456	91
9	Short 3/4	22	22	72	1,584	88
	3/4	26	26	72	1,872	104
10	Short 3/4	22	22	90	1,980	99
	3/4	26	26	90	2,340	117
11	3/4	26	26	110	2,860	130
12	3/4	26	26	132	3,432	143

Scoring Data

Part II: Mitchell Games

Tables	Type of Game	Boards in Play	Boards Played	Board Check Total	Grand Check Total	Average
7		21	21	21	441	63
		28	28	21	588	84
7 1/2	Bye Stand	24	N-S 24	21	504	72
			E-W 21	21	504	63
8	Skip	24	21	21	504	63
	Bye Stand	24	24	28	672	84
8 1/2	1 1/2 Appendix	21	N-S 21	28	588	73 1/2
			E-W 18-21	28	588	63-73 1/2
		27	N-S 27	28	756	94 1/2
			E-W 24	28	756	84
9		27	27	36	972	108
9 1/2	Bye Stand	20	N-S 20	36	720	80
			E-W 18	36	720	72
	1 1/2 Appendix	24	N-S 24	36	864	96
	With Skip		E-W 21-24	36	864	84-96
10	Skip	20	18	36	720	72
	Skip	30	27	36	1,080	108
10 1/2		22	N-S 22	45	990	99
			E-W 20	45	990	90
	1 1/2 Appendix	27	N-S 27	45	1,215	121 1/2
			E-W 24-27	45	1,215	108-121 1/2
11		22	22	55	1,210	110
11 1/2	Bye Stand	24	N-S 24	55	1,320	120
			E-W 22	55	1,320	110
	1 1/2 Appendix	30	N-S 30	55	1,650	150
			E-W 27-30	55	1,650	135-150
12	Skip	24	22	55	1,320	110
	Bye Stand	24	24	66	1,584	132
12 1/2		26	N-S 26	66	1,716	143
			E-W 24	66	1,716	132
13		26	26	78	2,028	156
13 1/2	Bye Stand	28	N-S 28	78	2,184	168
			E-W 26	78	2,184	156
14	Bye Stand	28	28	91	2,548	182
	Skip	28	26	78	2,184	156
14 1/2		28	N-S 26	78	2,184	156
			E-W 24	78	2,184	144-156
15		30	26	78	2,340	156
16	Skip	32	26	78	2,496	156

Part III: Individual Games

Players	Boards in Play	Boards Played	Board Check Total	Grand Check Total	Average
8	21	21	2	84	10 1/2
9	27	27	2	108	12
10	20	20	2	80	8
12	22	22	6	264	22
	33	33	6	396	33
13	26	26	6	312	24
16	24	24	12	576	36
	30	30	12	720	45
20	30	30	20	1,200	60
	20	19	Bds.1-15 20 Bds.16-20 12	720	36
24	21	21	30	1,260	52 1/2
25	25	25	20	1,200	48
	50	50	30	3,000	120
28	21	21	42	1,764	63
	28	27	Bds. 1-21 42 Bds.22-28 30	2,184	78
32	24	21	42	2,016	63
	24	24	56	2,688	84
36	27	27	72	3,888	108
40	30	24	56	3,360	84
	30	27	72	4,320	108
	30	30	90	5,400	135
44	22	22	110	4,840	110
48	24	22	110	5,280	110
	24	24	132	6,336	132
52	26	26	156	8,112	156

PART IV

Percentage Tables

THE PERCENTAGE TABLES shown here give the percentages for various match point scores, based on the average score for the field.

To use these tables, the director must first determine the average score for the game or the field. He should then find the column headed by that average score. Running down each column, he will first find the percentage for a half match point. Below that he will find percentages for from 1 through 9 match points. Thereafter, percentages will appear for 10 through 210 match points, by tens, and from 300 through 500 match points, by hundreds, wherever these numbers are likely to have any significance.

All percentages are given in five significant figures, or to three decimal places. This is probably one decimal place more than most directors will find they need.

To determine the percentage for any match point score, it is simply necessary to find the appropriate column, then to jot down the percentage for the number of hundreds in the score, the percentage for the number of tens, the percentage for the number of digits and, if need be, the percentage for a half match point. The total of these percentages will be the percentage for the match point score.

Suppose, for example, a four-table Howell game of 21 boards is being played. The director will first determine, either by calculation or by referring to the scoring data table, at the start of this Appendix, that the average score is 31 1/2 match points. He will then consult the column for a 31 1/2 average score, and determine the percentage for each pair. If, for instance, the winning pair scored 42 1/2 points, he will see that the percentage for the half point is .794%; the percentage for 2 points is 3.174%; and going on down the column, he will find that the percentage for 40 points is

63.492%. If he wishes, he can set down these percentages in this fashion, and add them:

For 1/2 point	.794%
For 2 points	3.174
For 40 points	63.492
Total	67.460%

The percentage for the winning score of 42 1/2 points is thus 67.460%. Suppose the second place pair in the same game scored 37 match points. Their percentage is similarly found:

For 7 points	11.109%
For 30 points	47.619
Total	58.728%

Now let us consider the example of a larger game, with an average of 156, in which the winning pair has a match point score of 207 1/2 points. Their percentage is found by consulting the column for the 156 average, and adding as follows:

For 1/2 point	.161%
For 7 points	2.244
For 200 points	64.103
Total	66.508%

Match Points	Avg. 20	22	24	25	31 1/2	33	36	40
1/2	1.250	1.136	1.042	1.000	.794	.757	.694	.625
1	2.500	2.273	2.083	2.000	1.587	1.515	1.389	1.250
2	5.000	4.546	4.166	4.000	3.174	3.030	3.778	2.500
3	7.500	6.819	6.249	6.000	4.761	4.545	4.167	3.750
4	10.000	9.092	8.332	8.000	6.348	6.060	5.556	5.000
5	12.500	11.365	10.415	10.000	7.935	7.575	6.945	6.250
6	15.000	13.638	12.498	12.000	9.522	9.090	8.334	7.500
7	17.500	15.911	14.581	14.000	11.109	10.605	9.723	8.750
8	20.000	18.184	16.664	16.000	12.696	12.120	11.112	10.000
9	22.500	20.457	18.747	18.000	14.283	13.635	12.501	11.250
10	25.000	22.727	20.833	20.000	15.873	15.151	13.889	12.500
20	50.000	45.454	41.666	40.000	31.746	30.302	27.778	25.000
30	75.000	68.181	62.499	60.000	47.619	45.453	41.667	37.500
40			83.332	80.000	63.492	60.604	55.556	50.000
50					79.365	75.755	69.445	62.500
60							83.335	75.000

Percentage Tables

Match Points	Avg. 42	45	48	52 1/2	54	55	60	63
1/2	.595	.555	.521	.476	.463	.455	.417	.397
1	1.190	1.111	1.042	.952	.926	.909	.833	.794
2	2.380	2.222	2.084	1.904	1.852	1.818	1.667	1.588
3	3.570	3.333	3.126	2.856	2.778	2.727	2.500	2.382
4	4.760	4.444	4.168	3.808	3.704	3.636	3.333	3.176
5	5.950	5.555	5.210	4.760	4.630	4.545	4.167	3.970
6	7.140	6.666	6.252	5.712	5.556	5.454	5.000	4.764
7	8.330	7.777	7.294	6.664	6.482	6.363	5.833	5.558
8	9.520	8.888	8.336	7.616	7.408	7.272	6.667	6.352
9	10.710	9.999	9.378	8.568	8.334	8.181	7.500	7.146
10	11.905	11.111	10.417	9.524	9.259	9.091	8.333	7.937
20	23.810	22.222	20.834	19.048	18.518	18.182	16.667	15.874
30	35.715	33.333	31.251	28.572	27.777	27.273	25.000	23.811
40	47.620	44.444	41.668	38.096	37.036	36.364	33.333	31.748
50	59.525	55.555	52.085	47.620	46.295	45.455	41.667	39.685
60	71.430	66.666	62.502	57.144	55.554	54.546	50.000	47.622
70		77.777	72.919	66.667	64.813	63.637	58.333	55.559
80				76.192	74.074	72.728	66.667	63.496
90							75.000	71.433
100								79.365

Match Points	Avg. 66	67 1/2	72	73 1/2	77	78	80	84
1/2	.379	.370	.347	.340	.325	.321	.312	.298
1	.758	.741	.694	.680	.649	.641	.625	.595
2	1.516	1.482	1.388	1.360	1.298	1.282	1.250	1.190
3	2.274	2.223	2.082	2.040	1.948	1.923	1.875	1.786
4	3.032	2.964	2.776	2.720	2.597	2.564	2.500	2.381
5	3.790	3.705	3.470	3.400	3.246	3.205	3.125	2.976
6	4.548	4.446	4.164	4.080	3.896	3.846	3.750	3.572
7	5.306	5.187	4.858	4.760	4.545	4.487	4.375	4.167
8	6.064	5.928	5.552	5.440	5.194	5.128	5.000	4.762
9	6.822	6.669	6.246	6.120	5.843	5.769	5.625	5.357
10	7.576	7.407	6.944	6.803	6.494	6.410	6.250	5.952
20	15.152	14.814	13.888	13.605	12.987	12.821	12.500	11.904
30	22.728	22.221	20.832	20.408	19.481	19.231	18.750	17.857
40	30.304	29.628	27.776	27.211	25.974	25.641	25.000	23.809
50	37.880	37.035	34.720	34.013	32.468	32.051	31.250	29.761
60	45.456	44.442	41.664	40.816	38.962	38.462	37.500	35.714
70	53.032	51.849	48.608	47.619	45.456	44.872	43.750	41.667
80	60.608	59.256	55.552	54.422	51.948	51.282	50.000	47.619
90	68.184	66.663	62.496	61.225	58.442	57.692	56.250	53.571
100	75.757	74.074	69.444	68.027	64.935	64.103	62.500	59.524
110			76.388	74.830	71.429	70.513	68.750	65.476
120							75.000	71.428

Match Points	Avg. 88	90	91	94 1/2	96	99	104	108
1/2	.284	.278	.275	.265	.260	.253	.240	.232
1	.568	.556	.549	.529	.521	.505	.481	.463
2	1.136	1.111	1.099	1.058	1.042	1.010	.962	.926
3	1.705	1.667	1.648	1.587	1.562	1.515	1.442	1.389
4	2.273	2.222	2.198	2.116	2.083	2.020	1.923	1.852
5	2.841	2.778	2.747	2.645	2.604	2.525	2.404	2.315
6	3.409	3.333	3.297	3.174	3.124	3.030	2.884	2.778
7	3.977	3.889	3.845	3.703	3.645	3.535	3.365	3.241
8	4.545	4.444	4.396	4.232	4.166	4.040	3.846	3.704
9	5.114	5.000	4.945	4.761	4.687	4.545	4.327	4.167
10	5.682	5.556	5.495	5.291	5.208	5.051	4.808	4.630
20	11.364	11.111	10.989	10.582	10.417	10.101	9.615	9.259
30	17.046	16.667	16.484	15.873	15.625	15.152	14.423	13.889
40	22.727	22.222	21.978	21.164	20.833	20.202	19.231	18.518
50	28.409	27.778	27.473	26.455	26.041	25.253	24.039	23.149
60	34.092	33.333	32.968	31.746	31.250	30.303	28.846	27.778
70	39.774	38.889	38.463	37.037	36.458	35.354	33.654	32.407
80	45.454	44.444	43.956	42.328	41.667	40.404	38.462	37.036
90	51.136	50.000	49.451	47.619	46.874	45.455	43.269	41.667
100	56.818	55.556	54.945	52.910	52.083	50.505	48.077	46.296
110	62.500	61.111	60.440	58.201	57.292	55.556	52.884	50.926
120	68.182	66.667	65.934	63.492	62.500	60.606	57.692	55.556
130	73.864	72.223	71.429	68.783	67.708	65.657	62.500	60.185
140				74.074	72.917	70.707	67.308	64.815
150							72.116	69.444
160								74.074

Percentage Tables

Match Points	Avg. 110	117	120	121 1/2	130	132	135	143
1/2	.227	.214	.208	.206	.192	.189	.185	.175
1	.455	.427	.417	.412	.385	.379	.370	.350
2	.909	.855	.833	.823	.769	.758	.741	.699
3	1.364	1.282	1.250	1.235	1.154	1.136	1.111	1.049
4	1.818	1.709	1.667	1.646	1.538	1.515	1.482	1.399
5	2.273	2.137	2.083	2.058	1.923	1.894	1.852	1.748
6	2.727	2.564	2.500	2.469	2.308	2.273	2.222	2.098
7	3.182	2.991	2.917	2.881	2.692	2.652	2.593	2.448
8	3.636	3.418	3.333	3.292	3.077	3.030	2.963	2.798
9	4.091	3.845	3.750	3.704	3.461	3.409	3.333	3.148
10	4.545	4.274	4.167	4.115	3.846	3.788	3.704	3.497
20	9.091	8.547	8.333	8.230	7.692	7.576	7.407	6.993
30	13.636	12.821	12.500	12.346	11.539	11.364	11.111	10.490
40	18.182	17.094	16.667	16.461	15.385	15.152	14.815	13.986
50	22.727	21.368	20.833	20.576	19.231	18.940	18.519	17.483
60	27.272	25.642	25.000	24.691	23.077	22.727	22.222	20.979
70	31.817	29.916	29.167	28.806	26.923	26.515	25.926	24.476
80	36.363	34.188	33.333	32.922	30.770	30.303	29.630	27.972
90	40.909	38.462	37.500	37.037	34.616	34.091	33.333	31.469
100	45.454	42.735	41.667	41.152	38.462	37.879	37.037	34.965
110	50.000	47.008	45.833	45.267	42.308	41.667	40.741	38.462
120	54.545	51.282	50.000	49.382	46.154	45.455	44.444	41.958
130	59.091	55.556	54.167	53.498	50.000	49.242	48.148	45.455
140	63.636	59.829	58.333	57.613	53.846	53.030	51.852	48.951
150	68.182	64.102	62.500	61.728	57.692	56.818	55.556	52.448
160	72.727	68.376	66.667	65.843	61.539	60.606	59.259	55.944
170		72.651	70.833	69.958	65.385	64.394	62.963	59.441
180				74.074	69.231	68.182	66.667	62.937
190					73.077	71.970	70.370	66.434
200								69.930
210								73.427

Match Points	Avg. 144	150	156	168	182	325
1/2	.174	.167	.161	.149	.137	.077
1	.347	.333	.321	.298	.275	.154
2	.694	.666	.641	.595	.549	.308
3	1.042	1.000	.962	.893	.824	.461
4	1.389	1.333	1.282	1.190	1.099	.615
5	1.736	1.667	1.603	1.488	1.374	.769
6	2.083	2.000	1.923	1.786	1.648	.923
7	2.430	2.333	2.244	2.083	1.923	1.077
8	2.778	2.667	2.564	2.381	2.198	1.230
9	3.125	3.000	2.885	2.678	2.472	1.384
10	3.472	3.333	3.205	2.976	2.747	1.538
20	6.944	6.667	6.410	5.952	5.495	3.077
30	10.417	10.000	9.615	8.929	8.242	4.615
40	13.889	13.333	12.820	11.905	10.989	6.154
50	17.361	16.667	16.026	14.881	13.736	7.692
60	20.833	20.000	19.231	17.857	16.484	9.230
70	24.305	23.333	22.436	20.833	19.231	10.769
80	27.778	26.667	25.641	23.810	21.978	12.307
90	31.250	30.000	28.846	26.786	24.725	13.846
100	34.722	33.333	32.051	29.762	27.473	15.385
110	38.194	36.667	35.256	32.738	30.220	16.923
120	41.667	40.000	38.462	35.714	32.967	18.461
130	45.139	43.333	41.667	38.691	35.714	20.000
140	48.611	46.667	44.872	41.667	38.462	21.538
150	52.083	50.000	48.077	44.643	41.209	23.077
160	55.556	53.333	51.282	47.619	43.956	24.615
170	59.028	56.667	54.487	50.595	46.703	26.154
180	62.500	60.000	57.692	53.571	49.451	27.692
190	65.972	63.333	60.897	56.548	52.198	29.230
200	69.444	66.667	64.103	59.524	54.945	30.769
210	72.917	70.000	67.308	62.500	57.692	32.307
300			96.154	89.285	82.418	46.154
400						61.538
500						76.923

Appendix B

TABLE OF PREFERRED MOVEMENTS

The following tabulation shows the types of movements preferred, according to the number of tables in play. When there is a possible variation in the number of boards that can be played, a corresponding variation is shown in the number of boards per round. In certain movements, some of the players will play fewer boards, and this smaller number of boards is shown in parentheses.

Tables	Boards	Boards per Round	Movement
2	18-21	6-7	Howell
2 1/2-3	20-25	4-5	Howell
3 1/2-4	21-28	3-4	Howell
4 1/2-5	18-27	2-3	Howell
5 1/2-6	22	2	Howell
6 1/2-7	24-26	2	Howell
7	21-28	3-4	Mitchell
7 1/2-8	(21) 24	3	Mitchell, with bye stand
8	21	3	Mitchell, with skip
8 1/2	(18) 21	3	Mitchell, with appendix table
8 1/2-9	(24) 27	3	Mitchell
9 1/2	(18) 20	2	Mitchell, with bye stand
9 1/2	(21) 24	3	Skip Mitchell, with appendix table
10	18-27	2-3	Mitchell, with skip
6-10	22	2	Short three-quarter Howell
10 1/2	(24) 27	3	Mitchell, with appendix table
10 1/2-11	(20) 22	2	Mitchell
11 1/2	(27) 30	3	Mitchell, with appendix table
11 1/2-12	(22) 24	2	Mitchell, with bye stand
12	22	2	Mitchell, with skip
8-12	26	2	Three-quarter Howell
12 1/2-13	(24) 26	2	Mitchell
13 1/2-14	(26) 28	2	Mitchell, with bye stand
14	26	2	Mitchell, with skip
14 1/2-15	(24) 26	2	Mitchell
15 1/2	(24) 26	2	Mitchell -- Rover
16	26	2	Mitchell, with skip

With more than 16 tables in play, it is advisable to split the game into two or more sections. See Pages 83-84, Chapter 6, for a discussion of multiple section games.

ADDING LATE PAIRS

Original Movement	Changes in Adding Late Pair
Howell, with half table	Fill the half table. Maintain Howell movement. Finish game with late play.
Howell, with full tables	Have the late pair replace Pair 2. Make original Pair 2 stationary in its position, assigning it new number just above highest pair number. When original Pair 2 starts against a stationary pair, have late pair replace the lowest numbered pair that does not start against a stationary pair. Tell all pairs to sit out during round in which they reach the position taken by the new stationary pair. Factor scores.
Straight Mitchell, with half table	Fill the half table. Maintain straight Mitchell movement. Finish game with late play.
Straight Mitchell, with:	
A. 7 full tables	1. Use 7 1/2-table Rover. 2. Change to bye stand movement. Place bye stand and set of boards between Tables 4 and 5. Announce to players that one set of boards will be out of order. 3. Change to skip Mitchell.
B. 9 full tables	1. Change to skip Mitchell, if either 18 or 27 boards are satisfactory. 2. Change to 1 1/2-table appendix Mitchell. Remove boards from Table 9. Set up relay between Tables 1 and 9. Finish game with late play. 3. Use 9 1/2-table Rover, if eight rounds of play are adequate (an irregularity makes ninth round impossible in this movement).

Original Movement	Changes in Adding Late Pair
C. 11 full tables	1. Use 11 1/2-table Rover. 2. Change to bye stand movement. Place bye stand and set of boards between Tables 6 and 7. Announce to players that one set of boards will be out of order. 3. Change to skip Mitchell.
D. 13 full tables	1. Use 13 1/2-table Rover. 2. Change to skip Mitchell.
E. 15 full tables	1. Use 15 1/2-table Rover. 2. Change to skip Mitchell.
Bye Stand Mitchell, with half table	Fill the half table. Set up relay between Table 1 and last table. Finish game with late play.
Bye Stand Mitchell, with 8, 12 or 14 full tables	1. Change to straight Mitchell, with sit-out. Move cards from bye stand to highest full table. Place additional set of boards at half table. Announce to players that boards will be out of order. Reshuffle and replay any cards played by higher numbered table in original relay. Finish game with late play. 2. Use appropriate Rover.
Skip Mitchell, with half table (movement is not recommended)	Fill the half table. Maintain the skip Mitchell movement.
Skip Mitchell, with full tables	1. Add a table and new set of boards. Change to straight Mitchell, with sit-out. 2. Use appropriate Rover, maintaining the skip Mitchell movement.
1 1/2-Table Appendix Mitchell, with:	
A. 8 1/2 tables	Change to straight Mitchell. Place additional boards on two highest tables. Reshuffle and replay any cards played by Table 8 in original relay. Finish game with late play.

Original Movement	Changes in Adding Late Pair
B. 9 1/2 tables	Change to skip Mitchell. Place additional boards on two highest tables. Reshuffle and replay any cards played by Table 9 in original relay. Finish game with late play.
C. 10 1/2 tables	Change to straight Mitchell. Place additional boards on two highest tables. Reshuffle and replay any cards played by Table 10 in original relay. Finish game with late play.
D. 11 1/2 tables (an unlikely movement)	Change to Appendix Mitchell. Change Table 11 to Table 12, maintaining its relay with Table 1. Make new table Table 11. Assign new pair numbers at affected tables, correcting traveling scores. Make East-West pair at Table 1 stationary. Make North-South pair at Table 12 stationary. Tell East-West pairs at Tables 2-12 to move up one table at each change, skipping Table 1. Tell North-South pairs at Tables 1-11 to move up two tables at each change, skipping Table 12. Finish game with late play.

Appendix C

HOWELL SCHEDULES AND MASTER SHEETS

SCHEDULE FOR 3-TABLE HOWELL

	Table 1			Table 2			Table 3		
Rd.	Bds.	N-S	E-W	Bds.	N-S	E-W	Bds.	N-S	E-W
1	1-5*	6	1	6-10	3	4	16-20	5	2
2	6-10	6	2	11-15	4	5	16-20	1	3
3	11-15	6	3	6-10	5	1	1-5	2	4
4	16-20	6	4	11-15	1	2	1-5	3	5
5	21-25R	6	5	21-25R	2	3	21-25R	4	1

*For a 20-board game, use only four boards per round; sets will be numbered 1-4, 5-8, 9-12, 13-16, 17-20.

R - Relay

Board Check Total: 6 Grand Check Total: 150 Average Score: 25

SCHEDULE FOR 3-TABLE HOWELL (NO RELAY)

	Table 1			Table 2			Table 3		
Rd.	Bds.	N-S	E-W	Bds.	N-S	E-W	Bds.	N-S	E-W
1	1-4	6	1	11-12, 15-16	2	5	5-6, 17-18	3	4
2	5-8	6	2	15-16, 19-20	3	1	9-10, 1-2	4	5
3	9-12	6	3	19-20, 3-4	4	2	13, 14, 5-6	5	1
4	13-16	6	4	3-4, 7-8	5	3	17-18, 9-10	1	2
5	17-20	6	5	7-8, 11-12	1	4	1-2, 13-14	2	3

Board Check Total: 6 Grand Check Total: 120 Average Score: 20

(The three-table movements form an exception to the regular movement of boards -- the director should watch that the boards are played in the proper order.)

SCHEDULE FOR 4-TABLE HOWELL

	Table 1			Table 2			Table 3			Table 4		
Rd.	Bds.	N-S	E-W	Bds.	N-S	E-W	Bds.	N-S	E-W	Bds.	N-S	E-W
1	1-3*	8	1	10-12	6	3	16-18	7	2	19-21	4	5
2	4-6	8	2	13-15	7	4	19-21	1	3	1-3	5	6
3	7-9	8	3	16-18	1	5	1-3	2	4	4-6	6	7
4	10-12	8	4	19-21	2	6	4-6	3	5	7-9	7	1
5	13-15	8	5	1-3	3	7	7-9	4	6	10-12	1	2
6	16-18	8	6	4-6	4	1	10-12	5	7	13-15	2	3
7	19-21	8	7	7-9	5	2	13-15	6	1	16-18	3	4

*Use four boards per round for a 28-board game; sets will be numbered 1-4, 5-8, 9-12, 13-16, 17-20, 21-24, 25-28.

Board Check Total: 12 Grand Check Total: 252 Average Score: 31 1/2

SCHEDULE FOR CURTAILED 4-TABLE HOWELL

	Table 1			Table 2			Table 3			Table 4		
Rd.	Bds.	N-S	E-W	Bds.	N-S	E-W	Bds.	N-S	E-W	Bds.	N-S	E-W
1	1-3*R	8	1	1-3R	7	5	7-9	6	2	4-6	3	4
2	4-6R	8	2	4-6R	7	6	10-12	1	3	7-9	4	5
3	7-9R	8	3	7-9R	7	1	13-15	2	4	10-12	5	6
4	10-12R	8	4	10-12R	2	7	16-18	3	5	13-15	6	1
5	13-15R	8	5	13-15R	3	7	1-3	4	6	16-18	1	2
6	16-18R	8	6	16-18R	4	7	4-6	5	1	1-3	2	3

*Use four boards per round for a 24-board game; sets will be numbered 1-4, 5-8, 9-12 13-16, 17-20, 21-24.

R-Relay

Board Check Total: 12 Grand Check Total: 216 Average Score: 27

Howell Movements

HOWELL SCHEDULE FOR 5 TABLES -- 18-27 BOARDS

	Table 1			Table 2			Table 3		
Rd.	Bds.	N-S	E-W	Bds.	N-S	E-W	Bds.	N-S	E-W
1	1-3*	7	3	4-6	5	2	7-9	10	1
2	4-6	8	4	7-9	6	3	10-12	10	2
3	7-9	9	5	10-12	7	4	13-15	10	3
4	10-12	1	6	13-15	8	5	16-18	10	4
5	13-15	2	7	16-18	9	6	19-21	10	5
6	16-18	3	8	19-21	1	7	22-24	10	6
7	19-21	4	9	22-24	2	8	25-27	10	7
8	22-24	5	1	25-27	3	9	1-3	10	8
9	25-27	6	2	1-3	4	1	4-6	10	9

	Table 4			Table 5		
Rd.	Bds.	N-S	E-W	Bds.	N-S	E-W
1	10-12	9	8	13-15	4	6
2	13-15	1	9	16-18	5	7
3	16-18	2	1	19-21	6	8
4	19-21	3	2	22-24	7	9
5	22-24	4	3	25-27	8	1
6	25-27	5	4	1-3	9	2
7	1-3	6	5	4-6	1	3
8	4-6	7	6	7-9	2	4
9	7-9	8	7	10-12	3	5

*Use two boards per round for an 18-board game; sets will be numbered 1-2, 3-4, 5-6, 7-8, 9-10, 11-12, 13-14, 15-16, 17-18.

Board Check Total: 20 Grand Check Total: 540 Average Score: 54

HOWELL MASTER SHEET FOR 5 TABLES, CURTAILED -- 21 BOARDS

Rd.	Bds. 1-3	4-6	7-9	10-12	13-15	16-18	19-21	Table
1	10-1		2-7	5-6		4-8	3-9	
2	9-4	10-2		3-1	6-7		8-5	5
3	6-8	9-5	10-3		4-2	7-1		4
4		7-8	9-6	10-4		5-3	1-2	Bye
5	2-3		8-1	7-9	10-5		6-4	3
6	7-5	3-4		8-2	1-9	10-6		2
7		1-6	4-5		3-8	2-9	10-7	Bye
	Table	Bye	2	3	Bye	4	5	1

Board Check Total: 20 Grand Check Total: 420 Average Score: 42

HOWELL MASTER SHEET FOR 5 TABLES, CURTAILED -- 24 BOARDS

Rd.	Bds. 1-3	4-6	7-9	10-12	13-15	16-18	19-21	22-24	Table
1	10-1 9-5	4-7		2-3	6-8				
2		10-2 9-6	5-8		3-4	7-1			Bye
3			10-3 9-7	6-1		4-5	8-2		Bye
4				10-4 9-8	7-2		5-6	1-3	Bye
5	2-4				10-5 1-9	8-3		6-7	4
6	7-8	3-5				10-6 2-9	1-4		3
7		8-1	4-6				10-7 3-9	2-5	Bye
8	3-6		1-2	5-7				10-8 4-9	2
	Table	2	Bye	3	4	Bye	Bye	Bye	1 R 5

R - Relay

Board Check Total: 20 Grand Check Total: 480 Average Score: 48

HOWELL MASTER SHEET FOR 6 TABLES -- 22 BOARDS

Rd.	Bds. 1-2	3-4	5-6	7-8	9-10	11-12	13-14	15-16	17-18	19-20	21-22	Table
1	12-1			6-7		11-4		3-9	2-5		10-8	
2	11-9	12-2			7-8		1-5		4-10	3-6		6
3		1-10	12-3			8-9		2-6		5-11	4-7	Bye
4	5-8		2-11	12-4			9-10		3-7		6-1	5
5	7-2	6-9		3-1	12-5			10-11		4-8		4
6		8-3	7-10		4-2	12-6			11-1		5-9	Bye
7	6-10		9-4	8-11		5-3	12-7			1-2		3
8		7-11		10-5	9-1		6-4	12-8			2-3	Bye
9	3-4		8-1		11-6	10-2		7-5	12-9			2
10		4-5		9-2		1-7	11-3		8-6	12-10		Bye
11			5-6		10-3		2-8	1-4		9-7	12-11	Bye
	Table	Bye	Bye	2	Bye	3	Bye	4	5	Bye	6	1

Board Check Total: 30   Grand Check Total: 660   Average Score: 55

HOWELL MASTER SHEET FOR 6 TABLES -- 24 BOARDS

Rd.	Bds. 1-3	4-6	7-9	10-12	13-15	16-18	19-21	22-24	Table
1	12-1	11-8	10-6	5-9	7-4	3-2			
2		12-2	11-1	10-7	6-9	8-5	4-3		Bye
3			12-3	11-2	8-10	9-7	1-6	5-4	Bye
4	6-5			12-4	11-3	1-10	9-8	2-7	6
5	3-8	7-6			12-5	4-11	2-10	1-9	5
6	2-9	4-1	8-7			12-6	5-11	3-10	4
7	10-4	9-3	5-2	1-8			12-7	6-11	3
8	7-11	10-5	9-4	6-3	2-1			12-8	2
	Table	2	3	4	5	6	Bye	Bye	1

Board Check Total: 30 Grand Check Total: 720 Average Score: 60

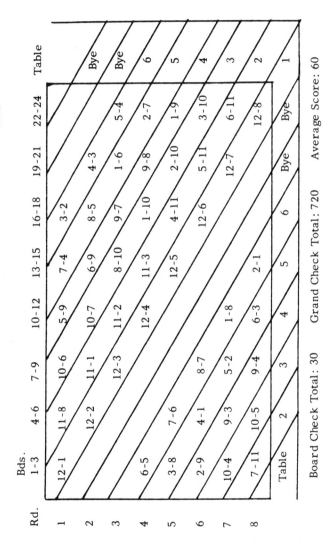

HOWELL MASTER SHEET FOR 6 TABLES -- 18 OR 27 BOARDS

Rd.	Bds. 1-3*	4-6	7-9	10-12	13-15	16-18	19-21	22-24	25-27	Table
1	12-1	11-4	10-8	2-7	9-6	5-3				
2		12-2	11-5	10-9	3-8	1-7	6-4			Bye
3			12-3	11-6	1-10	4-9	2-8	7-5		Bye
4				12-4	7-11	2-10	5-1	3-9	8-6	Bye
5	9-7				12-5	8-11	10-3	6-2	4-1	6
6	5-2	1-8				12-6	11-9	10-4	7-3	5
7	8-4	6-3	2-9				12-7	11-1	5-10	4
8	6-10	9-5	7-4	3-1				12-8	2-11	3
9	3-11	7-10	1-6	8-5	4-2				12-9	2
	Table	2	3	4	5	6	Bye	Bye	Bye	1

* Use two boards per round for an 18-board game; sets will be numbered 1-2, 3-4, 5-6, 7-8, 9-10, 11-12, 13-14, 15-16, 17-18.

Board Check Total: 30   Grand Check Total: 810   Average Score: 67 1/2

HOWELL MASTER SHEET FOR 7 TABLES - 26 BOARDS

Rd.	Bds. 1-2	3-4	5-6	7-8	9-10	11-12	13-14	15-16	17-18	19-20	21-22	23-24	25-26	Table
1	14-1	10-5		9-3	11-2					8-6	13-12		7-4	
2	8-5	14-2	11-6		10-4	12-3					9-7	1-13		
3		9-6	14-3	12-7		11-5	13-4					10-8	2-1	7
4	3-2		10-7	14-4	13-8		12-6	1-5					11-9	Bye
5	12-10	4-3		11-8	14-5	1-9		13-7	2-6					6
6		13-11	5-4		12-9	14-6	2-10		1-8	3-7				5
7			1-12	6-5		13-10	14-7	3-11		2-9	4-8			Bye
8				2-13	7-6		1-11	14-8	4-12		3-10	5-9		Bye
9					3-1	8-7		2-12	14-9	5-13		4-11	6-10	Bye
10	7-17					4-2	9-8		3-13	14-10	6-1		5-12	Bye
11	6-13	8-12					5-3	10-9		4-1	14-11	7-2		4
12		7-1	9-13					6-4	11-10		5-2	14-12	8-3	3
13	9-4		8-2	10-1					7-5	12-11		6-3	14-13	Bye
														2
	Table 2		Bye	3	4	Bye	Bye	Bye	Bye	5	6	Bye	7	1

Board Check Total: 42   Grand Check Total: 1092   Average Score: 78

(Movement by Olof Hanner)

3/4 HOWELL MASTER SHEET FOR 8 TABLES -- 26 BOARDS

Rd.	Bds. 1-2	3-4	5-6	7-8	9-10	11-12	13-14	15-16	17-18	19-20	21-22	23-24	25-26	Table
1	16-1	4-15	11-13	14-7	10-9	5-12	3-8	2-6						
2		16-2	5-15	12-1	14-8	11-10	6-13	4-9	3-7					Bye
3			16-3	6-15	13-2	14-9	12-11	7-1	5-10	4-8				Bye
4				16-4	7-15	1-3	14-10	13-12	8-2	6-11	5-9			Bye
5					16-5	8-15	2-4	14-11	1-13	9-3	7-12	6-10		Bye
6						16-6	9-15	3-5	14-12	2-1	10-4	8-13	7-11	Bye
7	8-12						16-7	10-15	4-6	14-13	3-2	11-5	9-1	8
8	10-2	9-13						16-8	15-11	5-7	1-14	4-3	12-6	7
9	13-7	11-3	10-1						16-9	15-12	6-8	2-14	5-4	6
10	6-5	1-8	12-4	11-2						16-10	15-13	7-9	3-14	5
11	4-14	7-6	2-9	13-5	12-3						16-11	15-1	8-10	4
12	9-11	5-14	8-7	3-10	1-6	13-4						16-12	15-2	3
13	15-3	10-12	6-14	9-8	4-11	2-7	1-5						16-13	2
	Table	2	3	4	5	6	7	8	Bye	Bye	Bye	Bye	Bye	1

Board Check Total: 56 | Grand Check Total: 1456 | Average Score: 91

3/4 HOWELL MASTER SHEET FOR 9 TABLES -- 26 BOARDS

Rd.	Bds. 1-2	3-4	5-6	7-8	9-10	11-12	13-14	15-16	17-18	19-20	21-22	23-24	25-26	Table
1	18-1	17-12	8-5	2-10	13-9	7-16	15-6	11-4	14-3					
2		18-2	17-13	9-6	3-11	1-10	8-16	15-7	12-5	14-4				Bye
3			18-3	17-1	10-7	4-12	2-11	9-16	8-15	13-6	14-5			Bye
4				18-4	17-2	11-8	5-13	3-12	10-16	9-15	1-7	14-6		Bye
5					18-5	17-3	12-9	6-1	4-13	16-11	10-15	2-8	14-7	Bye
6	8-14					18-6	17-4	13-10	7-2	5-1	16-12	15-11	3-9	9
7	4-10	9-14					18-7	17-5	1-11	8-3	6-2	16-13	15-12	8
8	13-15	5-11	10-14					18-8	6-17	2-12	9-4	7-3	16-1	7
9	16-2	1-15	6-12	11-14					18-9	7-17	3-13	10-5	8-4	6
10	9-5	16-3	15-2	7-13	12-14					18-10	8-17	4-1	11-6	5
11	12-7	10-6	4-16	15-3	8-1	13-14					18-11	9-17	5-2	4
12	6-3	13-8	11-7	5-16	15-4	9-2	14-1					18-12	10-17	3
13	11-17	7-4	1-9	12-8	6-16	15-5	10-3	14-2					18-13	2
	Table	2	3	4	5	6	7	8	9	Bye	Bye	Bye	Bye	1

Board Check Total: 72 Grand Check Total: 1872 Average Score: 104

3/4 HOWELL MASTER SHEET FOR 10 TABLES -- 26 BOARDS

Rd.	Bds. 1-2	3-4	5-6	7-8	9-10	11-12	13-14	15-16	17-18	19-20	21-22	23-24	25-26	Table
1	20-1	6-19	18-8	13-17	3-7	12-16	15-2	11-5	14-10	9-4				
2		20-2	7-19	9-18	17-1	4-8	13-16	15-3	12-6	14-11	10-5			Bye
3			20-3	19-8	10-18	17-2	5-9	16-1	15-4	13-7	14-12	11-6		Bye
4				20-4	19-9	11-18	3-17	6-10	16-2	15-5	1-8	13-14	12-7	Bye
5	13-8				20-5	19-10	12-18	4-17	7-11	16-3	15-6	2-9	1-14	10
6	2-14	1-9				20-6	11-19	18-13	17-5	8-12	4-16	15-7	3-10	9
7	4-11	3-14	2-10				20-7	12-19	18-1	17-6	9-13	5-16	15-8	8
8	9-15	5-12	4-14	3-11				20-8	13-19	18-2	7-17	10-1	16-6	7
9	16-7	10-15	6-13	5-14	4-12				20-9	1-19	3-18	17-8	11-2	6
10	12-3	16-8	11-15	7-1	14-6	5-13				20-10	19-2	4-18	17-9	5
11	10-17	13-4	9-16	12-15	8-2	14-7	6-1				20-11	19-3	5-18	4
12	18-6	11-17	1-5	10-16	13-15	9-3	14-8	7-2				20-12	19-4	3
13	19-5	18-7	12-17	2-6	11-16	1-15	10-4	14-9	8-3				20-13	2
	Table	2	3	4	5	6	7	8	9	10	Bye	Bye	Bye	1

Board Check Total: 90 Grand Check Total: 2340 Average Score: 117

3/4 HOWELL MASTER SHEET FOR 11 TABLES -- 26 BOARDS

Rd.	Bds. 1-2	3-4	5-6	7-8	9-10	11-12	13-14	15-16	17-18	19-20	21-22	23-24	25-26	Table
1	7-8	22-1	21-3	20-5	2-19	10-18	12-17	4-16	15-11	13-14	6-9			
2		8-9	22-2	21-4	20-6	3-19	11-18	17-13	5-16	15-12	1-14	7-10		Bye
3			9-10	22-3	21-5	20-7	19-4	18-12	17-1	16-6	15-13	14-2	8-11	Bye
4	9-12			10-11	22-4	21-6	8-20	19-5	13-18	2-17	16-7	1-15	14-3	11
5	4-14	10-13			11-12	22-5	7-21	9-20	6-19	18-1	3-17	16-8	2-15	10
6	3-15	5-14	11-1			12-13	22-6	8-21	10-20	19-7	18-2	4-17	9-16	9
7	10-16	15-4	6-14	12-2			13-1	22-7	9-21	11-20	8-19	3-18	5-17	8
8	6-17	11-16	15-5	14-7	13-3			1-2	22-8	21-10	12-20	19-9	18-4	7
9	18-5	7-17	16-12	15-6	14-8	1-4			2-3	22-9	21-11	20-13	19-10	6
10	19-11	6-18	17-8	16-13	7-15	14-9	2-5			3-4	22-10	12-21	20-1	5
11	20-2	12-19	7-18	17-9	1-16	8-15	14-10	3-6			4-5	22-11	13-21	4
12	1-21	20-3	13-19	18-8	17-10	2-16	9-15	11-14	4-7			5-6	22-12	3
13	22-13	2-21	4-20	1-19	18-9	17-11	16-3	10-15	12-14	5-8			6-7	2
	Table	2	3	4	5	6	7	8	9	10	11	Bye	Bye	1

Board Check Total: 110 Grand Check Total: 2860 Average Score: 130

3/4 HOWELL MASTER SHEET FOR 12 TABLES -- 26 BOARDS

Rd.	Bds. 1-2	3-4	5-6	7-8	9-10	11-12	13-14	15-16	17-18	19-20	21-22	23-24	25-26	Table
1	7-8	22-1	21-3	20-5	2-19	10-18	12-17	4-16	15-11	14-13	24-9 6-23			
2		8-9	22-2	21-4	20-6	3-19	11-18	13-17	5-16	15-12	14-1	24-10 7-23		Bye
3			9-10	22-3	21-5	20-7	4-19	12-18	1-17	6-16	15-13	14-2	24-11 8-23	Bye
4	24-12 9-23			10-11	22-4	21-6	20-8	5-19	13-18	2-17	7-16	15-1	14-3	11 12 R
5	14-4	13-24 10-23			11-12	22-5	21-7	20-9	6-19	1-18	3-17	8-16	15-2	10
6	15-3	14-5	1-24 11-23			12-13	22-6	21-8	20-10	7-19	2-18	4-17	9-16	9
7	10-16	15-4	14-6	2-24 12-23			13-1	22-7	21-9	20-11	8-19	3-18	5-17	8
8	17-6	16-11	5-15	7-14	3-24 23-13			1-2	22-8	10-21	12-20	19-9	18-4	7
9	18-5	17-7	16-12	6-15	8-14	4-24 23-1			2-3	22-9	11-21	13-20	19-10	6
10	19-11	18-6	17-8	16-13	7-15	9-14	5-24 23-2			3-4	22-10	12-21	1-20	5
11	2-20	19-12	18-7	17-9	16-1	8-15	10-14	24-6 23-3			4-5	22-11	13-21	4
12	21-1	3-20	19-13	18-8	17-10	16-2	9-15	11-14	24-7 23-4			5-6	22-12	3
13	22-13	21-2	4-20	19-1	18-9	17-11	16-3	10-15	12-14	24-8 23-5			6-7	2
	Table	2	3	4	5	6	7	8	9	10	11 12 R	Bye	Bye	1

Board Check Total: 132 Grand Check Total: 3432 Average Score: 143

SHORT 3/4 HOWELL MASTER SHEET FOR 7 TABLES -- 22 BOARDS

Rd	Bds 1-2	3-4	5-6	7-8	9-10	11-12	13-14	15-16	17-18	19-20	21-22	Table
1	14-1	4-6	9-10	7-3	12-2	11-13	5-8					
2		14-2	5-7	10-11	8-4	12-3	1-13	6-9				Bye
3			14-3	6-8	11-1	9-5	12-4	2-13	7-10			Bye
4				14-4	7-9	1-2	10-6	12-5	13-3	8-11		Bye
5					14-5	8-10	2-3	11-7	12-6	13-4	9-1	Bye
6	10-2					14-6	9-11	3-4	1-8	12-7	13-5	7
7	13-6	11-3					14-7	10-1	4-5	2-9	8-12	6
8	9-12	7-13	1-4					14-8	11-2	5-6	3-10	5
9	4-11	10-12	8-13	2-5					14-9	1-3	6-7	4
10	7-8	5-1	11-12	9-13	3-6					14-10	2-4	3
11	3-5	8-9	6-2	1-12	10-13	4-7					14-11	2
	Table	2	3	4	5	6	7	Bye	Bye	Bye	Bye	1

Board Check Total: 42 Grand Check Total: 924 Average Score: 66

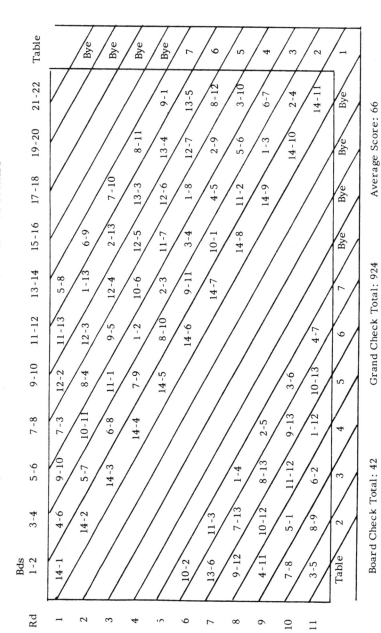

SHORT 3/4 HOWELL MASTER SHEET FOR 8 TABLES -- 22 BOARDS

Rd.	Bds. 1-2	3-4	5-6	7-8	9-10	11-12	13-14	15-16	17-18	19-20	21-22	Table
1	16-1	4-15	11-13	14-10	9-8	5-7	3-12	2-6				
2		16-2	5-15	1-13	14-11	10-9	6-8	4-12	3-7			Bye
3			16-3	6-15	2-13	1-14	11-10	7-9	5-12	4-8		Bye
4				16-4	7-15	13-3	2-14	1-11	8-10	6-12	5-9	Bye
5	6-10				16-5	8-15	13-4	3-14	2-1	9-11	12-7	8
6	12-8	7-11				16-6	9-15	13-5	4-14	3-2	10-1	7
7	11-2	12-9	8-1				16-7	15-10	6-13	5-14	4-3	6
8	5-4	1-3	12-10	9-2				16-8	15-11	7-13	6-14	5
9	14-7	6-5	2-4	12-11	10-3				16-9	15-1	8-13	4
10	13-9	14-8	7-6	3-5	1-12	11-4				16-10	15-2	3
11	15-3	13-10	14-9	8-7	4-6	2-12	1-5				16-11	2
	Table	2	3	4	5	6	7	8	Bye	Bye	Bye	1

Board Check Total: 56 Grand Check Total: 1232 Average Score: 77

SHORT 3/4 HOWELL MASTER SHEET FOR 9 TABLES -- 22 BOARDS

Rd.	Bds. 1-2	3-4	5-6	7-8	9 10	11-12	13-14	15-16	17-18	19-20	21-22	Table
1	18-1	17-5	16-11	2-10	15 9	7-8	6-14	4-13	3-12			
2		18-2	17-6	16-1	3-11	15-10	8-9	7-14	5-13	12-4		Bye
3			18-3	17-7	16-2	4-1	11-15	9-10	8-14	13-6	12-5	Bye
4	12-6			18-4	17-8	3-16	5-2	1-15	10-11	14-9	13-7	9
5	13-8	12-7			18-5	17-9	4-16	6-3	2-15	11-1	14-10	8
6	14-11	13-9	8-12			18-6	17-10	5-16	7-4	15-3	1-2	7
7	2-3	14-1	10-13	9-12			18-7	11-17	6-16	8-5	15-4	6
8	15-5	3-4	2-14	13-11	12-10			18-8	1-17	7-16	9-6	5
9	10-7	15-6	4-5	14-3	13-1	11-12			18-9	2-17	16-8	4
10	16-9	11-8	7-15	5-6	14-4	2-13	12-1			18-10	3-17	3
11	4-17	16-10	1-9	8-15	6-7	5-14	3-13	2-12			18-11	2
	Table	2	3	4	5	6	7	8	9	Bye	Bye	1

Board Check Total: 72 Grand Check Total: 1584 Average Score: 88

SHORT 3/4 HOWELL MASTER SHEET FOR 10 TABLES -- 22 BOARDS

Rd.	Bds. 1-2	3-4	5-6	7-8	9-10	11-12	13-14	15-16	17-18	19-20	21-22	Table
1	18-1	17-5	1-11	19-10 20-2	9-15	7-8	6-14	4-13	3-12			
2		18-2	17-6	16-1	19-11 20-3	10-15	8-9	14-7	5-13	12-4		Bye
3			18-3	17-7	2-16	19-1 20-4	15-11	9-10	14-8	6-13	5-12	Bye
4	12-6			18-4	8-17	3-16	19-2 20-5	15-1	10-11	9-14	13-7	10
5	8-13	7-12			18-5	9-17	16-4	19-3 6-20	15-2	11-1	10-14	9
6	14-11	13-9	8-12			18-6	10-17	16-5	19-4 7-20	3-15	1-2	8
7	2-3	14-1	13-10	9-12			18-7	17-11	6-16	5-19 8-20	4-15	7
8	5-15	3-4	2-14	13-11	12-10			18-8	17-1	7-16	6-19 9-20	6
9	7-19 10-20	15-6	4-5	3-14	1-13	12-11			18-9	17-2	16-8	5 4R
10	16-9	8-19 20-11	15-7	5-6	14-4	13-2	12-1			18-10	3-17	3
11	4-17	10-16	9-19 20-1	8-15	6-7	14-5	3-13	2-12			18-11	2
	Table	2	3	4 5R	6	7	8	9	10	Bye	Bye	1

Board Check Total: 90 Grand Check Total: 1980 Average Score: 99

Appendix D

MITCHELL MASTER SHEETS

MITCHELL MASTER SHEET FOR 11 TABLES -- 22 BOARDS

Rd.	Bds. 1-2	3-4	5-6	7-8	9-10	11-12	13-14	15-16	17-18	19-20	21-22	Table
1	1-1	2-2	3-3	4-4	5-5	6-6	7-7	8-8	9-9	10-10	11-11	
2	11-10	1-11	2-1	3-2	4-3	5-4	6-5	7-6	8-7	9-8	10-9	11
3	10-8	11-9	1-10	2-11	3-1	4-2	5-3	6-4	7-5	8-6	9-7	10
4	9-6	10-7	11-8	1-9	2-10	3-11	4-1	5-2	6-3	7-4	8-5	9
5	8-4	9-5	10-6	11-7	1-8	2-9	3-10	4-11	5-1	6-2	7-3	8
6	7-2	8-3	9-4	10-5	11-6	1-7	2-8	3-9	4-10	5-11	6-1	7
7	6-11	7-1	8-2	9-3	10-4	11-5	1-6	2-7	3-8	4-9	5-10	6
8	5-9	6-10	7-11	8-1	9-2	10-3	11-4	1-5	2-6	3-7	4-8	5
9	4-7	5-8	6-9	7-10	8-11	9-1	10-2	11-3	1-4	2-5	3-6	4
10	3-5	4-6	5-7	6-8	7-9	8-10	9-11	10-1	11-2	1-3	2-4	3
11	2-3	3-4	4-5	5-6	6-7	7-8	8-9	9-10	10-11	11-1	1-2	2
	Table	2	3	4	5	6	7	8	9	10	11	1

Board Check Total: 55 Grand Check Total: 1210 Average Score: 110

SKIP MITCHELL MASTER SHEET FOR 12 TABLES -- 24 BOARDS

Rd.	Bds. 1-2	3-4	5-6	7-8	9-10	11-12	13-14	15-16	17-18	19-20	21-22	23-24	Table
1	1-1	2-2	3-3	4-4	5-5	6-6	7-7	8-8	9-9	10-10	11-11	12-12	
2	12-11	1-12	2-1	3-2	4-3	5-4	6-5	7-6	8-7	9-8	10-9	11-10	12
3	11-9	12-10	1-11	2-12	3-1	4-2	5-3	6-4	7-5	8-6	9-7	10-8	11
4	10-7	11-8	12-9	1-10	2-11	3-12	4-1	5-2	6-3	7-4	8-5	9-6	10
5	9-5	10-6	11-7	12-8	1-9	2-10	3-11	4-12	5-1	6-2	7-3	8-4	9
6	8-3	9-4	10-5	11-6	12-7	1-8	2-9	3-10	4-11	5-12	6-1	7-2	8
7	7-12	8-1	9-2	10-3	11-4	12-5	1-6	2-7	3-8	4-9	5-10	6-11	7
8	6-10	7-11	8-12	9-1	10-2	11-3	12-4	1-5	2-6	3-7	4-8	5-9	6
9	5-8	6-9	7-10	8-11	9-12	10-1	11-2	12-3	1-4	2-5	3-6	4-7	5
10	4-6	5-7	6-8	7-9	8-10	9-11	10-12	11-1	12-2	1-3	2-4	3-5	4
11	3-4	4-5	5-6	6-7	7-8	8-9	9-10	10-11	11-12	12-1	1-2	2-3	3
	Table	3	4	5	6	7	8	9	10	11	12	1	2

EAST-WEST PAIRS SKIP ONE TABLE

Board Check Total: 55   Grand Check Total: 1320   Average Score: 110

BYE STAND MITCHELL MASTER SHEET FOR 8 TABLES -- 24 BOARDS

Relay Tables 1 and 8 -- Bye Stand between Tables 4 and 5

Rd.	Bds. 1-3	4-6	7-9	10-12	13-15	16-18	19-21	22-24	Table
1	1-1 8-8	2-2	3-3	4-4		5-5	6-6	7-7	
2	7-6	1-8 8-7	2-1	3-2	4-3		5-4	6-5	7
3	6-4	7-5	1-7 8-6	2-8	3-1	4-2		5-3	6
4	5-2	6-3	7-4	1-6 8-5	2-7	3-8	4-1		5
5		5-1	6-2	7-3	1-5 8-4	2-6	3-7	4-8	Bye
6	4-7		5-8	6-1	7-2	1-4 8-3	2-5	3-6	4
7	3-5	4-6		5-7	6-8	7-1	1-3 8-2	2-4	3
8	2-3	3-4	4-5		5-6	6-7	7-8	1-2 8-1	2
	Table	2	3	4	Bye	5	6	7	1R 8

Board Check Total: 28 Grand Check Total: 672 Average Score: 84

1 1/2 TABLE APPENDIX MITCHELL MASTER SHEET FOR 9 1/2 TABLES -- 24 BOARDS

Relay Tables 1 and 9

Rd.	Bds. 1-3	4-6	7-9	10-12	13-15	16-18	19-21	22-24	Table
1	1-1 9-9	2-2	3-3	4-4	5-5	6-6	7-7	8-8	
2	8-7	1-10 9-8	2-1	3-2	4-3	5-4	6-5	7-6	8
3	7-5	8-6	1-9 9-7	2-10	3-1	4-2	5-3	6-4	7
4	6-3	7-4	8-5	1-8 9-6	2-9	3-10	4-1	5-2	6
5	5-10	6-1	7-2	8-3	1-6 9-4	2-7	3-8	4-9	5
6	4-8	5-9	6-10	7-1	8-2	1-5 9-3	2-6	3-7	4
7	3-6	4-7	5-8	6-9	7-10	8-1	1-4 9-2	2-5	3
8	2-4	3-5	4-6	5-7	6-8	7-9	8-10	1-3 9-1	2
	Table	2	3	4	5	6	7	8	1 R 9

EAST-WEST PAIRS SKIP ONE TABLE

Board Check Total: 36 Grand Check Total: 864 Average Score: N-S, E-W 1 and E-W 6: 96; Remaining E-W: 84

Mitchell Movements

INTERWOVEN MOVEMENT MASTER SHEET FOR 7 TABLES

FIRST SESSION -- SCRAMBLED MITCHELL -- 21 BOARDS

Rd.	Bds. 1-3	4-6	7-9	10-12	13-15	16-18	19-21	Table
1	1-14	2-8	3-9	4-10	5-11	6-12	7-13	
2	7-12	1-13	2-14	3-8	4-9	5-10	6-11	7
3	6-10	7-11	1-12	2-13	3-14	4-8	5-9	6
4	8-5	9-6	10-7	11-1	12-2	13-3	14-4	5
5	13-4	14-5	8-6	9-7	10-1	11-2	12-3	4
6	11-3	12-4	13-5	14-6	8-7	9-1	10-2	3
	Table	3	4	5	6	7	1	2

Board Check Total: 30 Grand Check Total: 630 Average Score: 45

SECOND SESSION -- INTERWOVEN HOWELL -- 21 BOARDS

Rd.	Bds. 1-3	4-6	7-9	10-12	13-15	16-18	19-21	Table
1	8-1	4-5 11-12	2-7 9-14		3-6 10-13			
2		9-2	5-6 12-13	3-1 10-8		4-7 11-14		Bye
3			10-3	6-7 13-14	4-2 11-9		5-1 12-8	Bye
4	6-2 13-9			11-4	7-1 14-8	5-3 12-10		7R 6
5		7-3 14-10			12-5	1-2 8-9	6-4 13-11	Bye
6	7-5 14-12		1-4 8-11			13-6	2-3 9-10	5R 4
7	3-4 10-11	1-6 8-13		2-5 9-12			14-7	3R 2
	Table	3R 2	5R 4	Bye	7R 6	Bye	Bye	1

Board Check Total: 42 Grand Check Total: 882 Average Score: 63

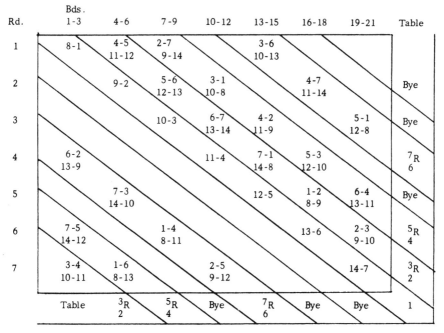

INTERWOVEN MOVEMENT MASTER SHEET FOR 8 TABLES

FIRST SESSION -- SCRAMBLED BYE STAND MITCHELL -- 24 BOARDS

Relay Tables 1 and 8 -- Bye Stand between Tables 4 and 5

Rd. / Bds.	1-3	4-6	7-9	10-12	13-15	16-18	19-21	22-24	Table
1	8-15 1-16	2-9	3-10	4-11		5-12	6-13	7-14	
2	7-13	8-14 1-15	2-16	3-9	4-10		5-11	6-12	7
3	6-11	7-12	8-13 1-14	2-15	3-16	4-9		5-10	6
4	5-9	6-10	7-11	8-12 1-13	2-14	3-15	4-16		5
5		16-5	9-6	10-7	11-8 12-1	3-2	14-3	15-4	Bye
6	14-4		15-5	16-6	9-7	10-8 11-1	12-2	13-3	4
7	12-3	13-4		14-5	15-6	16-7	9-8 10-1	11-2	3
8	10-2	11-3	12-4		13-5	14-6	15-7	16-8 9-1	2
	Table	2	3	4	Bye	5	6	7	8R 1

Board Check Total: 56 Grand Check Total: 1344 Average Score: 84

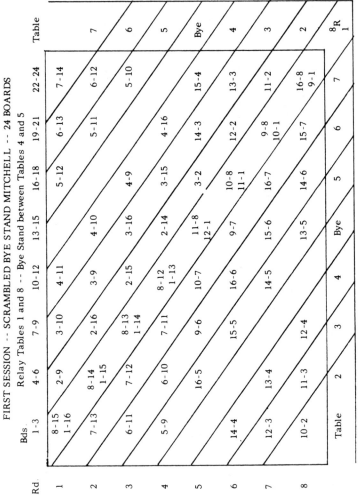

SECOND SESSION -- INTERWOVEN HOWELL -- 21 BOARDS

Rd.	Bds 1-3	4-6	7-9	10-12	13-15	16-18	19-21	Table
1	16-9 8-1	12-13	10-15	3-6	11-14	2-7	4-5	
2	5-6	16-10 8-2	13-14	11-9	4-7	12-15	3-1	7
3	4-2	6-7	16-11 8-3	14-15	12-10	5-1	13-9	6
4	14-10	5-3	7-1	16-12 8-4	15-9	13-11	6-2	5
5	7-3	15-11	6-4	1-2	13-16 8-5	9-10	14-12	4
6	15-13	1-4	9-12	7-5	2-3	14-16 8-6	10-11	3
7	11-12	9-14	2-5	10-13	1-6	3-4	15-16 8-7	2
	Table	2	3	4	5	6	7	8R 1

Board Check Total: 56 Grand Check Total: 1176 Average Score: 73 1/2

INTERWOVEN MOVEMENT MASTER SHEET FOR 9 TABLES

FIRST SESSION -- SCRAMBLED MITCHELL -- 27 BOARDS

Rd.	Bds 1-3	4-6	7-9	10-12	13-15	16-18	19-21	22-24	25-27	Table
1	1-18	2-10	3-11	4-12	5-13	6-14	7-15	8-16	9-17	
2	9-16	1-17	2-18	3-10	4-11	5-12	6-13	7-14	8-15	9
3	8-14	9-15	1-16	2-17	3-18	4-10	5-11	6-12	7-13	8
4	7-12	8-13	9-14	1-15	2-16	3-17	4-18	5-10	6-11	7
5	10-6	11-7	12-8	13-9	14-1	15-2	16-3	17-4	18-5	6
6	17-5	18-6	10-7	11-8	12-9	13-1	14-2	15-3	16-4	5
7	15-4	16-5	17-6	18-7	10-8	11-9	12-1	13-2	14-3	4
8	13-3	14-4	15-5	16-6	17-7	18-8	10-9	11-1	12-2	3
	Table	3	4	5	6	7	8	9	1	2

Board Check Total: 56 Grand Check Total: 1512 Average Score: 84

SECOND SESSION -- INTERWOVEN HOWELL -- 27 BOARDS

Rd.	Bds. 1-3	4-6	7-9	10-12	13-15	16-18	19-21	22-24	25-27	Table
1	10-1	17-18	2-5 13-15		8-9	3-7		4-6 12-16	11-14	
2	12-15	11-2	18-10	3-6 14-16		9-1	4-8		5-7 13-17	9
3	6-8 14-18	13-16	12-3	10-11	4-7 15-17		1-2	5-9		$^{8}R_{7}$
4		7-9 15-10	14-17	13-4	11-12	5-8 16-18		2-3	6-1	Bye
5	7-2		8-1 16-11	15-18	14-5	12-13	6-9 17-10		3-4	6
6	4-5	8-3		9-2 17-12	16-10	15-6	13-14	7-1 18-11		5
7		5-6	9-4		1-3 18-13	17-11	16-7	14-15	8-2 10-12	Bye
8	9-3 11-13		6-7	1-5		2-4 10-14	18-12	17-8	15-16	$^{4}R_{3}$
9	16-17	1-4 12-14		7-8	2-6		3-5 11-15	10-13	18-9	2
	Table	2	$^{4}R_{3}$	Bye	5	6	Bye	$^{8}R_{7}$	9	1

Board Check Total: 72 Grand Check Total: 1944 Average Score: 108

INTERWOVEN MOVEMENT MASTER SHEET FOR 10 TABLES

FIRST SESSION -- SCRAMBLED SKIP MITCHELL --30 BOARDS

Rd.	Bds. 1-3	4-6	7-9	10-12	13-15	16-18	19-21	22-24	25-27	28-30	Table
1	1-20	2-11	3-12	4-13	5-14	6-15	7-16	8-17	9-18	10-19	
2	10-18	1-19	2-20	3-11	4-12	5-13	6-14	7-15	8-16	9-17	10
3	9-16	10-17	1-18	2-19	3-20	4-11	5-12	6-13	7-14	8-15	9
4	8-14	9-15	10-16	1-17	2-18	3-19	4-20	5-11	6-12	7-13	8
5	7-12	8-13	9-14	10-15	1-16	2-17	3-18	4-19	5-20	6-11	7
			EAST-WEST PAIRS SKIP ONE TABLE								
6	19-6	20-7	11-8	12-9	13-10	14-1	15-2	16-3	17-4	18-5	6
7	17-5	18-6	19-7	20-8	11-9	12-10	13-1	14-2	15-3	16-4	5
8	15-4	16-5	17-6	18-7	19-8	20-9	11-10	12-1	13-2	14-3	4
9	13-3	14-4	15-5	16-6	17-7	18-8	19-9	20-10	11-1	12-2	3
	Table	3	4	5	6	7	8	9	10	1	2

Board Check Total: 72 Grand Check Total: 2160 Average Score: 108

SECOND SESSION -- INTERWOVEN HOWELL -- 27 BOARDS

Rd.	Bds. 1-3	4-6	7-9	10-12	13-15	16-18	19-21	22-24	25-27	Table
1	14-16 7-3	5-2	10-1	9-8	4-6	17-13	15-12	20-11	19-18	
2	11-19	15-17 8-4	6-3	10-2	1-9	5-7	18-14	16-13	20-12	9
3	20-13	12-11	16-18 9-5	7-4	10-3	2-1	6-8	19-15	17-14	8
4	18-15	20-14	13-12	17-19 1-6	8-5	10-4	3-2	7-9	11-16	7
5	12-17	19-16	20-15	14-13	18-11 2-7	9-6	10-5	4-3	8-1	6
6	9-2	13-18	11-17	16-20	15-14	19-12 3-8	1-7	10-6	5-4	5
7	6-5	1-3	14-19	12-18	17-20	16-15	11-13 4-9	2-8	10-7	4
8	10-8	7-6	2-4	15-11	13-19	18-20	17-16	12-14 5-1	3-9	3
9	4-1	10-9	8-7	3-5	16-12	14-11	19-20	18-17	13-15 6-2	2
	Table	2	3	4	5	6	7	8	9	10R 1

Board Check Total: 90 Grand Check Total: 2430 Average Score: 121 1/2

Appendix E

ROVER MOVEMENTS

7 1/2 Tables
21 Boards

Rd.	Table	Bds.
1	Bye	
2	2	7-9
3	4	16-18
4	6	4-6
5	1	13-15
6	3	1-3
7	5	10-12

8 1/2 Tables
21 Boards*

Rd.	Table	Bds.
1	Bye	
2	2	7-9
3	4	16-18
4	6	1-3
E-W Pairs Skip		
5	3	19-21
6	5	4-6
7	7	13-15

* IMPORTANT: 24 boards in play, 3 on each of the 8 tables

** 9 1/2 Tables
27 Boards

Rd.	Table	Bds.
1	Bye	
2	2	7-9
3	4	16-18
4	6	25-27
5	9	10-12
6	3	22-24
7	5	4-6
8	7	13-15
9	8	19-21

10 1/2 Tables
27 Boards

Rd.	Table	Bds.
1	Bye	
2	2	7-9
3	4	16-18
4	6	25-27
5	8	4-6
E-W Pairs Skip		
6	3	22-24
7	5	1-3
8	7	10-12
9	9	19-21

11 1/2 Tables
22 Boards

Rd.	Table	Bds.
1	Bye	
2	2	5-6
3	4	11-12
4	6	17-18
5	8	1-2
6	10	7-8
7	1	13-14
8	3	19-20
9	5	3-4
10	7	9-10
11	9	15-16

12 1/2 Tables
24 Boards

Rd.	Table	Bds.
1	Bye	
2	2	5-6
3	10	23-24
4	8	21-22
5	6	19-20
6	4	17-18
E-W Pairs Skip		
7	1	13-14
8	11	11-12
9	9	9-10
10	5	3-4
11	3	1-2

**This movement requires two irregularities in movement of East-West pairs: E-W Pair 6 moves as follows -- Tables 6, 7, 2, 9, 1, 5, 3, 4 and 8; E-W Pair 9 moves as follows -- Tables 9, 1, 8, 3, 4, 2, 6, 7 and 5.

13 1/2 Tables
26 Boards

Rd.	Table	Bds.
1	Bye	
2	2	5-6
3	4	11-12
4	6	17-18
5	8	23-24
6	10	3-4
7	12	9-10
8	1	15-16
9	3	21-22
10	5	1-2
11	7	7-8
12	9	13-14
13	11	19-20

14 1/2 Tables
28 Boards

Rd.	Table	Bds.
1	Bye	
2	2	5-6
3	4	11-12
4	6	17-18
5	8	23-24
6	10	1-2
7	12	7-8
E-W Pairs Skip		
8	3	19-20
9	5	25-26
10	7	3-4
11	9	9-10
12	11	15-16
13	13	21-22

15 1/2 Tables
30 Boards

Rd.	Table	Bds.
1	Bye	
2	2	5-6
3	4	11-12
4	6	17-18
5	8	23-24
6	10	29-30
7	13	7-8
8	15	13-14
9	3	21-22
10	5	27-28
11	7	3-4
12	9	9-10
13	11	15-16

16 1/2 Tables
32 Boards

Rd.	Table	Bds.
1	Bye	
2	2	5-6
3	4	11-12
4	6	17-18
5	8	23-24
6	10	29-30
7	12	3-4
8	14	9-10
E-W Pairs Skip		
9	3	21-22
10	5	27-28
11	7	1-2
12	9	7-8
13	11	13-14

17 1/2 Tables
34 Boards

Rd.	Table	Bds.
1	Bye	
2	2	5-6
3	4	11-12
4	6	17-18
5	8	23-24
6	10	29-30
7	12	1-2
8	14	7-8
9	16	13-14
10	1	19-20
11	3	25-26
12	5	31-32
13	7	3-4

18 1/2 Tables
36 Boards

Rd.	Table	Bds
1	Bye	
2	2	5-6
3	4	11-12
4	6	17-18
5	8	23-24
6	10	29-30
7	12	35-36
8	15	7-8
9	17	13-14
E-W Pairs Skip		
10	5	27-28
11	7	33-34
12	9	3-4
13	11	9-10

Appendix F

INDIVIDUAL MOVEMENTS

SCHEDULE FOR 8-PLAYER INDIVIDUAL -- 21 BOARDS

Table 1

Rds.	Bds.	N	S	E	W
1	1-3R*	8	1	6	2
2	4-6R	8	2	7	3
3	7-9R	8	3	1	4
4	10-12R	8	4	2	5
5	13-15R	8	5	3	6
6	16-18R	8	6	4	7
7	19-21R	8	7	5	1

Table 2

Rds.	Bds.	N	S	E	W
1	1-3R	5	7	3	4
2	4-6R	6	1	4	5
3	7-9R	7	2	5	6
4	10-12R	1	3	6	7
5	13-15R	2	4	7	1
6	16-18R	3	5	1	2
7	19-21R	4	6	2	3

*For a 28-board game, play four boards to a round; sets will be numbered 1-4, 5-8, 9-12, 13-16, 17-20, 21-24, 25-28.

Board Check Total: 2 Grand Check Total: 84
Average Score: 10 1/2

SCHEDULE FOR 9-PLAYER INDIVIDUAL -- 27 BOARDS

	Table 1						Table 2					Sit-
Rd.	Bds.	N	S	E	W	Rd.	Bds.	N	S	E	W	Out
1	1-3R	2	3	4	7	1	1-3R	6	8	5	9	1
2	4-6R	3	4	5	8	2	4-6R	7	9	6	1	2
3	7-9R	4	5	6	9	3	7-9R	8	1	7	2	3
4	10-12R	5	6	7	1	4	10-12R	9	2	8	3	4
5	13-15R	6	7	8	2	5	13-15R	1	3	9	4	5
6	16-18R	7	8	9	3	6	16-18R	2	4	1	5	6
7	19-21R	8	9	1	4	7	19-21R	3	5	2	6	7
8	22-24R	9	1	2	5	8	22-24R	4	6	3	7	8
9	25-27R	1	2	3	6	9	25-27R	5	7	4	8	9

Board Check Total: 2 Grand Check Total: 108 Average Score: 12

SCHEDULE FOR 10-PLAYER INDIVIDUAL -- 20 (30) BOARDS

	Table 1						Table 2						
Rd.	Bds.	N	S	E	W	Rd.	Bds.	N	S	E	W	Sitout	
1	1-2R	1	2	4	6	1	1-2R	9	3	7	10	5	8
2	3-4R	2	3	5	7	2	3-4R	10	4	8	1	6	9
3	5-6R	3	4	6	8	3	5-6R	1	5	9	2	7	10
4	7-8R	4	5	7	9	4	7-8R	2	6	10	3	8	1
5	9-10R	5	6	8	10	5	9-10R	3	7	1	4	9	2
6	11-12R	6	7	9	1	6	11-12R	4	8	2	5	10	3
7	13-14R	7	8	10	2	7	13-14R	5	9	3	6	1	4
8	15-16R	8	9	1	3	8	15-16R	6	10	4	7	2	5
9	17-18R	9	10	2	4	9	17-18R	7	1	5	8	3	6
10	19-20R	10	1	3	5	10	19-20R	8	2	6	9	4	7

Board Check Total: 2 **Grand Check Total (20 Boards):** 80

Average Score: 8

(Movement by Olof Hanner)

SCHEDULE FOR 12-PLAYER INDIVIDUAL -- 33 BOARDS

Table 1

Rd.	Bds.	N	S	E	W
1	1-3R	12	1	5	11
2	4-6R	12	2	6	1
3	7-9R	12	3	7	2
4	10-12R	12	4	8	3
5	13-15R	12	5	9	4
6	16-18R	12	6	10	5
7	19-21R	12	7	11	6
8	22-24R	12	8	1	7
9	25-27R	12	9	2	8
10	28-30R	12	10	3	9
11	31-33R	12	11	4	10

Table 2

Rd.	Bds.	N	S	E	W
1	1-3R	4	3	10	7
2	4-6R	5	4	11	8
3	7-9R	6	5	1	9
4	10-12R	7	6	2	10
5	13-15R	8	7	3	11
6	16-18R	9	8	4	1
7	19-21R	10	9	5	2
8	22-24R	11	10	6	3
9	25-27R	1	11	7	4
10	28-30R	2	1	8	5
11	31-33R	3	2	9	6

Table 3

Rd.	Bds.	N	S	E	W
1	1-3R	2	9	6	8
2	4-6R	3	10	7	9
3	7-9R	4	11	8	10
4	10-12R	5	1	9	11
5	13-15R	6	2	10	1
6	16-18R	7	3	11	2
7	19-21R	8	4	1	3
8	22-24R	9	5	2	4
9	25-27R	10	6	3	5
10	28-30R	11	7	4	6
11	31-33R	1	8	5	7

Board Check Total: 6 Grand Check Total: 396 Average Score: 33

SCHEDULE FOR 12-PLAYER INDIVIDUAL --22 BOARDS

Table 1

Rd.	Bds.	N	S	E	W
1	1-2	12	1	5	10
2	3-4	12	2	6	11
3	5-6	12	3	7	1
4	7-8	12	4	8	2
5	9-10	12	5	9	3
6	11-12	12	6	10	4
7	13-14	12	7	11	5
8	15-16	12	8	1	6
9	17-18	12	9	2	7
10	19-20	12	10	3	8
11	21-22	12	11	4	9

Table 2

Rd.	Bds.	N	S	E	W
1	11-12	7	11	8	9
2	13-14	8	1	9	10
3	15-16	9	2	10	11
4	17-18	10	3	11	1
5	19-20	11	4	1	2
6	21-22	1	5	2	3
7	1-2	2	6	3	4
8	3-4	3	7	4	5
9	5-6	4	8	5	6
10	7-8	5	9	6	7
11	9-10	6	10	7	8

Table 3

Rd.	Bds.	N	S	E	W
1	13-14	2	4	3	6
2	15-16	3	5	4	7
3	17-18	4	6	5	8
4	19-20	5	7	6	9
5	21-22	6	8	7	10
6	1-2	7	9	8	11
7	3-4	8	10	9	1
8	5-6	9	11	10	2
9	7-8	10	1	11	3
10	9-10	11	2	1	4
11	11-12	1	3	2	5

Board Check Total: 6 Grand Check Total: 264 Average Score: 22

SCHEDULE FOR 13-PLAYER INDIVIDUAL -- 26 BOARDS

	Table 1						Table 2						Table 3					
Rd.	Bds.	N	S	E	W	Rd.	Bds.	N	S	E	W	Rd.	Bds.	N	S	E	W	Out
1	1-2	5	7	9	10	1	11-12	11	3	4	8	1	23-24	6	13	12	2	1
2	3-4	6	8	10	11	2	13-14	12	4	5	9	2	25-26	7	1	13	3	2
3	5-6	7	9	11	12	3	15-16	13	5	6	10	3	1-2	8	2	1	4	3
4	7-8	8	10	12	13	4	17-18	1	6	7	11	4	3-4	9	3	2	5	4
5	9-10	9	11	13	1	5	19-20	2	7	8	12	5	5-6	10	4	3	6	5
6	11-12	10	12	1	2	6	21-22	3	8	9	13	6	7-8	11	5	4	7	6
7	13-14	11	13	2	3	7	23-24	4	9	10	1	7	9-10	12	6	5	8	7
8	15-16	12	1	3	4	8	25-26	5	10	11	2	8	11-12	13	7	6	9	8
9	17-18	13	2	4	5	9	1-2	6	11	12	3	9	13-14	1	8	7	10	9
10	19-20	1	3	5	6	10	3-4	7	12	13	4	10	15-16	2	9	8	11	10
11	21-22	2	4	6	7	11	5-6	8	13	1	5	11	17-18	3	10	9	12	11
12	23-24	3	5	7	8	12	7-8	9	1	2	6	12	19-20	4	11	10	13	12
13	25-26	4	6	8	9	13	9-10	10	2	3	7	13	21-22	5	12	11	1	13

Board Check Total: 6 Grand Check Total: 312 Average Score: 24

SCHEDULE FOR 14-PLAYER INDIVIDUAL -- 28 BOARDS

	Table 1						Table 2						Table 3						
Rd.	Bds.	N	S	E	W	Rd.	Bds.	N	S	E	W	Rd.	Bds.	N	S	E	W	Out	
1	1-2	2	6	3	8	1	3-4	11	10	13	5	1	15-16	4	7	12	14	1	9
2	3-4	3	7	4	9	2	5-6	12	11	14	6	2	17-18	5	8	13	1	2	10
3	5-6	4	8	5	10	3	7-8	13	12	1	7	3	19-20	6	9	14	2	3	11
4	7-8	5	9	6	11	4	9-10	14	13	2	8	4	21-22	7	10	1	3	4	12
5	9-10	6	10	7	12	5	11-12	1	14	3	9	5	23-24	8	11	2	4	5	13
6	10-11	7	11	8	13	6	13-14	2	1	4	10	6	25-26	9	12	3	5	6	14
7	13-14	8	12	9	14	7	15-16	3	2	5	11	7	27-28	10	13	4	6	7	1
8	15-16	9	13	10	1	8	17-18	4	3	6	12	8	1-2	11	14	5	7	8	2
9	17-18	10	14	11	2	9	19-20	5	4	7	13	9	3-4	12	1	6	8	9	3
10	19-20	11	1	12	3	10	21-22	6	5	8	14	10	5-6	13	2	7	9	10	4
11	21-22	12	2	13	4	11	23-24	7	6	9	1	11	7-8	14	3	8	10	11	5
12	23-24	13	3	14	5	12	25-26	8	7	10	2	12	9-10	1	4	9	11	12	6
13	25-26	14	4	1	6	13	27-28	9	8	11	3	13	11-12	2	5	10	12	13	7
14	27-28	1	5	2	7	14	1-2	10	9	12	4	14	13-14	3	6	11	13	14	8

Board Check Total: 6 Grand Check Total: 336 Average Score: 24

(Movement by Olof Hanner)

SCHEDULE FOR 16-PLAYER INDIVIDUAL -- 24 BOARDS

	Table 1					Table 2					Table 3					Table 4				
Rd.	Bds.	N	S	E	W	Bds.	N	S	E	W	Bds.	N	S	E	W	Bds.	N	S	E	W
1	1-2	16	1	6	10	3-4R	4	5	13	3	3-4R	8	15	12	9	5-6	7	2	11	14
2	3-4	16	2	7	11	5-6R	5	6	13	4	5-6R	9	15	1	10	7-8	8	3	12	14
3	5-6	16	3	8	12	7-8R	6	7	13	5	7-8R	10	15	2	11	9-10	9	4	1	14
4	7-8	16	4	9	1	9-10R	7	8	13	6	9-10R	11	15	3	12	11-12	10	5	2	14
5	9-10	16	5	10	2	11-12R	8	9	13	7	11-12R	12	15	4	1	13-14	11	6	3	14
6	11-12	16	6	11	3	13-14R	9	10	13	8	13-14R	1	15	5	2	15-16	12	7	4	14
7	13-14	16	7	12	4	15-16R	10	11	13	9	15-16R	2	15	6	3	17-18	1	8	5	14
8	15-16	16	8	1	5	17-18R	11	12	13	10	17-18R	3	15	7	4	19-20	2	9	6	14
9	17-18	16	9	2	6	19-20R	12	1	13	11	19-20R	4	15	8	5	21-22	3	10	7	14
10	19-20	16	10	3	7	21-22R	1	2	13	12	21-22R	5	15	9	6	23-24	4	11	8	14
11	21-22	16	11	4	8	23-24R	2	3	13	1	23-24R	6	15	10	7	1-2	5	12	9	14
12	23-24	16	12	5	9	1-2R	3	4	13	2	1-2R	7	15	11	8	3-4	6	1	10	14

Board Check Total: 12 Grand Check Total: 576 Average Score: 36

SCHEDULE FOR 16-PLAYER INDIVIDUAL -- 30 BOARDS

	Table 1					Table 2					Table 3					Table 4				
Rd.	Bds.	N	S	E	W	Bds.	N	S	E	W	Bds.	N	S	E	W	Bds.	N	S	E	W
1	1-2	16	1	2	3	5-6	4	13	10	9	7-8	14	8	5	7	9-10	15	11	6	12
2	3-4	16	2	14	15	1-2	13	9	5	6	23-24	10	3	1	4	25-26	11	12	7	8
3	5-6	16	3	15	7	11-12	1	14	13	8	13-14	2	12	10	6	3-4	4	9	5	11
4	7-8	16	4	13	1	9-10	2	10	9	3	1-2	15	12	14	7	5-6	11	6	5	8
5	9-10	16	5	1	8	7-8	15	9	12	10	21-22	6	7	2	4	19-20	3	13	11	14
6	11-12	16	6	7	10	13-14	8	3	13	15	15-16	4	14	9	12	17-18	5	1	11	2
7	13-14	16	7	4	5	5-6	1	2	12	14	11-12	3	15	9	11	3-4	13	10	6	8
8	15-16	16	8	3	6	17-18	7	13	15	10	11-12	5	2	4	12	13-14	1	11	9	14
9	17-18	16	9	6	14	27-28	8	4	15	2	29-30	12	3	5	13	15-16	10	1	7	11
10	19-20	16	10	5	12	21-22	8	15	1	9	23-24	7	2	13	11	25-26	6	4	3	14
11	21-22	16	11	12	13	27-28	9	5	7	3	29-30	14	2	8	10	19-20	6	1	4	15
12	23-24	16	12	8	9	25-26	10	5	15	1	7-8	3	11	2	6	9-10	7	4	14	13
13	25-26	16	13	9	2	1-2	11	8	10	4	3-4	12	7	3	1	23-24	14	5	6	15
14	27-28	16	14	10	11	29-30	9	6	1	7	15-16	5	15	2	13	17-18	12	8	4	3
15	29-30	16	15	11	4	21-22	14	10	3	5	27-28	13	6	12	1	19-20	9	7	8	2

Board Check Total: 12 Grand Check Total: 720 Average Score: 45

SCHEMATIC SCHEDULE FOR 20-PLAYER INDIVIDUAL (RAINBOW) -- 30 BOARDS

Rd.	Table 1	Table 2	Table 3	Table 4	Table 5
1	4 1 A* 3 2	8 5 B 7 6	12 9 C 11 10	16 13 D 15 14	20 17 E 19 18
2	4 9 B 15 18	8 13 C 19 2	12 17 D 3 6	16 1 E 7 10	20 5 A 11 14
3	4 17 C 7 14	8 1 D 11 18	12 5 E 15 2	16 9 A 19 6	20 13 B 3 10
4	4 5 D 19 10	8 9 E 3 14	12 13 A 7 18	16 17 B 11 2	20 1 C 15 6
5	4 13 E 11 6	8 17 A 15 10	12 1 B 19 14	16 5 C 3 18	20 9 D 7 2

*Boards are in sets A, B, C, D and E. For 30-board game, set A will include Boards 1-6 (two for each partnership); set B, 7-12; C, 13-18; D, 19-24 and E, 25-30. For 15-board game, set A will include 1-3; B, 4-6; C, 7-9; D, 10-12 and E, 13-15.

Board Check Total: 20 Grand Check Total (30 Boards): 1200
Average Score: 60

MASTER SHEET FOR 20-PLAYER INDIVIDUAL -- 4 STANZAS, 19 BOARDS

	Bd. 1				2				3				4				5			
Rd.	N	S	E	W	N	S	E	W	N	S	E	W	N	S	E	W	N	S	E	W
1	5	9	12	18	1	10	13	19	2	6	14	20	3	7	15	16	4	8	11	17
2	13	20	4	7	14	16	5	8	15	17	1	9	11	18	2	10	12	19	3	6
3	17	14	10	3	18	15	6	4	19	11	7	5	20	12	8	1	16	13	9	2
4	8	2	19	15	9	3	20	11	10	4	16	12	6	5	17	13	7	1	18	14
	6				7				8				9				10			
5	1	11	20	10	2	12	19	9	3	13	18	8	4	14	17	7	5	15	16	6
6	14	2	6	18	15	3	10	17	11	4	9	16	12	5	8	20	13	1	7	19
7	7	16	12	3	6	20	13	4	10	19	14	5	9	18	15	1	8	17	11	2
8	19	8	4	15	18	7	5	11	17	6	1	12	16	10	2	13	20	9	3	14
9	9	17	5	13	8	16	1	14	7	20	2	15	6	19	3	11	10	18	4	12
	11				12				13				14				15			
10	1	20	10	11	2	19	9	12	3	18	8	13	4	17	7	14	5	16	6	15
11	18	2	14	6	17	3	15	10	16	4	11	9	20	5	12	8	19	1	13	7
12	7	12	3	16	6	13	4	20	10	14	5	19	9	15	1	18	8	11	2	17
13	15	8	19	4	11	7	18	5	12	6	17	1	13	10	16	2	14	9	20	3
14	9	13	17	5	8	14	16	1	7	15	20	2	6	11	19	3	10	12	18	4
	16 (1)				17 (2)				18 (3)				19 (4)				20 (5)			
15	1	4	3	2	6	9	8	7	11	14	13	12	16	19	18	17	(5	10	15	20)
16	(1	6	11	16)	2	5	4	3	7	10	9	8	12	15	14	13	17	20	19	18
17	18	16	20	19	(2	7	12	17)	3	1	5	4	8	6	10	9	13	11	15	14
18	14	12	11	15	19	17	16	20	(3	8	13	18)	4	2	1	5	9	7	6	10
19	10	8	7	6	15	13	12	11	20	18	17	16	(4	9	14	19)	5	3	2	1

Boards 1-15 Check Total: 20   Grand Check Total: 720   Average Score: 36
Boards 16-20 Check Total: 12

MASTER SHEET FOR 24-PLAYER INDIVIDUAL -- 21 BOARDS

Rd.		Bds. 1-3	4-6	7-9	10-12	13-15	16-18	19-21	Table
1	N-S E-W	1 5 6 16	3 22 14 19	15 17 21 13	7 23 10 20	24 4 12 18		8 9 11 2	
2	N-S E-W	9 10 12 3	2 6 7 17	4 8 20 22	16 18 15 14	11 23 1 21	24 5 13 19		6
3	N-S E-W		10 13 11 4	3 7 1 18	21 5 9 22	17 19 16 8	15 23 2 12	24 6 14 20	Bye
4	N-S E-W	24 7 8 21		11 12 14 5	4 1 2 19	6 22 10 15	18 20 17 9	3 23 13 16	5
5	N-S E-W	14 23 4 17	24 1 9 15		12 13 6 8	5 2 3 20	16 7 11 22	19 21 18 10	4
6	N-S E-W	20 15 19 11	18 5 8 23	24 2 10 16		13 9 14 7	6 3 4 21	17 1 12 22	3
7	N-S E-W	2 22 13 18	21 16 20 12	9 6 19 23	24 3 11 17		14 8 10 1	7 4 5 15	2
	Table		2	3	4	5	Bye	6	1

Board Check Total: 30 Grand Check Total: 1260 Average Score: 52 1/2

MASTER SHEET FOR 25-PLAYER INDIVIDUAL -- 5 STANZAS, 25 BOARDS

Bd.	1 (1-2R)*				2 (3-4)				3 (5-6)				4 (7-8)				5 (9-10)				26-30 (1-10R)				Out
Rd.	N	S	E	W	N	S	E	W	N	S	E	W	N	S	E	W	N	S	E	W	N	S	E	W	
1	25	1	16	6	24	5	17	7	8	18	23	4	3	22	9	19	20	10	2	21	13	12	14	11	15
2	18	7	3	21	25	2	19	8	24	1	20	9	10	16	23	5	4	22	6	17	14	13	15	12	11
3	5	22	8	20	16	9	4	21	25	3	17	10	24	2	18	6	7	19	23	1	15	14	11	13	12
4	9	71	23	2	1	22	10	18	19	6	5	21	25	4	20	7	24	3	16	8	11	15	12	14	13
5	24	4	19	10	6	20	23	3	2	22	7	16	17	8	1	21	25	5	18	9	12	11	13	15	14
	6 (11-12R)				7 (13-14)				8 (15-16)				9 (17-18)				10 (19-20)				26-30 (11-20R)				
6	25	6	11	16	21	10	12	17	18	13	24	9	8	23	19	14	15	20	17	22	3	2	4	1	5
7	13	17	8	22	25	7	14	18	21	6	15	19	20	11	24	10	9	23	16	12	4	3	5	2	1
8	10	23	18	15	11	19	9	22	25	8	12	20	21	7	13	16	17	14	24	6	5	4	1	3	2
9	19	12	24	7	6	23	20	13	14	16	10	22	25	9	15	17	21	8	11	18	1	5	2	4	3
10	21	9	14	20	16	15	24	8	7	23	17	11	12	18	6	22	25	10	13	19	2	1	3	5	4
	11 (21-22R)				12 (23-24)				13 (25-26)				14 (27-28)				15 (29-30)				26-30 (21-30R)				
11	25	11	6	1	22	15	7	2	3	8	21	14	13	23	4	9	10	5	12	24	18	17	19	16	20
12	8	2	13	24	25	12	9	3	22	11	10	4	5	6	21	15	14	23	1	7	19	18	20	17	16
13	15	23	3	10	6	4	14	24	25	13	7	5	22	12	8	1	2	9	21	11	20	19	16	18	17
14	4	7	21	12	11	23	5	8	9	1	15	24	25	14	10	2	22	13	6	3	16	20	17	19	18
15	22	14	9	5	1	10	21	13	12	23	2	6	7	3	11	24	25	15	8	4	17	16	18	20	19

	16 (31-33R)	17 (33-34)	18 (35-36)	19 (37-38)	20 (39-40)	26-30 (31-40R)	
16	25 16 1 11	23 20 2 12	13 3 21 19	18 24 14 4	5 15 17 22	8 7 9 6	10
17	3 12 18 22	25 17 4 13	23 16 5 14	15 1 21 20	19 24 11 2	9 8 10 7	6
18	20 24 13 5	1 14 19 22	25 18 2 15	23 17 3 11	12 4 21 16	10 9 6 8	7
19	21 17 2 14	3 15 16 24	20 22 11 4	25 19 5 12	13 1 23 18	6 10 7 9	8
20	4 15 19 23	18 21 11 5	1 12 17 24	16 22 13 2	25 20 3 14	7 6 8 10	9

	21 (41-42R)	22(43-44)	23 (45-46)	24 (47-48)	25 (49-50)	26-30 (41-50R)	
21	10 12 3 19	6 11 2 18	1 17 15 7	16 5 8 14	13 9 20 4	25 21 24 22	23
22	18 1 9 14	17 5 10 13	6 12 4 16	7 11 3 20	8 15 2 19	25 22 23 24	21
23	4 17 11 8	9 15 3 16	14 10 20 2	1 19 13 6	7 12 5 18	25 23 22 21	24
24	16 2 7 13	12 8 20 1	11 9 19 5	4 18 15 10	17 3 6 14	25 24 21 23	22
25	20 5 6 15	14 7 19 4	18 3 8 13	2 17 12 9	10 11 1 16	24 21 22 23	25

*Single-session game will use one board per round;
two-session game will use board numbers shown in parentheses.

Board Check Total: 20
Board Check Total (Two Sessions): 30

Grand Check Total -- One Session: 1200
Grand Check Total -- Two Sessions: 3000

Average Score: 48
Average Score (Two Sessions): 120

MASTER SHEET FOR 28-PLAYER INDIVIDUAL -- 4 STANZAS, 27 BOARDS

*Sets

	1				2				3				4				5				6				7			
Rd.	N	S	E	W	N	S	E	W	N	S	E	W	N	S	E	W	N	S	E	W	N	S	E	W	N	S	E	W
1	22	1	15	8	23	2	16	9	24	3	17	10	25	4	18	11	26	5	19	12	27	6	20	13	28	7	21	14
2	28	2	20	11	22	3	21	12	23	4	15	13	24	5	16	14	25	6	17	8	26	7	18	9	27	1	19	10
3	14	18	27	3	8	19	28	4	9	20	22	5	10	21	23	6	11	15	24	7	12	16	25	1	13	17	26	2
4	10	16	26	4	11	17	27	5	12	18	28	6	13	19	22	7	14	20	23	1	8	21	24	2	9	15	25	3
5	13	21	25	5	14	15	26	6	8	16	27	7	9	17	28	1	10	18	22	2	11	19	23	3	12	20	24	4
6	24	6	19	9	25	7	20	10	26	1	21	11	27	2	15	12	28	3	16	13	22	4	17	14	23	5	18	8
7	23	7	17	12	24	1	18	13	25	2	19	14	26	3	20	8	27	4	21	9	28	5	15	10	22	6	16	11

	8				9				10				11				12				13				14			
8	22	8	1	15	23	9	2	16	24	10	3	17	25	11	4	18	26	12	5	19	27	13	6	20	28	14	7	21
9	6	18	9	28	7	19	10	22	1	20	11	23	2	21	12	24	3	15	13	25	4	16	14	26	5	17	8	27
10	4	21	10	27	5	15	11	28	6	16	12	22	7	17	13	23	1	18	14	24	2	19	8	25	3	20	9	26
11	2	17	11	26	3	18	12	27	4	19	13	28	5	20	14	22	6	21	8	23	7	15	9	24	1	16	10	25
12	25	12	7	20	26	13	1	21	27	14	2	15	28	8	3	16	22	9	4	17	23	10	5	18	24	11	6	19
13	24	13	5	16	25	14	6	17	26	8	7	18	27	9	1	19	28	10	2	20	22	11	3	21	23	12	4	15
14	3	19	14	23	4	20	8	24	5	21	9	25	6	15	10	26	7	16	11	27	1	17	12	28	2	18	13	22

	15	16	17	18	19	20	21
15	28 16 13 4	22 17 14 5	23 18 8 6	24 19 9 7	25 20 10 1	26 21 11 2	27 15 12 3
16	27 17 11 7	28 18 12 1	22 19 13 2	23 20 14 3	24 21 8 4	25 15 9 5	26 16 10 6
17	26 18 9 3	27 19 10 4	28 20 11 5	22 21 12 6	23 15 13 7	24 16 14 1	25 17 8 2
18	6 14 25 19	7 8 26 20	1 9 27 21	2 10 28 15	3 11 22 16	4 12 23 17	5 13 24 18
19	2 12 20 24	3 13 21 25	4 14 15 26	5 8 16 27	6 9 17 28	7 10 18 22	1 11 19 23
20	23 21 10 5	24 15 11 6	25 16 12 7	26 17 13 1	27 18 14 2	28 19 8 3	22 20 9 4

	22 (15)	23 (16)	24 (17)	25 (18)	26(19)	27 (20)	28 (21)
21	1 6 22 26	3 4 8 12	16 19 25 27	23 24 11 13	15 20 9 10	5 2 17 18	(7 14 21 28)
22	(1 8 15 22)	2 7 23 27	4 5 9 13	17 20 26 28	24 25 12 14	16 21 10 11	6 3 18 19
23	7 4 19 20	(2 9 16 23)	3 1 24 28	5 6 10 14	18 21 27 22	25 26 13 8	17 15 11 12
24	18 16 12 13	1 5 20 21	(3 10 17 24)	4 2 25 22	6 7 11 8	19 15 28 23	26 27 14 9
25	27 28 8 10	19 17 13 14	2 6 21 15	(4 11 18 25)	5 3 26 23	7 1 12 9	20 16 22 24
26	21 17 23 25	28 22 9 11	20 18 14 8	3 7 15 16	(5 12 19 26)	6 4 27 24	1 2 13 10
27	2 3 14 11	15 18 24 26	22 23 10 12	21 19 8 9	4 1 16 17	(6 13 20 27)	7 5 28 25

*For a one-session game, play one board to a set;
for a two-session game, play two boards to a set, two stanzas to a session.

Board check total-sets 1-21: 42 — Grand check total-one session: 2184 — Average score: 81
Board check total-sets 22-28: 30 — Grand check total-two sessions: 4368 — Average score: 81

Sets 22-28 will be played only six times with a five point top. Thus, the scores for these boards must be factored up 1/5 to give the s[illegible] w[illegible]ht to every board played.

MASTER SHEET FOR 28-PLAYER INDIVIDUAL (RAINBOW) -- 21 BOARDS

Rd.		Bds. 1-3	4-6	7-9	10-12	13-15	16-18	19-21	Table
1	N-S	1 15	2 16	3 17	4 18	5 19	6 20	7 21	
	E-W	22 8	23 9	24 10	25 11	26 12	27 13	28 14	
2	N-S	7 20	1 21	2 15	3 16	4 17	5 18	6 19	7
	E-W	26 9	27 10	28 11	22 12	23 13	24 14	25 8	
3	N-S	6 18	7 19	1 20	2 21	3 15	4 16	5 17	6
	E-W	23 10	24 11	25 12	26 13	27 14	28 8	22 9	
4	N-S	5 16	6 17	7 18	1 19	2 20	3 21	4 15	5
	E-W	27 11	28 12	22 13	23 14	24 8	25 9	26 10	
5	N-S	4 21	5 15	6 16	7 17	1 18	2 19	3 20	4
	E-W	24 12	25 13	26 14	27 8	28 9	22 10	23 11	
6	N-S	3 19	4 20	5 21	6 15	7 16	1 17	2 18	3
	E-W	28 13	22 14	23 8	24 9	25 10	26 11	27 12	
7	N-S	2 17	3 18	4 19	5 20	6 21	7 15	1 16	2
	E-W	25 14	26 8	27 9	28 10	22 11	23 12	24 13	
	Table		2	3	4	5	6	7	1

Board Check Total: 42 Grand Check Total: 1764 Average Score: 63

MASTER SHEET FOR 32-PLAYER INDIVIDUAL -- 24 BOARDS

Rd.		Bds. 1-3	4-6	7-9	10-12	13-15	16-18	19-21	22-24	Table
1	N-S	1 17	2 18	3 19	4 20	5 21	6 22	7 23	8 24	
	E-W	25 9	26 10	27 11	28 12	29 13	30 14	31 15	32 16	
2	N-S	2 20	1 19	4 18	3 17	6 24	5 23	8 22	7 21	8
	E-W	30 15	29 16	32 13	31 14	26 11	25 12	28 9	27 10	
3	N-S	3 23	4 24	1 21	2 22	7 19	8 20	5 17	6 18	7
	E-W	32 10	31 9	30 12	29 11	28 14	27 13	26 16	25 15	
4	N-S	4 22	3 21	2 24	1 23	8 18	7 17	6 20	5 19	6
	E-W	27 16	28 15	25 14	26 13	31 12	32 11	29 10	30 9	
5	N-S	28 11	27 12	26 9	25 10	32 15	31 16	30 13	29 14	5
	E-W	18 5	17 6	20 7	19 8	22 1	21 2	24 3	23 4	
6	N-S	31 13	32 14	29 15	30 16	27 9	28 10	25 11	26 12	4
	E-W	19 6	20 5	17 8	18 7	23 2	24 1	21 4	22 3	
7	N-S	29 12	30 11	31 10	32 9	25 16	26 15	27 14	28 13	3
	E-W	24 7	23 8	22 5	21 6	20 3	19 4	18 1	17 2	
8	N-S	26 14	25 13	28 16	27 15	30 10	29 9	32 12	31 11	2
	E-W	21 8	22 7	23 6	24 5	17 4	18 3	19 2	20 1	
	Table		2	3	4	5	6	7	8	1

Board Check Total: 56 Grand Check Total: 2688 Average Score: 84

MASTER SHEET FOR 32-PLAYER INDIVIDUAL (APPENDIX RAINBOW) -- 24 BOARDS

Rd.		Bds. 1-3	4-6	7-9	10-12	13-15	16-18	19-21	Table	(Table 8) 22-24
1	N-S	29 15	2 16	3 31	4 18	5 19	6 20	7 21		1 25
	E-W	8 22	30 23	10 24	11 32	12 26	13 27	14 28		17 9
2	N-S	4 19	29 20	6 21	7 31	1 16	2 17	3 18	7	5 27
	E-W	13 23	14 24	30 25	9 26	10 32	11 28	12 22		15 8
3	N-S	7 16	1 17	29 18	3 19	4 31	5 21	6 15	6	2 22
	E-W	11 24	12 25	13 26	30 27	8 28	9 32	10 23		20 14
4	N-S	3 20	4 21	5 15	29 16	7 17	1 31	2 19	5	6 24
	E-W	9 25	10 26	11 27	12 28	30 22	14 23	8 32		18 13
5	N-S	6 17	7 18	1 19	2 20	29 21	4 15	5 31	4	3 26
	E-W	14 32	8 27	9 28	10 22	11 23	30 24	13 25		16 12
6	N-S	2 31	3 15	4 16	5 17	6 18	29 19	1 20	3	7 28
	E-W	12 27	13 32	14 22	8 23	9 24	10 25	30 26		21 11
7	N-S	5 18	6 31	7 20	1 21	2 15	3 16	29 17	2	4 23
	E-W	30 28	11 22	12 32	13 24	14 25	8 26	9 27		19 10
		Table	2	3	4	5	6	7	1	

Board Check Total: 42 Grand Check Total: 2016 Average Score: 63

INDIVIDUAL MASTER SHEET FOR GROUPS OF 8 PLAYERS EACH -- 21 BOARDS

Rd.	Bds. 1-3	4-6	7-9	10-12	15-17	18-21	19-21
1	8-1 6-2 5-7 3-4	18-11 16-12 15-17 13-14	28-21 26-22 25-27 23-24	38-31 36-32 35-37 33-34	48-41 46-42 45-47 43-44	58-51 56-52 55-57 53-54	68-61 66-62 65-67 63-64
2	68-62 67-63 66-61 64-65	8-2 7-3 6-1 4-5	18-12 17-13 16-11 14-15	28-22 27-23 26-21 24-25	38-32 37-33 36-31 34-35	48-42 47-43 46-41 44-45	58-52 57-53 56-51 54-55
3	58-53 51-54 57-52 55-56	68-63 61-64 67-62 65-66	8-3 1-4 7-2 5-6	18-13 11-14 17-12 15-16	28-23 21-24 27-22 25-26	38-33 31-34 37-32 35-36	48-43 41-44 47-42 45-46
4	48-44 42-45 41-43 46-47	58-54 52-55 51-53 56-57	68-64 62-65 61-63 66-67	8-4 2-5 1-3 6-7	18-14 12-15 11-13 16-17	28-24 22-25 21-23 26-27	38-34 32-35 31-33 36-37
5	38-35 33-36 32-34 37-31	48-45 43-46 42-44 47-41	58-55 53-56 52-54 57-51	68-65 63-66 62-64 67-61	8-5 3-6 2-4 7-1	18-15 13-16 12-14 17-11	28-25 23-26 22-24 27-21
6	28-26 24-27 23-25 21-22	38-36 34-37 33-35 31-32	48-46 44-47 43-45 41-42	58-56 54-57 53-55 51-52	68-66 64-67 63-65 61-62	8-6 4-7 3-5 1-2	18-16 14-17 13-15 11-12
7	18-17 15-11 14-16 12-13	28-27 25-21 24-26 22-23	38-37 35-31 34-36 32-33	48-47 45-41 44-46 42-43	58-57 55-51 54-56 52-53	68-67 65-61 64-66 62-63	8-7 5-1 4-6 2-3
	4 3R	6 5R	8 7R	10 9R	12 11R	14 13R	2 1R

Right margin: 14 13R, 12 11R, 10 9R, 8 7R, 6 5R, 4 3R

Board Check Total (7 Groups) 182 Grand Check Total: 7644 Average Score: 136 1/2

MASTER SHEET FOR 13 TEAMS OF FOUR,
AMERICAN WHIST LEAGUE MOVEMENT -- 26 BOARDS

Rd.	Bds. 1-2	3-4	5-6	7-8	9-10	11-12	13-14	15-16	17-18	19-20	21-22	23-24	25-26	Table
1	13-2	1-3	2-4	3-5	4-6	5-7	6-8	7-9	8-10	9-11	10-12	11-13	12-1	12
2	12-3	13-4	1-5	2-6	3-7	4-8	5-9	6-10	7-11	8-12	9-13	10-1	11-2	11
3	11-4	12-5	13-6	1-7	2-8	3-9	4-10	5-11	6-12	7-13	8-1	9-2	10-3	10
4	10-5	11-6	12-7	13-8	1-9	2-10	3-11	4-12	5-13	6-1	7-2	8-3	9-4	9
5	9-6	10-7	11-8	12-9	13-10	1-11	2-12	3-13	4-1	5-2	6-3	7-4	8-5	8
6	8-7	9-8	10-9	11-10	12-11	13-12	1-13	2-1	3-2	4-3	5-4	6-5	7-6	7
7	7-8	8-9	9-10	10-11	11-12	12-13	13-1	1-2	2-3	3-4	4-5	5-6	6-7	6
8	6-9	7-10	8-11	9-12	10-13	11-1	12-2	13-3	1-4	2-5	3-6	4-7	5-8	5
9	5-10	6-11	7-12	8-13	9-1	10-2	11-3	12-4	13-5	1-6	2-7	3-8	4-9	4
10	4-11	5-12	6-13	7-1	8-2	9-3	10-4	11-5	12-6	13-7	1-8	2-9	3-10	3
11	3-12	4-13	5-1	6-2	7-3	8-4	9-5	10-6	11-7	12-8	13-9	1-10	2-11	2
12	2-13	3-1	4-2	5-3	6-4	7-5	8-6	9-7	10-8	11-9	12-10	13-11	1-12	1
	Table	2	3	4	5	6	7	8	9	10	11	12	13	

MASTER SHEET FOR 8 TEAMS OF FOUR, SPLIT MOVEMENT -- 24 BOARDS

Rd.	Bds. 1-3	4-6	7-9	10-12	13-15	16-18	19-21	22-24
1	8-2	1-3	2-4	3-5	4-6	5-7	6-8	7-1
			CROSS-OVER					
2	2-8	3-1	4-2	5-3	6-4	7-5	8-6	1-7
		SPLIT -- RETURN BOARDS TO ORIGINAL SEQUENCE						
3	7-4	8-5	1-6	2-7	3-8	4-1	5-2	6-3
4	6-5	7-6	8-7	1-8	2-1	3-2	4-3	5-4
5	5-6	6-7	7-8	8-1	1-2	2-3	3-4	4-5
6	4-7	5-8	6-1	7-2	8-3	1-4	2-5	3-6
7	3-7 7-3	4-8 8-4	New boards shuffled and relayed				1-5 5-1	2-6 6-2

East-West pairs move down four tables after the cross-over.
East-West pairs move up one table after the split.

MASTER SHEET FOR 10 TEAMS OF FOUR, SPLIT MOVEMENT -- 30 BOARDS

Rd.	Bds. 1-3	4-6	7-9	10-12	13-15	16-18	19-21	22-24	25-27	28-30
1	10-2	1-3	2-4	3-5	4-6	5-7	6-8	7-9	8-10	9-1
2	9-3	10-4	1-5	2-6	3-7	4-8	5-9	6-10	7-1	8-2
				CROSS-OVER						
3	3-9	4-10	5-1	6-2	7-3	8-4	9-5	10-6	1-7	2-8
4	2-10	3-1	4-2	5-3	6-4	7-5	8-6	9-7	10-8	1-9
			SPLIT -- RETURN BOARDS TO ORIGINAL SEQUENCE							
5	8-5	9-6	10-7	1-8	2-9	3-10	4-1	5-2	6-3	7-4
6	7-6	8-7	9-8	10-9	1-10	2-1	3-2	4-3	5-4	6-5
7	6-7	7-8	8-9	9-10	10-1	1-2	2-3	3-4	4-5	5-6
8	5-8	6-9	7-10	8-1	9-2	10-3	1-4	2-5	3-6	4-7
9	4-9 9-4	5-10 10-5	New boards shuffled and relayed					1-6 6-1	2-7 7-2	3-8 8-3

East-West pairs move normally after the cross-over.
East-West pairs move up one table after the split.

MASTER SHEET FOR 12 TEAMS OF FOUR -- SPLIT MOVEMENT -- 24 BOARDS

Rd.	Bds. 1-2	3-4	5-6	7-8	9-10	11-12	13-14	15-16	17-18	19-20	21-22	23-24
1	12-2	1-3	2-4	3-5	4-6	5-7	6-8	7-9	8-10	9-11	10-12	11-1
2	11-3	12-4	1-5	2-6	3-7	4-8	5-9	6-10	7-11	8-12	9-1	10-2
						CROSS - OVER						
3	3-11	4-12	5-1	6-2	7-3	8-4	9-5	10-6	11-7	12-8	1-9	2-10
4	2-12	3-1	4-2	5-3	6-4	7-5	8-6	9-7	10-8	11-9	12-10	1-11
				SPLIT -- RETURN BOARDS TO ORIGINAL SEQUENCE								
5	10-5	11-6	12-7	1-8	2-9	3-10	4-11	5-12	6-1	7-2	8-3	9-4
6	9-6	10-7	11-8	12-9	1-10	2-11	3-12	4-1	5-2	6-3	7-4	8-5
7	8-7	9-8	10-9	11-10	12-11	1-12	2-1	3-2	4-3	5-4	6-5	7-6
8	7-8	8-9	9-10	10-11	11-12	12-1	1-2	2-3	3-4	4-5	5-6	6-7
9	6-9	7-10	8-11	9-12	10-1	11-2	12-3	1-4	2-5	3-6	4-7	5-8
10	5-10	6-11	7-12	8-1	9-2	10-3	11-4	12-5	1-6	2-7	3-8	4-9
11	4-10 10-4	5-11 11-5	6-12 12-6			New boards shuffled and relayed				1-7 7-1	2-8 8-2	3-9 9-3

East-West pairs move down four tables after the cross-over.
East-West pairs move up three tables after the split.

MASTER SHEET FOR 14 TEAMS OF FOUR -- SPLIT MOVEMENT

Rd.	Sets 1	2	3	4	5	6	7	8	9	10	11	12	13	14
1	14-2	1-3	2-4	3-5	4-6	5-7	6-8	7-9	8-10	9-11	10-12	11-13	12-14	13-1
2	13-3	14-4	1-5	2-6	3-7	4-8	5-9	6-10	7-11	8-12	9-13	10-14	11-1	12-2
3	12-4	13-5	14-6	1-7	2-8	3-9	4-10	5-11	6-12	7-13	8-14	9-1	10-2	11-3
					CROSS-OVER									
4	4-12	5-13	6-14	7-1	8-2	9-3	10-4	11-5	12-6	13-7	14-8	1-9	2-10	3-11
5	3-13	4-14	5-1	6-2	7-3	8-4	9-5	10-6	11-7	12-8	13-9	14-10	1-11	2-12
6	2-14	3-1	4-2	5-3	6-4	7-5	8-6	9-7	10-8	11-9	12-10	13-11	14-12	1-13
			SPLIT -- RETURN BOARDS TO ORIGINAL SEQUENCE											
7	11-6	12-7	13-8	14-9	1-10	2-11	3-12	4-13	5-14	6-1	7-2	8-3	9-4	10-5
8	10-7	11-8	12-9	13-10	14-11	1-12	2-13	3-14	4-1	5-2	6-3	7-4	8-5	9-6
9	9-8	10-9	11-10	12-11	13-12	14-13	1-14	2-1	3-2	4-3	5-4	6-5	7-6	8-7
10	8-9	9-10	10-11	11-12	12-13	13-14	14-1	1-2	2-3	3-4	4-5	5-6	6-7	7-8
11	7-10	8-11	9-12	10-13	11-14	12-1	13-2	14-3	1-4	2-5	3-6	4-7	5-8	6-9
12	6-11	7-12	8-13	9-14	10-1	11-2	12-3	13-4	14-5	1-6	2-7	3-8	4-9	5-10
13	5-12 12-5	6-13 13-6	7-14 14-7		New boards shuffled and relayed						1-8 8-1	2-9 9-2	3-10 10-3	4-11 11-4

East-West pairs move normally after the cross-over.
East-West pairs move up three tables after the split.

MASTER SHEET FOR 16 TEAMS OF FOUR -- SPLIT MOVEMENT

Rd.	Sets 1	2	3	4	5	6	7	8	9	10	11	12	13	14	15	16
1	16-2	1-3	2-4	3-5	4-6	5-7	6-8	7-9	8-10	9-11	10-12	11-13	12-14	13-15	14-16	15-1
2	15-3	16-4	1-5	2-6	3-7	4-8	5-9	6-10	7-11	8-12	9-13	10-14	11-15	12-16	13-1	14-2
3	14-4	15-5	16-6	1-7	2-8	3-9	4-10	5-11	6-12	7-13	8-14	9-15	10-16	11-1	12-2	13-3
	CROSS-OVER															
4	4-14	5-15	6-16	7-1	8-2	9-3	10-4	11-5	12-6	13-7	14-8	15-9	16-10	1-11	2-12	3-13
5	3-15	4-16	5-1	6-2	7-3	8-4	9-5	10-6	11-7	12-8	13-9	14-10	15-11	16-12	1-13	2-14
6	2-16	3-1	4-2	5-3	6-4	7-5	8-6	9-7	10-8	11-9	12-10	13-11	14-12	15-13	16-14	1-15
	SPLIT--RETURN BOARDS TO ORIGINAL SEQUENCE															
7	13-6	14-7	15-8	16-9	1-10	2-11	3-12	4-13	5-14	6-15	7-16	8-1	9-2	10-3	11-4	12-5
8	12-7	13-8	14-9	15-10	16-11	1-12	2-13	3-14	4-15	5-16	6-1	7-2	8-3	9-4	10-5	11-6
9	11-8	12-9	13-10	14-11	15-12	16-13	1-14	2-15	3-16	4-1	5-2	6-3	7-4	8-5	9-6	10-7
10	10-9	11-10	12-11	13-12	14-13	15-14	16-15	1-16	2-1	3-2	4-3	5-4	6-5	7-6	8-7	9-8
11	9-10	10-11	11-12	12-13	13-14	14-15	15-16	16-1	1-2	2-3	3-4	4-5	5-6	6-7	7-8	8-9
12	8-11	9-12	10-13	11-14	12-15	13-16	14-1	15-2	16-3	1-4	2-5	3-6	4-7	5-8	6-9	7-10
13	7-12	8-13	9-14	10-15	11-16	12-1	13-2	14-3	15-4	16-5	1-6	2-7	3-8	4-9	5-10	6-11
14	6-13	7-14	8-15	9-16	10-1	11-2	12-3	13-4	14-5	15-6	16-7	1-8	2-9	3-10	4-11	5-12
15	5-13 13-5	6-14 14-6	7-15 15-7	8-16 16-8	New boards shuffled and relayed								1-9 9-1	2-10 10-2	3-11 11-3	4-12 12-4

East-West pairs move down four tables after the cross-over.
East-West pairs move up five tables after the split.

MASTER SHEET FOR 18 TEAMS OF FOUR -- SPLIT MOVEMENT

Rd.	Sets 1	2	3	4	5	6	7	8	9	10	11	12	13	14	15	16	17	18
1	18-2	1-3	2-4	3-5	4-6	5-7	6-8	7-9	8-10	9-11	10-12	11-13	12-14	13-15	14-16	15-17	16-18	17-1
2	17-3	18-4	1-5	2-6	3-7	4-8	5-9	6-10	7-11	8-12	9-13	10-14	11-15	12-16	13-17	14-18	15-1	16-2
3	16-4	17-5	18-6	1-7	2-8	3-9	4-10	5-11	6-12	7-13	8-14	9-15	10-16	11-17	12-18	13-1	14-2	15-3
4	15-5	16-6	17-7	18-8	1-9	2-10	3-11	4-12	5-13	6-14	7-15	8-16	9-17	10-18	11-1	12-2	13-3	14-4
	CROSS-OVER																	
5	5-15	6-16	7-17	8-18	9-1	10-2	11-3	12-4	13-5	14-6	15-7	16-8	17-9	18-10	1-11	2-12	3-13	4-14
6	4-16	5-17	6-18	7-1	8-2	9-3	10-4	11-5	12-6	13-7	14-8	15-9	16-10	17-11	18-12	1-13	2-14	3-15
7	3-17	4-18	5-1	6-2	7-3	8-4	9-5	10-6	11-7	12-8	13-9	14-10	15-11	16-12	17-13	18-14	1-15	2-16
8	2-18	3-1	4-2	5-3	6-4	7-5	8-6	9-7	10-8	11-9	12-10	13-11	14-12	15-13	16-14	17-15	18-16	1-17
	SPLIT -- RETURN BOARDS TO ORIGINAL SEQUENCE																	
9	14-7	15-8	16-9	17-10	18-11	1-12	2-13	3-14	4-15	5-16	6-17	7-18	8-1	9-2	10-3	11-4	12-5	13-6
10	13-8	14-9	15-10	16-11	17-12	18-13	1-14	2-15	3-16	4-17	5-18	6-1	7-2	8-3	9-4	10-5	11-6	12-7
11	12-9	13-10	14-11	15-12	16-13	17-14	18-15	1-16	2-17	3-18	4-1	5-2	6-3	7-4	8-5	9-6	10-7	11-8
12	11-10	12-11	13-12	14-13	15-14	16-15	17-16	18-17	1-18	2-1	3-2	4-3	5-4	6-5	7-6	8-7	9-8	10-9
13	10-11	11-12	12-13	13-14	14-15	15-16	16-17	17-18	18-1	1-2	2-3	3-4	4-5	5-6	6-7	7-8	8-9	9-10
14	9-12	10-13	11-14	12-15	13-16	14-17	15-18	16-1	17-2	18-3	1-4	2-5	3-6	4-7	5-8	6-9	7-10	8-11
15	8-13	9-14	10-15	11-16	12-17	13-18	14-1	15-2	16-3	17-4	18-5	1-6	2-7	3-8	4-9	5-10	6-11	7-12
16	7-14	8-15	9-16	10-17	11-18	12-1	13-2	14-3	15-4	16-5	17-6	18-7	1-8	2-9	3-10	4-11	5-12	6-13
17	6-15 15-6	7-16 16-7	8-17 17-8	9-18 18-9				New boards shuffled and relayed						1-10 10-1	2-11 11-2	3-12 12-3	4-13 13-4	5-14 14-5

East-West pairs move normally after the cross-over.
East-West pairs move up five tables after the split.

MASTER SHEET FOR 20 TEAMS OF FOUR -- SPLIT MOVEMENT

Rd.	Sets 1	2	3	4	5	6	7	8	9	10	11	12	13	14	15	16	17	18	19	20
1	20-2	1-3	2-4	3-5	4-6	5-7	6-8	7-9	8-10	9-11	10-12	11-13	12-14	13-15	14-16	15-17	16-18	17-19	18-20	19-1
2	19-3	20-4	1-5	2-6	3-7	4-8	5-9	6-10	7-11	8-12	9-13	10-14	11-15	12-16	13-17	14-18	15-19	16-20	17-1	18-2
3	18-4	19-5	20-6	1-7	2-8	3-9	4-10	5-11	6-12	7-13	8-14	9-15	10-16	11-17	12-18	13-19	14-20	15-1	16-2	17-3
4	17-5	18-6	19-7	20-8	1-9	2-10	3-11	4-12	5-13	6-14	7-15	8-16	9-17	10-18	11-19	12-20	13-1	14-2	15-3	16-4
	CROSS-OVER																			
5	5-17	6-18	7-19	8-20	9-1	10-2	11-3	12-4	13-5	14-6	15-7	16-8	17-9	18-10	19-11	20-12	1-13	2-14	3-15	4-16
6	4-18	5-19	6-20	7-1	8-2	9-3	10-4	11-5	12-6	13-7	14-8	15-9	16-10	17-11	18-12	19-13	20-14	1-15	2-16	3-17
7	3-19	4-20	5-1	6-2	7-3	8-4	9-5	10-6	11-7	12-8	13-9	14-10	15-11	16-12	17-13	18-14	19-15	20-16	1-17	2-18
8	2-20	3-1	4-2	5-3	6-4	7-5	8-6	9-7	10-8	11-9	12-10	13-11	14-12	15-13	16-14	17-15	18-16	19-17	20-18	1-19
	SPLIT -- RETURN BOARDS TO ORIGINAL SEQUENCE																			
9	16-7	17-8	18-9	19-10	20-11	1-12	2-13	3-14	4-15	5-16	6-17	7-18	8-19	9-20	10-1	11-2	12-3	13-4	14-5	15-6
10	15-8	16-9	17-10	18-11	19-12	20-13	1-14	2-15	3-16	4-17	5-18	6-19	7-20	8-1	9-2	10-3	11-4	12-5	13-6	14-7
11	14-9	15-10	16-11	17-12	18-13	19-14	20-15	1-16	2-17	3-18	4-19	5-20	6-1	7-2	8-3	9-4	10-5	11-6	12-7	13-8
12	13-10	14-11	15-12	16-13	17-14	18-15	19-16	20-17	1-18	2-19	3-20	4-1	5-2	6-3	7-4	8-5	9-6	10-7	11-8	12-9
13	12-11	13-12	14-13	15-14	16-15	17-16	18-17	19-18	20-19	1-20	2-1	3-2	4-3	5-4	6-5	7-6	8-7	9-8	10-9	11-10
14	11-12	12-13	13-14	14-15	15-16	16-17	17-18	18-19	19-20	20-1	1-2	2-3	3-4	4-5	5-6	6-7	7-8	8-9	9-10	10-11
15	10-13	11-14	12-15	13-16	14-17	15-18	16-19	17-20	18-1	19-2	20-3	1-4	2-5	3-6	4-7	5-8	6-9	7-10	8-11	9-12
16	9-14	10-15	11-16	12-17	13-18	14-19	15-20	16-1	17-2	18-3	19-4	20-5	1-6	2-7	3-8	4-9	5-10	6-11	7-12	8-13
17	8-15	9-16	10-17	11-18	12-19	13-20	14-1	15-2	16-3	17-4	18-5	19-6	20-7	1-8	2-9	3-10	4-11	5-12	6-13	7-14
18	7-16	8-17	9-18	10-19	11-20	12-1	13-2	14-3	15-4	16-5	17-6	18-7	19-8	20-9	1-10	2-11	3-12	4-13	5-14	6-15
19	6-16 16-6	7-17 17-7	8-18 18-8	9-19 19-9	10-20 20-10	New boards shuffled and relayed										1-11 11-1	2-12 12-2	3-13 13-3	4-14 14-4	5-15 15-5

East-West pairs move down four tables after the cross-over.
East-West pairs move up seven tables after the split.
To shorten movement after the split, rounds 9 and 18 may be omitted (but if either is omitted, both must be omitted); the relay round, as usual, may be omitted at any time.

MASTER SHEET FOR 10 TEAMS OF FOUR -- STAGGER MOVEMENT -- 30 BOARDS

FIRST STANZA

Rd.	Bds. 1-3	4-6	7-9	10-12	13-15	Table
1	5-7 10-2	1-3 6-8	2-4 7-9	3-5 8-10	4-6 9-1	
2	4-8 9-3	5-9 10-4	1-5 6-10	2-6 7-1	3-7 8-2	4 9R
3	3-9 8-4	4-10 9-5	5-1 10-6	1-7 6-2	2-8 7-3	3 8R
4	2-10 7-5	3-1 8-6	4-2 9-7	5-3 10-8	1-9 6-4	2 7R
	Table	2 7R	3 8R	4 9R	5 10R	1R

SECOND STANZA

Rd.	Bds. 16-18	19-21	22-24	25-27	28-30	Table
5	1-2 6-7	2-3 7-8	3-4 8-9	4-5 9-10	5-6 10-1	
6	5-8 10-3	1-4 6-9	2-5 7-10	3-6 8-1	4-7 9-2	5 10R
7	4-9 9-4	5-10 10-5	1-6 6-1	2-7 7-2	3-8 8-3	4 9R
8	3-10 8-5	4-1 9-6	5-2 10-7	1-8 6-3	2-9 7-4	3 8R
9	2-1 7-6	3-2 8-7	4-3 9-8	5-4 10-9	1-10 6-5	2 7R
	Table	2 7R	3 8R	4 9R	5 10R	1 6R

MASTER SHEET FOR 6 TEAMS OF FOUR --
NEW ENGLAND RELAY -- 24 BOARDS

Rd.	Bds. 1-4	5-8	9-12	13-16	17-20	21-24	Table
1		1-2 4-5		2-3 5-6		3-4 6-1	
2	3-5 6-2		1-3 4-6		2-4 5-1		3 6R
3		3-6 6-3		1-4 4-1		2-5 5-2	Bye
4	2-6 5-3		3-1 6-4		1-5 4-2		2 5R
5		2-1 5-4		3-2 6-5		1-6 4-3	Bye
	Table	Bye	2 5R	Bye	3 6R	Bye	1 4R

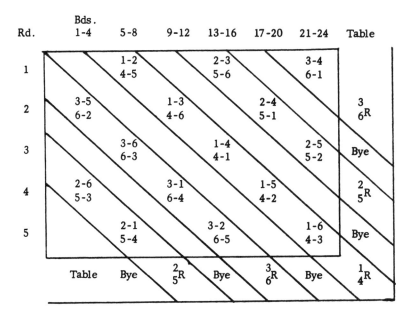

MASTER SHEET FOR 10 TEAMS OF FOUR -- NEW ENGLAND RELAY -- 30 BOARDS

Rd.	Bds. 1-3	4-6	7-9	10-12	13-15	16-18	19-21	22-24	25-27	28-30	Tables
1	1-2 6-7		2-3 7-8		3-4 8-9		4-5 9-10		5-6 10-1		
2		1-3 6-8		2-4 7-9		3-5 8-10		4-6 9-1		5-7 10-2	Bye
3	5-8 10-3		1-4 6-9		2-5 7-10		3-6 8-1		4-7 9-2		5 10R
4		5-9 10-4		1-5 6-10		2-6 7-1		3-7 8-2		4-8 9-3	Bye
5	4-9 9-4		5-10 10-5		1-6 6-1		2-7 7-2		3-8 8-3		4 9R
6		4-10 9-5		5-1 10-6		1-7 6-2		2-8 7-3		3-9 8-4	Bye
7	3-10 8-5		4-1 9-6		5-2 10-7		1-8 6-3		2-9 7-4		3 8R
8		3-1 8-6		4-2 9-7		5-3 10-8		1-9 6-4		2-10 7-5	Bye
9	2-1 7-6		3-2 8-7		4-3 9-8		5-4 10-9		1-10 6-5		2 7R
	Table	2 7R	Bye	3 8R	Bye	4 9R	Bye	5 10R	Bye	1 6R	Bye

Appendix H

TEAMS OF PAIRS MOVEMENTS

MASTER SHEET FOR TWO TEAMS OF 16 PAIRS -- GRUENTHER RELAY

FIRST STANZA

Rd.	Sets 1	2	3	4	5	6	7	8
1	1A-1B 9B-9A	2A-2B 10B-10A	3A-3B 11B-11A	4A-4B 12B-12A	5A-5B 13B-13A	6A-6B 14B-14A	7A-7B 15B-15A	8A-8B 16B-16A
2	8A-7B 16B-15A	1A-8B 9B-16A	2A-1B 10B-9A	3A-2B 11B-10A	4A-3B 12B-11A	5A-4B 13B-12A	6A-5B 14B-13A	7A-6B 15B-14A
3	7A-5B 15B-13A	8A-6B 16B-14A	1A-7B 9B-15A	2A-8B 10B-16A	3A-1B 11B-9A	4A-2B 12B-10A	5A-3B 13B-11A	6A-4B 14B-12A
4	6A-3B 14B-11A	7A-4B 15B-12A	8A-5B 16B-13A	1A-6B 9B-14A	2A-7B 10B-15A	3A-8B 11B-16A	4A-1B 12B-9A	5A-2B 13B-10A
	EAST-WEST PAIRS SKIP ONE TABLE.							
5	5A-8B 13B-16A	6A-1B 14B-9A	7A-2B 15B-10A	8A-3B 16B-11A	1A-4B 9B-12A	2A-5B 10B-13A	3A-6B 11B-14A	4A-7B 12B-15A
6	4A-6B 12B-14A	5A-7B 13B-15A	6A-8B 14B-16A	7A-1B 15B-9A	8A-2B 16B-10A	1A-3B 9B-11A	2A-4B 10B-12A	3A-5B 11B-13A
7	3A-4B 11B-12A	4A-5B 12B-13A	5A-6B 13B-14A	6A-7B 14B-15A	7A-8B 15B-16A	8A-1B 16B-9A	1A-2B 9B-10A	2A-3B 10B-11A

BOARDS ARE RELAYED THROUGHOUT THE MOVEMENT.

MASTER SHEET FOR TWO TEAMS OF 16 PAIRS -- GRUENTHER RELAY

SECOND STANZA

Rd.	Sets 9	10	11	12	13	14	15	16
8	1A-9B 1B-9A	2A-10B 2B-10A	3A-11B 3B-11A	4A-12B 4B-12A	5A-13B 5B-13A	6A-14B 6B-14A	7A-15B 7B-15A	8A-16B 8B-16A
9	8A-15B 8B-15A	1A-16B 1B-16A	2A-9B 2B-9A	3A-10B 3B-10A	4A-11B 4B-11A	5A-12B 5B-12A	6A-13B 6B-13A	7A-14B 7B-14A
10	7A-13B 7B-13A	8A-14B 8B-14A	1A-15B 1B-15A	2A-16B 2B-16A	3A-9B 3B-9A	4A-10B 4B-10A	5A-11B 5B-11A	6A-12B 6B-12A
11	6A-11B 6B-11A	7A-12B 7B-12A	8A-13B 8B-13A	1A-14B 1B-14A	2A-15B 2B-15A	3A-16B 3B-16A	4A-9B 4B-9A	5A-10B 5B-10A

EAST-WEST PAIRS SKIP ONE TABLE.

Rd.	9	10	11	12	13	14	15	16
12	5A-16B 5B-16A	6A-9B 6B-9A	7A-10B 7B-10A	8A-11B 8B-11A	1A-12B 1B-12A	2A-13B 2B-13A	3A-14B 3B-14A	4A-15B 4B-15A
13	4A-14B 4B-14A	5A-15B 5B-15A	6A-16B 6B-16A	7A-9B 7B-9A	8A-10B 8B-10A	1A-11B 1B-11A	2A-12B 2B-12A	3A-13B 3B-13A
14	3A-12B 3B-12A	4A-13B 4B-13A	5A-14B 5B-14A	6A-15B 6B-15A	7A-16B 7B-16A	8A-9B 8B-9A	1A-10B 1B-10A	2A-11B 2B-11A

BOARDS ARE RELAYED THROUGHOUT THE MOVEMENT.

SCHEDULE FOR TWO TEAMS OF 4 PAIRS -- BALDWIN

		Table 1		Table 2		Table 3		Table 4	
Rd.	Bds.	N-S	E-W	N-S	E-W	N-S	E-W	N-S	E-W
1	1-6	1A	1B	2A	2B	3B	3A	4B	4A
2	7-12	1A	2B	2A	3B	4B	3A	1B	4A
3	13-18	1A	3B	2A	4B	1B	3A	2B	4A
4	19-24	1A	4B	2A	1B	2B	3A	3B	4A

SCHEDULE FOR TWO TEAMS OF 4 PAIRS -- BALDWIN MODIFIED

	Table 1			Bye	Table 2		
Rd.	Bds.	N-S	E-W	Bds.	Bds.	N-S	E-W
1	1-6	1A	1B	19-24	13-18	2A	2B
2	7-12	1A	2B	1-6	19-24	2A	3B
3	13-18	1A	3B	7-12	1-6	2A	4B
4	19-24	1A	4B	13-18	7-12	2A	1B

Table 3			Table 4		
Bds.	N-S	E-W	Bds.	N-S	E-W
7-12	3B	3A	7-12	4B	4A
13-18	4B	3A	13-18	1B	4A
19-24	1B	3A	19-24	2B	4A
1-6	2B	3A	1-6	3B	4A

SCHEDULE FOR TWO TEAMS OF 6 PAIRS -- BALDWIN -- 24 BOARDS

	Table 1			Table 2			Table 3		
Rd.	Bds.	N-S	E-W	Bds.	N-S	E-W	Bds.	N-S	E-W
1	1-4	1A	1B	9-12	2A	2B	17-20	3A	3B
2	5-8	1A	2B	13-16	2A	3B	21-24	3A	4B
3	9-12	1A	3B	17-20	2A	4B	1-4	3A	5B
4	13-16	1A	4B	21-24	2A	5B	5-8	3A	6B
5	17-20	1A	5B	1-4	2A	6B	9-12	3A	1B
6	21-24	1A	6B	5-8	2A	1B	13-16	3A	2B

	Table 4			Table 5			Table 6		
Rd.	Bds	N-S	E-W	Bds.	N-S	E-W	Bds.	N-S	E-W
1	1-4	4B	4A	9-12	5B	5A	17-20	6B	6A
2	5-8	5B	4A	13-16	6B	5A	21-24	1B	6A
3	9-12	6B	4A	17-20	1B	5A	1-4	2B	6A
4	13-16	1B	4A	21-24	2B	5A	5-8	3B	6A
5	17-20	2B	4A	1-4	3B	5A	9-12	4B	6A
6	21-24	3B	4A	5-8	4B	5A	13-16	5B	6A

Teams of Pairs Movements

MASTER SHEET FOR TWO TEAMS OF 6 PAIRS -- BALDWIN -- 24 BOARDS

Rd.	Bds. 1-4	5-8	9-12	13-16	17-20	21-24	Table
1	1A-1B 4B-4A		2A-2B 5B-5A		3A-3B 6B-6A		
2		1A-2B 5B-4A		2A-3B 6B-5A		3A-4B 1B-6A	Bye
3	3A-5B 2B-6A		1A-3B 6B-4A		2A-4B 1B-5A		3 6^R
4		3A-6B 3B-6A		1A-4B 1B-4A		2A-5B 2B-5A	Bye
5	2A-6B 3B-5A		3A-1B 4B-6A		1A-5B 2B-4A		2 5^R
6		2A-1B 4B-5A		3A-2B 5B-6A		1A-6B 3B-4A	Bye
	Table	Bye	2 5^R	Bye	3 6^R	Bye	1 4^R

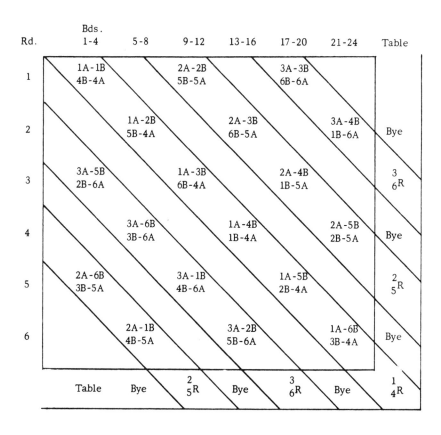

MASTER SHEET FOR FOUR TEAMS OF 3 PAIRS -- 24 BOARDS

Rd.	Bds. 1-4	5-8	9-12	13-16	17-20	21-24	Table
1	1A-3D	1B-2A	1C-3B	1D-2C	3A-2D	2B-3C	
2	2B-2D	1A-3C	1B-3D	1C-2A	1D-3B	3A-2C	6
3	3A-3B	2B-2C	1A-2D	1B-3C	1C-3D	1D-2A	5
		EAST-WEST PAIRS SKIP ONE TABLE					
4	1D-3C	3A-3D	2B-2A	1A-3B	1B-2C	1C-2D	4
		EAST-WEST PAIRS SKIP TWO TABLES					
5	1C-2A	1D-3B	3A-2C	2B-2D	1A-3C	1B-3D	3
		EAST-WEST PAIRS SKIP TWO TABLES					
6	1B-2C	1C-2D	1D-3C	3A-3D	2B-2A	1A-3B	2
	Table	2	3	4	5	6	1

Each team plays every other team six times.
Each team plays each board three times.
N-S--Pairs 1 on each team, Pair 3 on Team A, and Pair 2 on Team B -- remain stationary.
E-W--all other pairs--move as follows:

- Up one table after first round.
- Up one table after second round.
- Up two tables after third round.
- Up three tables after fourth round.
- Up three tables after fifth round.

Winners;

- High team on total match points.
- High N-S pair.
- High E-W pair.

Teams of Pairs Movements

MASTER SHEET FOR THREE TEAMS OF 4 PAIRS -- 24 BOARDS

Rd.	Bds. 1-4	5-8	9-12	13-16	17-20	21-24	Table
1	1A-3C	1B-3A	1C-3B	2A-4C	2B-4A	2C-4B	
2	2C-4A	1A-4B	1B-3C	1C-3A	2A-3B	2B-4C	6
		EAST-WEST PAIRS SKIP ONE TABLE					
3	2B-3A	2C-3B	1A-4C	1B-4A	1C-4B	2A-3C	5
4	2A-4B	2B-3C	2C-3A	1A-3B	1B-4C	1C-4A	4
		EAST-WEST PAIRS SKIP ONE TABLE					
5	1C-3B	2A-4C	2B-4A	2C-4B	1A-3C	1B-3A	3
		EAST-WEST PAIRS SKIP THREE TABLES					
6	1B-4C	1C-4A	2A-4B	2B-3C	2C-3A	1A-3B	2
	Table	2	3	4	5	6	1

Each team plays every other team 12 times.
Each team plays each board three times.
N-S -- Pairs 1 and 2 on each team -- remain stationary.
E-W -- Pairs 3 and 4 on each team -- move up one table after the first and third rounds, up two tables after the second and fourth rounds, and up four tables after the fifth round.

Winners: High team on total match points.
High N-S pair.
High E-W pair.

MASTER SHEET FOR FOUR TEAMS OF 4 PAIRS -- 32 BOARDS

Rd.	Bds. 1-4	5-8	9-12	13-16	17-20	21-24	25-28	29-32	Table
1	1A-3D	1B-3A	1C-3B	1D-3C	2A-4D	2B-4A	2C-4B	2D-4C	
2	2D-4B	1A-4C	1B-3D	1C-3A	1D-3B	2A-3C	2B-4D	2C-4A	8
3	2C-4D	2D-4A	1A-4B	1B-4C	1C-3D	1D-3A	2A-3B	2B-3C	7
			EAST-WEST PAIRS SKIP ONE TABLE						
4	2B-3A	2C-3B	2D-3C	1A-4D	1B-4A	1C-4B	1D-4C	2A-3D	6
5	2A-4C	2B-3D	2C-3A	2D-3B	1A-3C	1B-4D	1C-4A	1D-4B	5
6	1D-4A	2A-4B	2B-4C	2C-3D	2D-3A	1A-3B	1B-3C	1C-4D	4
	Table	4	5	6	7	8	1	2	3

Each team plays every other team 8 times.

Each team plays each board at least twice (and plays four sets of four boards each four times.)

N-S -- Pairs 1 and 2 on each team -- remain stationary.

E-W -- Pairs 3 and 4 on each team -- move up one table after each round, except after the third round, when they move up two tables.

Winners:

High team on total match points.
High N-S pair.
High E-W pair.

MASTER SHEET FOR FIVE TEAMS OF 4 PAIRS -- 30 BOARDS

Rd.	Bds. 1-3	4-6	7-9	10-12	13-15	16-18	19-21	22-24	25-27	28-30	Table
1	1A-3E	1B-3A	1C-3B	1D-3C	1E-3D	2A-4E	2B-4A	2C-4B	2D-4C	2E-4D	
2	2E-4C	1A-4D	1B-3E	1C-3A	1D-3B	1E-3C	2A-3D	2B-4E	2C-4A	2D-4B	10
3	2D-4A	2E-4B	1A-4C	1B-4D	1C-3E	1D-3A	1E-3B	2A-3C	2B-3D	2C-4E	9
4	2C-3D	2D-4E	2E-4A	1A-4B	1B-4C	1C-4D	1D-3E	1E-3A	2A-3B	2B-3C	8
				EAST-WEST PAIRS SKIP ONE TABLE							
5	2B-3A	2C-3B	2D-3C	2E-3D	1A-4E	1B-4A	1C-4B	1D-4C	1E-4D	2A-3E	7
6	2A-4D	2B-3E	2C-3A	2D-3B	2E-3C	1A-3D	1B-4E	1C-4A	1D-4B	1E-4C	6
7	1E-4B	2A-4C	2B-4D	2C-3E	2D-3A	2E-3B	1A-3C	1B-3D	1C-4E	1D-4A	5
8	1D-4E	1E-4A	2A-4B	2B-4C	2C-4D	2D-3E	2E-3A	1A-3B	1B-3C	1C-3D	4
	Table	4	5	6	7	8	9	10	1	2	3

Each team plays every other team 8 times.
Each team plays each board at least twice (and plays six sets of three boards each four times.)
N-S -- Pairs 1 and 2 on each team -- remain stationary.
E-W -- Pairs 3 and 4 on each team -- move up one table after each round, except after the third round, when they move up two tables.
Winners: High team on total match points.
High N-S pair.
High E-W pair.

MASTER SHEET FOR SIX TEAMS OF 4 PAIRS -- 24 BOARDS

Rd.	Bds. 1-2	3-4	5-6	7-8	9-10	11-12	13-14	15-16	17-18	19-20	21-22	23-24	Table
1	1A-3F	1B-3A	1C-3B	1D-3C	1E-3D	1F-3E	2A-4F	2B-4A	2C-4B	2D-4C	2E-4D	2F-4E	
2	2F-4D	1A-4E	1B-3F	1C-3A	1D-3B	1E-3C	1F-3D	2A-3E	2B-4F	2C-4A	2D-4B	2E-4C	12
3	2E-4B	2F-4C	1A-4D	1B-4E	1C-3F	1D-3A	1E-3B	1F-3C	2A-3D	2B-3E	2C-4F	2D-4A	11
4	2D-4F	2E-4A	2F-4B	1A-4C	1B-4D	1C-4E	1D-3F	1E-3A	1F-3B	2A-3C	2B-3D	2C-3E	10
5	2C-3D	2D-3E	2E-4F	2F-4A	1A-4B	1B-4C	1C-4D	1D-4E	1E-3F	1F-3A	2A-3B	2B-3C	9
					EAST-WEST PAIRS SKIP ONE TABLE								
6	2B-3A	2C-3B	2D-3C	2E-3D	2F-3E	1A-4F	1B-4A	1C-4B	1D-4C	1E-4D	1F-4E	2A-3F	8
7	2A-4E	2B-3F	2C-3A	2D-3B	2E-3C	2F-3D	1A-3E	1B-4F	1C-4A	1D-4B	1E-4C	1F-4D	7
8	1F-4C	2A-4D	2B-4E	2C-3F	2D-3A	2E-3B	2F-3C	1A-3D	1B-3E	1C-4F	1D-4A	1E-4B	6
9	1E-4A	1F-4B	2A-4C	2B-4D	2C-4E	2D-3F	2E-3A	2F-3B	1A-3C	1B-3D	1C-3E	1D-4F	5
10	1D-3E	1E-4F	1F-4A	2A-4B	2B-4C	2C-4D	2D-4E	2E-3F	2F-3A	1A-3B	1B-3C	1C-3D	4
	Table	4	5	6	7	8	9	10	11	12	1	2	3

Each team plays every other team 8 times.
Each team plays each board at least twice (eight sets of two boards each four times).
N-S -- Pairs 1 and 2 on each team -- remain stationary.
E-W -- Pairs 3 and 4 on each team -- move up one table after each round, except after the fifth round, when they move up two tables.
Winners: High team on total match points.
High N-S pair.
High E-W pair.

MASTER SHEET FOR SEVEN TEAMS OF 4 PAIRS -- 28 BOARDS

Rd.	Bds. 1-2	3-4	5-6	7-8	9-10	11-12	13-14	15-16	17-18	19-20	21-22	23-24	25-26	27-28	Table
1	1A-3G	1B-3A	1C-3B	1D-3C	1E-3D	1F-3E	1G-3F	2A-4G	2B-4A	2C-4B	2D-4C	2E-4D	2F-4E	2G-4F	
2	2G-4E	1A-4F	1B-3G	1C-3A	1D-3B	1E-3C	1F-3D	1G-3E	2A-3F	2B-4G	2C-4A	2D-4B	2E-4C	2F-4D	14
3	2F-4C	2G-4D	1A-4E	1B-4F	1C-3G	1D-3A	1E-3B	1F-3C	1G-3D	2A-3E	2B-3F	2C-4G	2D-4A	2E-4B	13
4	2E-4A	2F-4B	2G-4C	1A-4D	1B-4E	1C-4F	1D-3G	1E-3A	1F-3B	1G-3C	2A-3D	2B-3E	2C-3F	2D-4G	12
5	2D-3F	2E-4G	2F-4A	2G-4B	1A-4C	1B-4D	1C-4E	1D-4F	1E-3G	1F-3A	1G-3B	2A-3C	2B-3D	2C-3E	11
6	2C-3D	2D-3E	2E-3F	2F-4G	2G-4A	1A-4B	1B-4C	1C-4D	1D-4E	1E-4F	1F-3G	1G-3A	2A-3B	2B-3C	10
					EAST-WEST PAIRS SKIP ONE ROUND										
7	2B-3A	2C-3B	2D-3C	2E-3D	2F-3E	2G-3F	1A-4G	1B-4A	1C-4B	1D-4C	1E-4D	1F-4E	1G-4F	2A-3G	9
8	2A-4F	2B-3G	2C-3A	2D-3B	2E-3C	2F-3D	2G-3E	1A-3F	1B-4G	1C-4A	1D-4B	1E-4C	1F-4D	1G-4E	8
9	1G-4D	2A-4E	2B-4F	2C-3G	2D-3A	2E-3B	2F-3C	2G-3D	1A-3E	1B-3F	1C-4G	1D-4A	1E-4B	1F-4C	7
10	1F-4B	1G-4C	2A-4D	2B-4E	2C-4F	2D-3G	2E-3A	2F-3B	2G-3C	1A-3D	1B-3E	1C-3F	1D-4G	1E-4A	6
11	1E-4G	1F-4A	1G-4B	2A-4C	2B-4D	2C-4E	2D-4F	2E-3G	2F-3A	2G-3B	1A-3C	1B-3D	1C-3E	1D-3F	5
12	1D-3E	1E-3F	1F-4G	1G-4A	2A-4B	2B-4C	2C-4D	2D-4E	2E-4F	2F-3G	2G-3A	1A-3B	1B-3C	1C-3D	4
	Table	4	5	6	7	8	9	10	11	12	13	14	1	2	3

Each team plays every other team 8 times.
Each team plays each board at least twice (and plays 10 sets of two boards each four times.)
N-S -- Pairs 1 and 2 on each team -- remain stationary.
E-W -- Pairs 3 and 4 on each team -- move up one table after each round, except after the sixth round, when they move up two tables.
Winners: High team on total match points.
High N-S pair.
High E-W pair.

MASTER SHEET FOR EIGHT TEAMS OF 4 PAIRS -- 48 BOARDS

Rd.	Bds. 1-3	4-6	7-9	10-12	13-15	16-18	19-21	22-24	25-27	28-30	31-33	34-36	37-39	40-42	43-45	46-48	Table
1	1A-3H	1B-3A	1C-3B	1D-3C	1E-3D	1F-3E	1G-3F	1H-3G	2A-4H	2B-4A	2C-4B	2D-4C	2E-4D	2F-4E	2G-4F	2H-4G	
2	2H-4F	1A-4G	1B-3H	1C-3A	1D-3B	1E-3C	1F-3D	1G-3E	1H-3F	2A-3G	2B-4H	2C-4A	2D-4B	2E-4C	2F-4D	2G-4E	16
3	2G-4D	2H-4E	1A-4F	1B-4G	1C-3H	1D-3A	1E-3B	1F-3C	1G-3D	1H-3E	2A-3F	2B-3G	2C-4H	2D-4A	2E-4B	2F-4C	15
4	2F-4B	2G-4C	2H-4D	1A-4E	1B-4F	1C-4G	1D-3H	1E-3A	1F-3B	1G-3C	1H-3D	2A-3E	2B-3F	2C-3G	2D-4H	2E-4A	14
5	2E-4H	2F-4A	2G-4B	2H-4C	1A-4D	1B-4E	1C-4F	1D-4G	1E-3H	1F-3A	1G-3B	1H-3C	2A-3D	2B-3E	2C-3F	2D-3G	13
6	2D-3F	2E-3G	2F-4H	2G-4A	2H-4B	1A-4C	1B-4D	1C-4E	1D-4F	1E-4G	1F-3H	1G-3A	1H-3B	2A-3C	2B-3D	2C-3E	12
7	2C-3D	2D-3E	2E-3F	2F-3G	2G-4H	2H-4A	1A-4B	1B-4C	1C-4D	1D-4E	1E-4F	1F-4G	1G-3H	1H-3A	2A-3B	2B-3C	11
	Table	11	12	13	14	15	16	1	2	3	4	5	6	7	8	9	10

Each team plays every other team 4 times.
Each team plays each board at least once (and plays six sets of three boards each three times.)
N-S -- Pairs 1 and 2 on each team -- remain stationary.
E-W -- Pairs 3 and 4 on each team -- move up one table after each round.
Winners: High team on total match points
High N-S pair.
High E-W pair.

MASTER SHEET FOR EIGHT TEAMS OF 4 PAIRS -- 48 BOARDS

Rd	Bds. 1-3	4-6	7-9	10-12	13-15	16-18	19-21	22-24	25-27	28-30	31-33	34-36	37-39	40-42	43-45	46-48	Table
1	1A-3E	1B-3F	1C-3G	1D-3H	1E-3A	1F-3B	1G-3C	1H-3D	2A-4E	2B-4F	2C-4G	2D-4H	2E-4A	2F-4B	2G-4C	2H-4D	
2	2H-4C	1A-4D	1B-3E	1C-3F	1D-3G	1E-3H	1F-3A	1G-3B	1H-3C	2A-3D	2B-4E	2C-4F	2D-4G	2E-4H	2F-4A	2G-4B	16
3	2G-4A	2H-4B	1A-4C	1B-4D	1C-3E	1D-3F	1E-3G	1F-3H	1G-3A	1H-3B	2A-3C	2B-3D	2C-4E	2D-4F	2E-4G	2F-4H	15
4	2F-4G	2G-4H	2H-4A	1A-4B	1B-4C	1C-4D	1D-3E	1E-3F	1F-3G	1G-3H	1H-3A	2A-3B	2B-3C	2C-3D	2D-4E	2E-4F	14
5	2E-3D	2F-4E	2G-4F	2H-4G	1A-4H	1B-4A	1C-4B	1D-4C	1E-4D	1F-3E	1G-3F	1H-3G	2A-3H	2B-3A	2C-3B	2D-3C	13
6	2D-3B	2E-3C	2F-3D	2G-4E	2H-4F	1A-4G	1B-4H	1C-4A	1D-4B	1E-4C	1F-4D	1G-3E	1H-3F	2A-3G	2B-3H	2C-3A	12
7	2C-3H	2D-3A	2E-3B	2F-3C	2G-3D	2H-4E	1A-4F	1B-4G	1C-4H	1D-4A	1E-4B	1F-4C	1G-4D	1H-3E	2A-3F	2B-3G	11
	Table	11	12	13	14	15	16	1	2	3	4	5	6	7	8	9	10

EAST-WEST PAIRS SKIP ONE TABLE

Each team plays every other team four times.
Each team plays each board at least once (and plays twelve sets of three boards each twice.)
N-S -- Pairs 1 and 2 on each team -- remain stationary.
E-W -- Pairs 3 and 4 on each team -- move up one table after each round, except after the fourth round, when they move up two tables.
Winners: High team on total match points.
High N-S pair.
High E-W pair.

MASTER SHEET FOR FOUR TEAMS OF 5 PAIRS -- 20 BOARDS

Rd.	Bds. 1-2	3-4	5-6	7-8	9-10	11-12	13-14	15-16	17-18	19-20	Table
1	1A-5D	1B-4A	1C-3B	1D-5C	2A-4D	2B-5A	2C-4B	2D-3C	3A-3D	4C-5B	
2	4C-3D	1A-5B	1B-5D	1C-4A	1D-3B	2A-5C	2B-4D	2C-5A	2D-4B	3A-3C	10
3	3A-4D	4C-5A	1A-4B	1B-3C	1C-3D	1D-5B	2A-5D	2B-4A	2C-3B	2D-5C	9
4	2D-5B	3A-5D	4C-4A	1A-3B	1B-5C	1C-4D	1D-5A	2A-4B	2B-3C	2C-3D	8
5	2C-4B	2D-3C	3A-3D	4C-5B	1A-5D	1B-4A	1C-3B	1D-5C	2A-4D	2B-5A	7
6	2B-4A	2C-3B	2D-5C	3A-4D	4C-5A	1A-4B	1B-3C	1C-3D	1D-5B	2A-5D	6
7	2A-5C	2B-4D	2C-5A	2D-4B	3A-3C	4C-3D	1A-5B	1B-5D	1C-4A	1D-3B	5
8	1D-5A	2A-4B	2B-3C	2C-3D	2D-5B	3A-5D	4C-4A	1A-3B	1B-5C	1C-4D	4
9	1C-3B	1D-5C	2A-4D	2B-5A	2C-4B	2D-3C	3A-3D	4C-5B	1A-5D	1B-4A	3
10	1B-3C	1C-3D	1D-5B	2A-5D	2B-4A	2C-3B	2D-5C	3A-4D	4C-5A	1A-4B	2
	Table	2	3	4	5	6	7	8	9	10	1

Teams play each other an uneven number of times.
Each team plays each board five times.
N-S -- Pairs 1 and 2 on each team, Pair 3A and Pair 4C -- remain stationary.
E-W -- all other pairs -- move irregularly as follows:

Up one table after first round.
Up three tables after second round.
Up four tables after third round.
Up two tables after fourth round.
Up four tables after fifth round.
Down three tables after sixth round.
Down three tables after seventh round.
Up two tables after eighth round.
Up four tables after ninth round.

MASTER SHEET FOR SIX TEAMS OF 6 PAIRS -- 36 BOARDS

Rd.	Bds. 1-2	3-4	5-6	7-8	9-10	11-12	13-14	15-16	17-18	19-20	21-22	23-24	25-26	27-28	29-30	31-32	33-34	35-36	Table
1	1A-4F	1B-4A	1C-4B	1D-4C	1E-4D	1F-4E	2A-5F	2B-5A	2C-5B	2D-5C	2E-5D	2F-5E	3A-6F	3B-6A	3C-6B	3D-6C	3E-6D	3F-6E	
2	3F-6D	1A-6E	1B-4F	1C-4A	1D-4B	1E-4C	1F-4D	2A-4E	2B-5F	2C-5A	2D-5B	2E-5C	2F-5D	3A-5E	3B-6F	3C-6A	3D-6B	3E-6C	18
3	3E-6B	3F-6C	1A-6D	1B-6E	1C-4F	1D-4A	1E-4B	1F-4C	2A-4D	2B-4E	2C-5F	2D-5A	2E-5B	2F-5C	3A-5D	3B-5E	3C-6F	3D-6A	17
4	3D-6F	3E-6A	3F-6B	1A-6C	1B-6D	1C-6E	1D-4F	1E-4A	1F-4B	2A-4C	2B-4D	2C-4E	2D-5F	2E-5A	2F-5B	3A-5C	3B-5D	3C-5E	16
5	3C-5D	3D-5E	3E-6F	3F-6A	1A-6B	1B-6C	1C-6D	1D-6E	1E-4F	1F-4A	2A-4B	2B-4C	2C-4D	2D-4E	2E-5F	2F-5A	3A-5B	3B-5C	15
6	3B-5A	3C-5B	3D-5C	3E-5D	3F-5E	1A-6F	1B-6A	1C-6B	1D-6C	1E-6D	1F-6E	2A-4F	2B-4A	2C-4B	2D-4C	2E-4D	2F-4E	3A-5F	14
7	3A-4E	3B-5F	3C-5A	3D-5B	3E-5C	3F-5D	1A-5E	1B-6F	1C-6A	1D-6B	1E-6C	1F-6D	2A-6E	2B-4F	2C-4A	2D-4B	2E-4C	2F-4D	13
8	2F-4C	3A-4D	3B-4E	3C-5F	3D-5A	3E-5B	3F-5C	1A-5D	1B-5E	1C-6F	1D-6A	1E-6B	1F-6C	2A-6D	2B-6E	2C-4F	2D-4A	2E-4B	12
9	2E-4A	2F-4B	3A-4C	3B-4D	3C-4E	3D-5F	3E-5A	3F-5B	1A-5C	1B-5D	1C-5E	1D-6F	1E-6A	1F-6B	2A-6C	2B-6D	2C-6E	2D-4F	11
10	2D-6E	2E-4F	2F-4A	3A-4B	3B-4C	3C-4D	3D-4E	3E-5F	3F-5A	1A-5B	1B-5C	1C-5D	1D-5E	1E-6F	1F-6A	2A-6B	2B-6C	2C-6D	10
	Table	10	11	12	13	14	15	16	17	18	1	2	3	4	5	6	7	8	9

Each team plays every other team 12 times.
Each team plays each board at least twice (and plays 12 sets of 2 boards each four times).
N-S -- Pairs 1-3 on each team -- remain stationary.
E-W -- Pairs 4-6 on each team -- move up one table after each round, except after the fifth round, when they move up two tables.
Winners: High team on total match points.
High N-S pair.
High E-W pair.

MASTER SHEET FOR FOUR TEAMS OF 8 PAIRS -- 48 BOARDS

Rd.	Bds 1-3	4-6	7-9	10-12	13-15	16-18	19-21	22-24	25-27	28-30	31-33	34-36	37-39	40-42	43-45	46-48	Table
1	1A-5D	1B-5A	1C-5B	1D-5C	2A-6D	2B-6A	2C-6B	2D-6C	3A-7D	3B-7A	3C-7B	3D-7C	4A-8D	4B-8A	4C-8B	4D-8C	
2	4D-8B	1A-8C	1B-5D	1C-5A	1D-5B	2A-5C	2B-6D	2C-6A	2D-6B	3A-6C	3B-7D	3C-7A	3D-7B	4A-7C	4B-8D	4C-8A	16
3	4C-8D	4D-8A	1A-8B	1B-8C	1C-5D	1D-5A	2A-5B	2B-5C	2C-6D	2D-6A	3A-6B	3B-6C	3C-7D	3D-7A	4A-7B	4B-7C	15
4	4B-7A	4C-7B	4D-7C	1A-8D	1B-8A	1C-8B	1D-8C	2A-5D	2B-5A	2C-5B	2D-5C	3A-6D	3B-6A	3C-6B	3D-6C	4A-7D	14
5	4A-6C	4B-7D	4C-7A	4D-7B	1A-7C	1B-8D	1C-8A	1D-8B	2A-8C	2B-5D	2C-5A	2D-5B	3A-5C	3B-6D	3C-6A	3D-6B	13
6	3D-6A	4A-6B	4B-6C	4C-7D	4D-7A	1A-7B	1B-7C	1C-8D	1D-8A	2A-8B	2B-8C	2C-5D	2D-5A	3A-5B	3B-5C	3C-6D	12
7	3C-5B	3D-5C	4A-6D	4B-6A	4C-6B	4D-6C	1A-7D	1B-7A	1C-7B	1D-7C	2A-8D	2B-8A	2C-8B	2D-8C	3A-5D	3B-5A	11
8	3B-8C	3C-5D	3D-5A	4A-5B	4B-5C	4C-6D	4D-6A	1A-6B	1B-6C	1C-7D	1D-7A	2A-7B	2B-7C	2C-8D	2D-8A	3A-8B	10
9	3A-7C	3B-8D	3C-8A	3D-8B	4A-8C	4B-5D	4C-5A	4D-5B	1A-5C	1B-6D	1C-6A	1D-6B	2A-6C	2B-7D	2C-7A	2D-7B	9
	Table	9	10	11	12	13	14	15	16	1	2	3	4	5	6	7	8

Each team plays every other team 24 times.
Each team plays each board at least four times (and plays eight sets of three boards each five times).
N-S -- Pairs 1-4 on each team -- remain stationary.
E-W -- Pairs 5-8 on each team -- move up one table after each round, except after the third, sixth and seventh round, when they move up two tables, and after the eighth round, when they move up three tables.
Winners: High team on total match points.
High N-S pair.
High E-W pair.

Appendix I

Computer Scoring

A club that has a computer available and is comfortable with its use can simplify significantly the tasks of directing and scoring a duplicate game through the use of a scoring program. There are a number of such programs available; one that is proving popular is ACBL-Score, created for the American Contract Bridge League by Jim Lopushinsky.

ACBL-Score can be used in any IBM-compatible computer with a hard drive and a 640K RAM capacity. In addition to rapid calculation of club game results, the software program has a wide range of capabilities useful to the club management and director.

Its database can hold virtually any conceivable club records, such as the club franchise number, its unit affiliation, regular and special games, lists of all members, their addresses, phone numbers, and their masterpoint totals and classifications. It can maintain records of members' awards for the month or year. All this data can be recorded on diskettes or printed out, and mailing labels can be generated.

The program can display and print movements for Howell, Mitchell, and Rover games, as well as individual guide cards.

As the director enters scores, it can handle up to four sections at once, helping detect errors en route. As soon as all scores are correctly entered, the program can print out results for the entire game, including percentages and masterpoint awards. When scoring is done on pick-up slips, the program can print out standings before the final round is played.

All in all, the director who uses this or any other capable program can lighten his burdens substantially.

Appendix J

The Scrambled Mitchell Movement

A major improvement in "arrow switches" to achieve balance among pairs was developed by Dr. Lawrence Rosler in 1964. Since then, even better balance has been obtained through the use of computers by Professor Olof Hanner, of the Matematiska institutionen of G teborg University, G teborg, Sweden, as follows:

Tables	Arrow North	Arrow East
6	Rounds 1,2,3,4	5,6
7	Rounds 1,2,3,4,5	6,7
8	Rounds 1,2,3,5,6	4,7,8
9	Rounds 1,2,3,4,5,7	6,8,9
10	Rounds 1,2,3,5,7,8	4,6,9,10
11	Rounds 1,2,3,4,5,6,9	7,8,10,11
12	Rounds 1,2,3,4,6,8,9,10	5,7,11,12
13	Rounds 1,2,3,4,5,6,8,10,11	7,9,12,13
14	Rounds 1,2,3,4,5,6,8,12,13	7,9,10,11,14
15	Rounds 1,2,3,4,5,6,8,9,11,13	7,10,12,14,15
16	Rounds 1,2,3,4,5,9,10,11,14,15	6,7,8,12,13,16

Where there is an even number of tables and no half tables in the game, Prof. Hanner points out, there should be no arrow switching at Table 1, in order to assure that there will be at least some comparisons between all pairs in the game.

Index

ACKNOWLEDGEMENTS

The author wishes to thank Richard Goldberg and Tannah Hirsch for their invaluable editorial assistance, and Harry and Shirley Silverman for their aid and encouragement.

The Author

"WRITING CAN BE a joyful pastime, a pleasant diversion or a highly-developed form of self-flagellation, depending on the subject and the writer. But there must be a strong strain of masochism in the profession, because most writers tend to describe their work as self-inflicted torture. And that is the way I think of it, although it also has its hours of pleasure and diversion and its rare and fleeting moments of joy."

That is how Alex Groner describes his business. Although he is a devoted fan of bridge and duplicate bridge, as well as an accomplished duplicate director, his business is writing. He was asked to write DUPLICATE BRIDGE DIRECTION for that reason. While there are a number of people who thoroughly understand the complexities of duplicate movements, and quite a number who can expertly teach duplicate direction, it is rare to find someone who can combine these attributes with those of a professional writer.

He has had a long and varied career in writing. He started as a reporter for The Cleveland Press, where he was also a rewrite man, assistant financial editor and editorial writer. In Cleveland he was also the local correspondent for Time, Life and Fortune. He became a contributing editor of Time and subsequently, as Manager of Internal Communications for Time Inc., conducted a training program for writers for the company's magazines. He also started a duplicate bridge club at Time Inc. and has been its director for a number of years.

Mr. Groner is now president of his own firm, Writing Services Company, which concentrates in the area he describes as "corporate journalism." This consists in part, he says, of explaining complex subject matter, "mainly by reducing complexities to their ultimate simplicities -- a job that a writer must frequently do."

He has given a pretty good demonstration of that art in DUPLICATE BRIDGE DIRECTION.

This book is bound with an entirely new plastic adhesive which permits the pages to be opened flat. The pages will not come loose with frequent handling.